CHILTON'S Repair and Tune-Up Guide

Volvo 2

ILLUSTRATED

Prepared by the

Automotive Editorial Department

Chilton Book Company
Chilton Way
Radnor, Pa. 19089
215—687-8200

managing editor **JOHN D. KELLY;** assistant managing editor **PETER J. MEYER;** senior editor **STEPHEN J. DAVIS;** editor **RONALD L. SESSIONS;** technical editors **N Banks Spence Jr, Eugene P. Nicolo, William L. Jones**

CHILTON BOOK COMPANY   RADNOR, PENNSYLVANIA

Copyright © 1973 by Chilton Book Company
First Edition
All rights reserved
Published in Radnor, Pa. by Chilton Book Company
and simultaneously in Ontario, Canada,
by Thomas Nelson & Sons, Ltd.
Manufactured in the United States of America
Second Printing, December 1973
Third Printing, September 1975

Library of Congress Cataloging in Publication Data

Chilton Book Company. Automotive Editorial Dept.
   Chilton's repair and tune-up guide: Volvo 2.

   Continues the guide prepared by the Automotive
Book Dept. in 1971, published under title:
Chilton's repair and tune-up guide for the Volvo.
   1. Volvo automobile.   I. Title.   II. Title:
Repair and tune-up guide: Volvo 2.
TL215.V65C49   629.28′7′22   73-3398
ISBN 0-8019-5813-X
ISBN 0-8019-5850-4 (pbk)

ACKNOWLEDGMENT

The Chilton Book Company expresses its appreciation to AB Volvo, American Motors Corporation, and the Ford Motor Company for the technical information and illustrations contained within this manual.

The editor wishes to give special thanks to Mr. Les Fowler and Mr. Neal Van Name of Volvo of America Corporation, and Mr. Dave Myers and Mr. Joseph Schukis of Charles Burdumy Inc., whose time and efforts have helped in the production of this book.

Contents

General Information and Maintenance

Introduction

Since Volvo imported its first cars to this country in 1956, the company has enjoyed a reputation for building safe, reliable, durable and economical cars. Volvo is currently manufacturing three distinctly different series of cars. The 140 series, first produced in 1967, is a four cylinder, medium priced compact offered in a two-door sedan (142), four-door sedan (144), and station wagon (145) body styles. The 164, first produced in 1969, is a six cylinder, upper-medium priced luxury rendition of the 144, sharing the same sheet metal and mechanical components with the 144 from the firewall back. The 1800 series, first imported in 1964, is a four cylinder, medium priced sports model offered through 1972 in a two-door coupe version (P1800, 1800S, 1800E), and since 1972 in a two-door sportswagon version (1800ES).

Note on Special Tools

Although the repair procedures are written so that, in most cases, the use of special factory tools is avoided, it sometimes becomes necessary to use them when no other conventional tool will do. In many cases, the tool numbers are provided in the illustrations for reference use only. The SVO tool company in Sweden is the sole manufacturer of special tools for AB Volvo. If it is imperative that a special tool be obtained, contact your nearest dealer. The dealer will probably have the desired tool hanging up on the tool rack, but if not, it will have to be ordered.

Model Identification

1967–70 140 series—144 shown

1971–72 140 series—144 shown

1

1973 140 series—144 shown

1969–72 164

1973 164

1970–72 1800E

1972–73 1800ES

Serial Number Identification

In all correspondence with the dealer or when ordering spare parts, the vehicle type designation, chassis number, and, if applicable, the engine, transmission, and rear axle (final drive) numbers should be quoted for proper identification.

VEHICLE TYPE DESIGNATION AND CHASSIS NUMBER

Type designation (142, 164, 1800 etc.) and chassis number appear at several locations on every Volvo. On all 140 series and 164 model Volvos, they are stamped into the sheet metal of the right front door pillar. On all 1800 models, they are stamped into the sheet metal on the right side of the engine compartment. The type designation and the chassis number also appear on a metal plate (1) riveted to the engine side of the firewall. For 1972–73, they appear on the V.I.N. plate (3) located at the foot of the left door post.

Chassis Number Chart

Year	Model	Starting Chassis No.
1970	142	112400
	144	138700
	145	30900
	164	12200
	1800E	30001
1971	142	178960
	144	194140
	145	61600
	164	32400
	1800E	32800
1972	142	249930
	144	263070
	145	103380
	164	52790
	1800E	37550
	1800ES	1
1973	142	323400
	144	340100
	145	153730
	164	74450
	1800ES	3070

ENGINE, TRANSMISSION, AND FINAL DRIVE IDENTIFICATION

The engine type designation, part number, and serial number are given on the

Ty

Serial number identification—1972 144 shown

left side of the block (4). The last figures of the part number are stamped on a tab and are followed by the serial number stamped on the block.

The transmission type designation, serial number, and part number appear on a metal plate (5) riveted to the underside of the transmission.

The final drive reduction ratio, part number, and serial number are found on a metal plate (6) riveted to the left-hand side of the differential.

Engine Identification Chart

Type Number	Engine Type	Horsepower (SAE gross)	Vehicle Type
496929	B 20 B	118	142S, 144S, 145S
496930	B 20 B	118	142S, 144S, 145S, with BW 35
496940	B 20 E	130	1800E
496941	B 20 E	130	1800E with BW 35
496943	B 20 E	130	142E
496945	B 20 E	130	142E with BW 35
498282	B 20 F	125	1800E, 1800ES
498283	B 20 F	125	1800E, 1800ES, with BW 35
498284	B 20 F	125	142E, 144E, 145E
498285	B 20 F	125	142E, 144E, 145E, with BW 35
496953	B 30 A	145	164
496954	B 30 A	145	164 with BW 35
498100	B 30 F	160	164E
498101	B 30 F	160	164E with BW 35

Oil and Fuel Recommendations

FUEL RECOMMENDATIONS

It is imperative that you use fuel of the proper octane rating in your Volvo. Octane rating is based on the quantity of antiknock compounds added to the fuel and determines the speed at which the gas will burn; the lower the octane, the faster it burns. The higher the numerical octane rating, the slower the fuel will burn and the greater the percentage of compounds in the fuel to prevent spark ping (knock), detonation, and pre-ignition. As the temperature of the engine increases, the air-fuel mixture shows a tendency to ignite before the spark plug is fired and the exhaust valve is opened. This is especially critical in high-compression engines (any engine with a compression ratio greater than 9.0:1), where the use of low-octane gas will cause combustion to occur before the piston has completed its compression stroke, thereby forcing the piston down while it is still traveling up. Fuel of the proper octane rating for the compression ratio of your car will slow the combustion process sufficiently to allow the spark plug time to ignite the mixture completely and time for the exhaust valve to open. Spark ping, detonation, and pre-ignition, may result in damage to the top of the pistons and burned exhaust valves. The following compression ratio/octane rating chart is useful in selecting the proper fuel for your Volvo.

OIL RECOMMENDATIONS

It is imperative that oil of an equal quality to original equipment be used in your Volvo. Generally speaking, oil that has been rated SE, heavy-duty detergent

by the American Petroleum Institute is satisfactory.

Oil of the SE variety performs a multitude of functions in addition to its basic task of lubricating. Through a balanced formula of metallic detergents and polymeric dispersants, the oil prevents high-temperature and low-temperature deposits and also keeps sludge and dirt particles in suspension. Acids, particularly sulphuric acid, as well as other by-products of combustion, are neutralized by the oil. These acids, if permitted to concentrate, may cause corrosion and rapid wear of the internal parts of the engine.

It is important to choose an oil of the proper viscosity for climatic and operational conditions. The SAE viscosity rating is printed on the top of the oil container. For winter operation, a "W" is added after the SAE rating to indicate the oil's suitability for cold temperatures. The oil viscosity chart is useful in selecting the proper grade.

Oil Viscosity Chart

Temperature Range	Viscosity Rating
Above 10°F (infrequent high-speed operation)	20W–40
Above 10°F (frequent high-speed operation)	20W–50
Below 10°F down to −20°F	10W–30
Below −20°F (never use at temperatures above 32°F)	5W–20

Routine Maintenance

MAINTENANCE INTERVAL CHART

The numerals in the maintenance chart represent the suggested intervals between

Compression Ratio/Fuel Octane Chart

Year	Model	Engine	Compression Ratio	Octane
1970–72	142S, 144S, 145S	B 20 B	9.3 : 1	100 (premium)
1970–71	142E, 1800E	B 20 E	10.5 : 1	97 (premium)
1970–71	164	B 30 A	9.3 : 1	97 (premium)
1972–73	142E, 144E, 145E, 1800E, 1800ES	B 20 F	8.7 : 1	91 (regular)
1972–73	164E	B 30 F	8.7 : 1	91 (regular)

service in thousands of miles or numbers of months, whichever occurs first.

6,000 miles or 6 months	6
12,000 miles or 12 months	12
24,000 miles or 24 months	24
36,000 miles or 36 months	36

Body

Body lubrication	6
Headlight alignment	6

Chassis

Ball joints, steering rods, and seals check	12
Brake linings and hydraulic system check	6
Brake master cylinder fluid level check	weekly
Brake system overhaul and seal replacement	36
Clutch free-play adjustment	6
Drive shaft and universal joints check	6
Parking brake linkage lubrication	12
Power brake air filter change	36
Power steering fluid level check	6
Rear axle fluid level check	6
Steering box fluid level check	6
Tire pressure check	weekly
Tire wear pattern check	6
Transmission oil level check	6
Transmission oil change	24

Engine

Air filter change	24
Battery electrolyte level check	weekly
Battery state of charge check	6
Carburetor idle speed, fast idle, and choke adjustments	12
Carburetor oil level check	6
Contact point adjustment	6
Coolant level check	weekly
Coolant replacement and system pressure test	12
Distributor lubrication	6
Drive belt adjustment	6
Exhaust gas recirculation system cleaning	12①
Exhaust gas recirculation valve replacement	24①
Fuel evaporative control system filter change	24
Fuel filter cleaning (carbureted models)	6
Fuel filter replacement (injected models)	12
Fuel tank pick-up screen cleaning	12②
Ignition timing adjustment	6
Oil change and filter replacement	6
Oil level check	weekly
Positive crankcase ventilation (PCV) system service	12
Spark plug cleaning and adjustment	6
Spark plug replacement	12
Throttle linkage lubrication	12
Valve lash adjustment	12

① 1973 Automatic transmission equipped models only
② 1973 Fuel Injection models only

FLUID LEVEL CHECKS

Engine Oil

The oil level in the engine should be checked at fuel stops. The check should be made with the engine warm and switched off for a period of about one minute so that the oil has time to drain down into the crankcase. Pull out the dipstick, wipe it clean, and reinsert it. The level of the oil must be kept between the minimum and maximum marks on the dipstick. If the oil level is kept above the maximum mark, heavy oil consumption will result. If the level remains below the minimum mark, severe engine damage may result. When topping up, make sure that the new oil is of the same type and viscosity rating as the oil in the crankcase.

Carburetor Oil

On carbureted 1970–72 140 series and 164 models, the oil level in the center spindle of the carburetors must be checked every six months or 6,000 miles. Unscrew the black knob on top of each carburetor and remove each damping plunger. The oil level should be maintained at about ¼ in. from the edge of the spindle. Top up as necessary with automatic transmission fluid Type A, or Dexron.

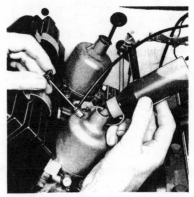

Checking center spindle oil level

Manual Transmission Fluid

At six-month or 6,000 mile intervals, the fluid level should be checked. After making sure that the vehicle is standing on level ground, unscrew the filler plug (1) and check to see that the fluid level is maintained at the bottom of the filler plug hole. Top up as necessary with SAE 80 gear oil, or SAE 30 motor oil if no gear oil is available.

Manual transmission drain plug locations—M40, M41 shown

Automatic Transmission Fluid

The fluid level of the automatic transmission should be checked every six months or 6,000 miles. Position the vehicle on level ground, place the selector lever in Park, and let the engine idle. Remove the dipstick from the filler tube on the right side of the engine, and wipe it clean with a chamois or similar lint-free cloth. Reinsert the dipstick, pull it straight out, and take the reading. Any transmission that has been driven for 5–7 miles is a warm transmission and its proper level is the upper range of marks on the dipstick. The proper level for a cold transmission is the lower range of marks. When necessary, top up with Type "F" automatic transmission fluid. The difference between the minimum and maximum marks is only one pint, so add the fluid slowly. Overfilling the transmission may cause it to overheat.

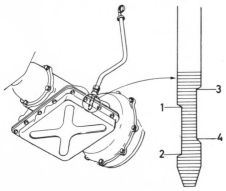

Checking automatic transmission fluid level

1. Max. oil level, cold transmission
2. Min. oil level, cold transmission
3. Max. oil level, warm transmission
4. Min. oil level, warm transmission

Brake Master Cylinder Fluid

The level of brake fluid in the master cylinder should be checked weekly by the driver. The master cylinder is located on the left (driver's) side of the engine compartment in front of the firewall. The level may be checked without removing the cap by simply observing whether or not the fluid is up to the maximum mark on the translucent reservoir. Top up as necessary with fluid of SAE 70R3 (J 1703) quality or better. Take care not to drop any foreign matter or dirt into the reservoir. Make sure that the vent hole in the reservoir cap is not blocked.

Coolant

The coolant level should be checked at fuel stops on all models. The level should appear between the maximum and minimum marks on the translucent expansion tank. Do not remove the filler cap except to top up as air might become trapped in the system and reduce cooling efficiency. Top up with a mixture of antifreeze and water equal to that remaining in the engine. When in doubt, top up with a mixture of 40–50 percent antifreeze and water, except in areas of the country where there is no danger of frost. If only water is added, it is wise to add rust inhibitor to the cooling system.

Expansion tank

Rear Axle Fluid

The level of lubricant in the rear axle should be checked every 6,000 miles. Top up with SAE 90 gear oil if the level is not up to the filler hole. Vehicles equipped with a limited-slip differential require a lubricant meeting American Military Standard MIL-L-2105B.

Rear axle drain plug locations

1. Filler plug   2. Drain plug

Steering gear filler plug location

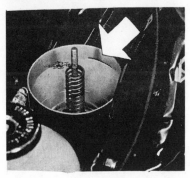

Power steering reservoir fluid level

Steering Gear (Manual) Fluid

Every 6,000 miles, check to see if the oil level in the steering box reaches the filler plug. Top up if necessary with SAE 80 Hypoid oil.

Power Steering Reservoir Fluid

On vehicles equipped with power (servo) steering, the fluid level in the reservoir should be checked every 6,000

Capacities

Year	Model	Engine Displacement Cu in. (cc)	Engine Crankcase (qt) With Filter	Without Filter	Transmission (pts) Manual 3 spd	4 spd *	Automatic	Drive Axle (pt)	Gasoline Tank (gal)	Cooling System (qt)
1970	142, 144, 145	122 (1990)	4.0	3.4	——	1.6 (3.4)	13.1	2.7	15.3	9.0
	164	183 (2978)	6.3	5.5	——	1.3 (3.0)	17.3	3.4	15.3	13.0
	1800	122 (1990)	4.0	3.4	——	(3.4)	——	2.7	12.0	9.0
1971	142, 144, 145	122 (1990)	4.0	3.4	——	1.6 (3.4)	13.1	2.7	15.3	10.5
	164	183 (2978)	6.3	5.5	——	1.3 (3.0)	17.3	3.4	15.3	13.0
	1800	122 (1990)	4.0	3.4	——	(3.4)	13.3	2.7	12.0	9.0
1972–73	142, 144, 145	122 (1990)	4.0	3.4	——	1.6 (3.4)	13.5	2.7	15.3	10.5
	164	183 (2978)	6.3	5.5	——	1.3 (3.0)	17.7	3.4	15.3	13.0
	1800	122 (1990)	4.0	3.4	——	(3.4)	13.5	2.7	12.0	9.0

* Figures in parentheses are for overdrive transmission.

miles. With the engine shut off, the fluid level should appear approximately ¼ in. above the level mark inside the reservoir. Top up as necessary while the engine is stopped with Type A automatic transmission fluid or Dexron.

Battery Electrolyte

At fuel stops, check the electrolyte level in the battery. If the level does not reach the slit tubes on the covers, top up with distilled water. Do not overfill as the highly corrosive electrolyte may splash out and damage components in the engine compartment.

CAUTION: *The gases formed inside the battery cells are highly explosive. Never check the level of the electrolyte by lighting a match.*

AIR CLEANER

The air cleaner should be serviced every 24,000 miles under normal driving conditions. When operating the vehicle in extremely dusty areas or in areas of high industrial pollution, the element should be changed sooner. Inspect the filter periodically. A clogged air cleaner will adversely affect the performance of your engine and will result in increased fuel consumption.

142S, 144S, 145S, AND 164

On carbureted 1970–72 Volvos, the element is removed from the air cleaner by disconnecting the hose clamp from the air preheating unit and the clips securing the air cleaner housing halves together. The old element is then lifted out and a new one is lowered in, making sure that the word "up" faces up. When securing the air cleaner housing halves together, take care not to damage the thermostat body for the intake air.

Air cleaner—142S, 144S, 145S, 164

142E, 144E, AND 145E

In order to remove the air cleaner from fuel-injected 140 series Volvos, you must: turn the front wheels fully to the right; position the expansion tank for the cooling system to one side; disconnect the inlet duct hose; and unfasten the attaching bolts for the air cleaner. On these models, the air cleaner is a one-piece disposable unit and must be replaced as a unit.

Air cleaner—142E, 144E, 145E

164E

On fuel-injected 164 series Volvos, the clips securing the cover to the air cleaner must be undone and the old element removed. When refitting the cover to the air cleaner, make sure that the arrow points coincide.

Air cleaner—164E

1800E AND 1800ES

On all 1800E and 1800ES models, the radiator grille must first be removed to gain access to the air cleaner. Remove the grille clips by inserting pliers between the

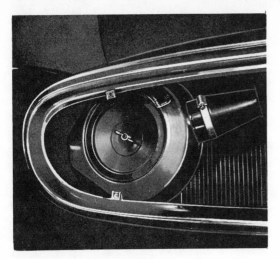

Air cleaner—1800E, 1800ES

ribs of the grille and lifting up on the front end of the clips. Push each clip into its hole and remove the grille. Unscrew the wing nut on the air cleaner cover and remove the element.

POSITIVE CRANKCASE VENTILATION (PCV) SYSTEM

Every 12 months or 12,000 miles, the PCV System is serviced. Remove and clean the nipple (3) on the intake manifold on carbureted versions, and on the inlet duct on injected versions. Remove the hoses (4 and 2) running from the breather cap to the nipple, and from the air cleaner insert (1) to the flame guard (5) respectively. Clean the hoses by running a kerosine-soaked rag through them until free of blowby material. The flame guard (5), which is located on the driver's side of the engine block, should also be removed and

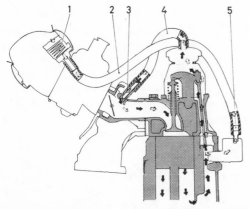

Positive crankcase ventilation system—B20B shown

cleaned. Replace any rubber hose that is in poor condition with a heat-treated, preferably factory replacement, hose.

FUEL EVAPORATIVE CONTROL SYSTEM CANISTER

The canister filter to the evaporative control system is replaced every 24 months or 24,000 miles. On 1970 140 series and 164 models, the canister is located on the left (driver's) side of the engine compartment. On 1971–73 140 series and 164 models, the canister is situated on the right (passenger's) side of the engine compartment. All 1800E and 1800ES models have an evaporative canister located behind the radiator grille.

To remove the canister filter, slacken the bracket screws, raise the venting filter body, and pull out the foam plastic filter from the bottom of the canister.

Fuel evaporative control system canister location —fuel injection engine shown

FUEL FILTER

On all carbureted 1970–72 Volvos, the fuel filter is removed and cleaned every six months or 6,000 miles. The filter is located integral with the fuel pump on the driver's side of the engine. To remove the filter on B20B engines, loosen the retaining screws and lift off the cover. To remove the filter on B30A engines, unscrew the plug and filter assembly on the side of the fuel pump. The filter is then cleaned in a low-volatility, petroleum-based solvent, such as kerosene. After replacing the cleaned element, and installing the cover and retain-

Fuel filter plug location—B20B

Fuel filter plug location—B30A

ing screw on B20B engines, and after installing the plug and filter assembly on B30A engines, run the engine at fast idle and check for fuel leaks. Replace the gasket if any fuel seepage is evident.

On all fuel-injected Volvos, the fuel filter is replaced every 12 months or 12,000 miles. The filter is located beneath the car, next to the fuel tank. Prior to removal of the filter, clean the fuel lines and the sur-

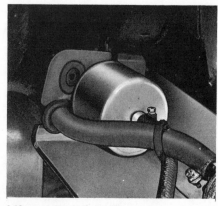

Fuel filter—1972 fuel injection type

rounding area to prevent dirt from entering the fuel system during the change. Remove the fuel lines from the filter one at a time and pinch each shut to prevent fuel from spilling out. Discard the old filter and replace it with a new one. When installing the new filter, make sure that the arrow on the filter points in the direction of flow. After installation, run the engine at fast idle and check for leaks.

FUEL TANK PICK-UP SCREEN

The fuel tank pick-up screen must be removed and cleaned every 12 months or 12,000 miles on 1973 models. The screen is accessible after removing the fuel tank's bottom countersunk plug with a drain plug wrench.

CAUTION: *It is advisable that the tank be as near to empty as possible, to avoid spillage of highly flammable gasoline. Have a container of sufficient size on hand.*

Pull the filter off the pick-up tube and soak it in solvent. When replacing the filter on the tube, make sure that it is centered on the tube so as not to restrict the fuel flow.

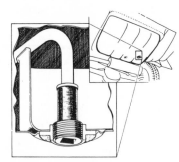

Fuel tank pick-up screen location—1973

COOLING SYSTEM

The engine coolant is drained and flushed every 12,000 miles, preferably in the autumn before the cold weather sets in. The cooling system is drained by opening the drain cock on the right side of the engine and disconnecting the lower radiator hose. The expansion tank is drained by inverting it or loosening the retaining brackets and lifting it sufficiently for the coolant to flow into the radiator. After the entire system has been drained it should be flushed with clean water.

The cooling system is filled with a mixture of 40–50 percent ethylene glycol anti-freeze and water. Set the heater control to maximum and after closing the drain cock and refitting the lower radiator hose, fill the radiator to the top through the filler opening. Fill the expansion tank to slightly above the "max" level. Run the engine for a short period to allow any trapped air to escape. Let the engine cool and recheck the coolant level. The radiator should be full and the coolant level in the expansion tank at "max."

TIRES

Tire Inflation Chart (cold pressures)

Model	Size Tire	Front *	Rear *
142, 144	6.85 x 15	24 (25)	26 (28)
	165R15	26 (27)	27 (31)
145	6.85 x 15	21 (23)	26 (38)
	165R15	25	28
164	6.85 x 15	24 (25)	26 (28)
	165R15	27 (29)	27 (34)
1800	165R15	26	28
	185HR15	25	27

* Figure in parentheses apply to fully loaded vehicles.

When prolonged high-speed driving is planned, the tire pressure should be increased by 4 psi. Never exceed 32 psi for 185HR15, 36 psi for 165R15, or 40 psi for 6.85 × 15.

BATTERY CARE

Every six months or 6,000 miles, the state of battery charge should be checked with a hydrometer. A fully charged battery should have a hydrometer reading of 1.260–1.310 specific gravity at 80° F electrolyte temperature. To correct readings for temperature variations, add 0.004 to the hydrometer reading for every 10° F that the electrolyte is above 80° F; subtract 0.004 for every 10° F below 80° F electrolyte temperature. The readings obtained in all six cells should be nearly equal. If any cell is markedly lower, it is defective. If this low reading is not improved by charging, the battery must be replaced. When charging a weak or sulphated (brownish color of electrolyte) battery, the slow charging method must be used. Never allow electrolyte temperature to exceed 120° F during charging.

At the same time the state of charge is checked, inspect the battery terminals for a tight fit on the poles, and check for corrosion. Remove any deposits with a wire brush, and coat the terminals with vaseline to prevent further corrosion.

DRIVE BELT ADJUSTMENT

Accessory drive belt tension is checked every six months or 6,000 miles. Loose belts can cause poor engine cooling and diminish alternator or power steering pump output. A belt that is too tight places a severe strain on the water pump, alternator, and power steering pump bearings.

Alternator drive belt tension is correct when the deflection made with light finger pressure on the belt at a point midway between the water pump and alternator is about ½ in. Power steering belt deflection at the midway point should be approximately ¼ in. Any belt that is glazed, frayed, or stretched so that it cannot be tightened sufficiently must be replaced.

Incorrect belt tension is corrected by moving the driven accessory (alternator or power steering pump) away from or toward the driving pulley. Loosen the mounting and adjusting bolts on the respective accessory and tighten them, once the belt tension is correct. Never position a metal pry bar on the rear end of the alternator housing or against the power steering pump reservoir; they can be deformed easily.

CHANGING ENGINE OIL AND FILTER

Except for the 1,500 mile break-in period of oil change, the normal interval for oil and filter change is six months or 6,000 miles. After the engine has reached operating temperature, shut it off, place a drip pan beneath the sump, and remove the drain plug. Allow the engine to drain thoroughly before replacing the drain plug. Place the drip pan beneath the oil filter. To remove the filter, turn it counterclockwise with a strap wrench. Wipe the contact surface of the new filter clean of all dirt and coat the rubber gasket with clean engine oil. Also wipe clean the adaptor on the block. To install, hand-turn the new filter clockwise until the gasket just contacts the cylinder block. Do not use a strap wrench to install. Then hand-turn the filter ½ additional turn. Unscrew the filler cap on the valve cover and fill the crankcase to the proper level on the dipstick with the recommended grade of oil. Replace the cap, start the engine, and operate at fast idle. Check the oil filter contact area and the drain plug for leaks.

NOTE: *Certain operating conditions may warrant more frequent changes. If the vehicle is used for short trips, water condensation and low-temperature deposits may make it necessary to change the oil sooner. If the vehicle is used mostly in stop-and-go city traffic, corrosive acids and high-temperature deposits may necessitate shorter oil changing intervals. The shorter intervals are also true for industrial or rural areas where high concentrations of dust contaminate the oil.*

CHANGING TRANSMISSION OIL

Manual Transmission

When breaking in a new or rebuilt transmission, the transmission oil should be changed after the first 1,500 miles to remove any metal particles. Thereafter, the oil is changed every 25,000 miles.

After the transmission has reached operating temperature (driven 5–7 miles), the oil may be changed. Place a drip pan beneath the vehicle and remove the drain plug and the filler plug. On vehicles equipped with overdrive, remove the six bolts and cover, allowing the unit to drain also. At this time, the prefilter and fine filter must be removed and cleaned in solvent. To remove the fine filter, SVO tool no. 2836 must be used to unscrew the filter housing. After blowing the filters dry with compressed air, install the fine filter in its socket with a new seal. Torque the plug

Overdrive unit cover

Overdrive fine filter assembly

1. Filter   2. Seal   3. Plug

for the filter housing with SVO tool no. 2836 to 16 ft lbs. Install the prefilter and the cover with a new gasket making sure that the magnet is in place. Replace the drain plug (2) in the transmission and fill up to the filler plug with the proper oil. All 140 series Volvos without overdrive equipped with the M40 gearbox use SAE 80 gear oil, or if none is available, SAE 30 engine oil. All 140 series Volvos with overdrive and all 1800 series Volvos equipped with the M41 gearbox, or 164 model Volvos with overdrive equipped with the M410 gearbox use SAE 30 or SAE 20W-40 engine oil. Model 164 Volvos, without overdrive, and equipped with the M400 gearbox use SAE 90 gear oil or SAE 40 engine oil.

Automatic Transmission

The oil fill in the Borg-Warner 35 automatic transmission need only be changed when the unit is torn down for repairs or rebuilding. Rebuilding of the automatic transmission is best referred to a Volvo agency.

CHANGING REAR AXLE OIL

The oil in the rear axle is changed after the first 1,500 miles, and thereafter only if the unit is rebuilt. When changing the oil after the break-in period, remove the filler plug (1) and the drain plug (2), allowing the warm oil to drain into a vessel. Be sure to wipe clean the magnet on the plug of all metal filings and foreign impurities. Install the drain plug (2) and fill the axle to the bottom of the filler hole with SAE 90 gear oil meeting American Military Standard MIL-L-2105B.

CHASSIS GREASING

Aside from the yearly greasing of all the joints for the throttle linkage, parking brake, and pedal linkages, no regular greasing of front-end components or universal joints is required. Use regular chassis lube on the above-mentioned joints once a year or if binding is noticed.

The upper and lower control arm ball joints as well as the tie rod and steering rod ball joints are lined with plastic (Teflon®) and do not require lubrication. However, every 12,000 miles, check the rubber seals of these ball joints for cracking or damage. Replace any damaged seal with a new one, making sure to pack the new seal with multipurpose chassis grease.

DISTRIBUTOR LUBRICATION

Every six months or 6,000 miles, the distributor shaft, cam lobes, and advance

Distributor lubrication

mechanism are lubricated. To lubricate the distributor shaft, fill the oil cup (3) on the side of the distributor with light engine oil. The cam lobes (2) are lightly smeared with Bosch Ft 1 v 4 or similar silicone cam lobe grease. The advance mechanism is lubricated by pouring two or three drops of SAE 10W engine oil on the wick (1) of the distributor shaft.

BODY LUBRICATION

In order to avoid rattles and unnecessary wear, lubricate the following body parts every 6,000 miles.

No.	Lubricating Point	Lubricant
1.	Hood lock	Paraffin wax
2.	Hood hinges	Light oil
3.	Ventilation window lock and hinges	Light oil
4.	Key holes	Lock oil with graphite
5.	Striker plate	Paraffin wax
6.	Door lock outer sliding surfaces	Paraffin wax
7.	Trunk lid hinges	Light oil
8.	Trunk lid lock	Light oil
	Trunk lid keyhole	Lock oil with graphite
9.	Door stop	Paraffin wax
10.	Door hinges	Polyethylene grease
11.	Front seat slide rails and latch devices	Paraffin wax, oil
12.	Window regulator, locking device	Light oil, silicon grease

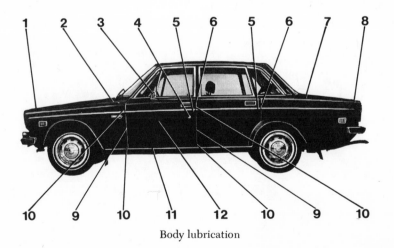

Body lubrication

Pushing, Towing, and Jump Starting

Pushing is not recommended for your Volvo as possible mismatching of bumper heights, especially over undulating road surfaces, may result in rear-end body damage.

Volvos may be towed, however, by attaching a tow line to the towing loop located beneath the car on the front axle member. The 140 series and 164 model Volvos may also be towed from the rear by the towing loop under the spare wheel housing. Never attach a tow line to the bumper.

If the car is equipped with an automatic transmission, special precautions must be taken. The car must be towed with the selector lever in the neutral (N) position. If the fluid level is correct in the transmission, the car may be towed a maximum distance of 20 miles at a maximum towing speed of 20 mph. If the transmission is faulty, or if it is necessary to tow the car for a distance greater than 20 miles, the driveshaft must be disconnected, or the car must be towed with the rear wheels raised.

Failure to observe these precautions may result in damage to the automatic transmission.

If your Volvo fails to start and is equipped with a manual transmission, it may be started by towing. The towing vehicle should start out smoothly and be driven at an even speed. Switch the ignition "on" and depress the clutch. On carbureted models, pull out the choke fully if the engine is cold. Do not pump the accelerator pedal. Place the transmission in third gear and, as the towing car picks up speed, gradually release the clutch. Once the engine fires, depress the clutch pedal and feather the gas, so as not to collide with the friend who is towing you.

Cars with automatic transmissions may not be started by towing. If the battery is dead, the car may be started with the use of jumper cables. Always connect the positive cable of the assist battery to the positive pole of the car battery and likewise for the negative cable and pole. Never use a high-speed battery charger as a starting aid on fuel-injected models, as serious damage to the electronic components may result. If the high-speed charger is used to recharge the battery, the engine must be turned off and the battery disconnected from the car's electrical system.

Chapter Two

Tune-up and Troubleshooting

Tune-Up Procedures

CAUTION: *When working with a running engine, make sure that there is proper ventilation. Also make sure that the transmission is in neutral, and the parking brake is firmly applied. Always keep hands, clothing, and tools well clear of the radiator fan.*

SPARK PLUG REMOVAL AND INSTALLATION

Every six months or 6,000 miles, the spark plugs should be removed for inspection. At this time they should be cleaned and regapped. At 12-month or 12,000-mile intervals, the plugs should be replaced.

Prior to removal, number each spark plug wire with a piece of masking tape bearing the cylinder number. Remove each spark plug wire by grasping its rubber boot on the end and twisting slightly to free the wire from the plug. Using a $^{13}/_{16}$ in. spark plug socket, turn the plugs counterclockwise to remove them. Do not allow any foreign matter to enter the cylinders through the spark plug holes.

Consult the spark plug inspection chart in step 4.6 of the "Troubleshooting" section when in doubt about plug condition. If the spark plugs are to be reused, check the porcelain insulator for cracks and the elec-trodes for excessive wear. Replace the entire set if one plug is damaged. Clean the reusable plugs with a stiff wire brush, or have them cleaned in a plug sandblasting machine (found in many service stations). Uneven wear of the center or ground electrode may be corrected by leveling off the unevenly worn section with a file.

The gap must be checked with a feeler gauge before installing the plug in the engine. With the ground electrode positioned parallel to the center electrode, a 0.030 in. wire gauge must pass through the opening with a slight drag. If the air gap between the two electrodes is not correct, the ground electrode must be bent to bring it to specifications.

After the plugs are gapped correctly, they may be inserted into their holes and hand-tightened. Be careful not to cross-thread the plugs. Torque the plugs to the

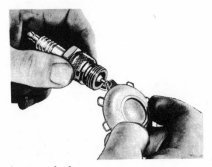

Checking spark plug gap

15

Tune-up Specifications

Year	Engine Type	Spark Plugs Type	Spark Plugs Gap (in.)	Distributor Point Dwell (deg)	Distributor Point Gap (in.)	Ignition Timing (deg) MT	Ignition Timing (deg) AT	Intake Valve Opens (deg)	Fuel Pump Pressure (psi)	Compression Pressure (psi)	Idle Speed (rpm) MT	Idle Speed (rpm) AT	Valve Clearance (in.) In	Valve Clearance (in.) Ex
1970–72	B 20 B	Bosch ③W200T35	0.030	59–65	②	10B	10B	TDC	1.56–3.55	170–200	800	700	0.020–0.022	0.020–0.022
1970–71	B 20 E	Bosch ④W225T35	0.030	59–65	0.016–0.020	10B	10B	5.5B	28	170–200	900	800	0.016–0.018	0.016–0.018
1972–73	B 20 F	⑤	0.030	59–65	0.014 min	10B	10B	5.5B	28	129–156	900	800	0.016–0.018	0.016–0.018
1970–72	B 30 A	Bosch W200T35	0.030	37–43	0.010 min	10B	10B	TDC	2.1–3.5	①	800	700	0.020–0.022	0.020–0.022
1972–73	B 30 F	Bosch W200T35	0.030	37–43	0.010 min	10B	10B	TDC	28	129–156	900	800	0.020–0.022	0.020–0.022

B Before Top Dead Center
① 1970 156–185
1971 170–200
1972 142–170
② 1972 0.014
1970–71 0.016–0.020
③ Severe service—W225T35
④ Severe service—W240T1
⑤ 1972 Bosch W225T35
1973 Bosch W200T35

proper specification with a $^{13}\!/_{16}$ in. socket and a torque wrench. Install each spark plug wire on its respective plug, making sure that each spark plug end is making good metal-to-metal contact in its wire socket.

BREAKER POINTS AND CONDENSER REMOVAL AND INSTALLATION

Volvo recommends that the breaker points be inspected and adjusted every six months or 6,000 miles. If, upon inspection, the points prove to be faulty, they must be replaced with the condenser as a unit.

CAUTION: *Make sure the ignition is off.*

Remove the distributor cap and rotor from the top of the distributor, taking note of their placement. On fuel-injected six cylinder models, remove the breaker point protective cover. Place a screwdriver against the breaker points and examine the condition of the contacts. Replace the points if the contacts are blackened, pitted, or worn excessively, if the breaker arm has lost its tension, or if the fiber rubbing block on the breaker has become worn or loose. Contact points that have become slightly burned (light gray) may be cleaned with a point file.

To replace the points and condenser, disconnect the electrical leads for both at the primary connection. Remove the lockscrew for the contact breakers and lift them straight up. Loosen the condenser bracket retaining screw and slide out the condenser. While the points are out, lubricate the breaker cam with a very light coating of silicone-based grease. Clean the distributor base plate with alcohol to free it of any oil film that might impede completion of the ground circuit. Also clean the contact point surfaces with the solvent. Install the new points and new condenser and tighten their retaining screws. Connect the electrical leads for both at the primary connection. Make sure that the point contacts are aligned horizontally and vertically. If the points are not aligned properly, bend the stationary arm to suit.

The breaker points must be correctly gapped before proceeding any further. Turn the engine until the rubbing block on the point assembly is resting on the high point of a breaker cam lobe. Loosen the point hold-down screw slightly and insert a feeler gauge of the proper thickness be-

Recess for adjusting contact points

tween the point contacts. Fine adjustment is made by inserting a screwdriver into the adjusting recess and turning the screwdriver until the proper size feeler gauge passes between the point contacts with a slight drag. Without disturbing the setting, tighten the breaker point retaining screw.

If a dwell meter is available, proceed to "Dwell Angle Setting." A dwell meter is considered a more accurate means of measuring point gap. If the meter is not available, except on fuel-injected six cylinder models, proceed to replace the rotor in top of the distributor shaft, making sure that the tab inside the rotor aligns with the slot on the distributor. Before replacing the rotor on fuel-injected six cylinder models, install the breaker point protective cover. Place the distributor cap on top of the distributor and snap the cap clasps into the slots on the cap. Make sure that all the spark plug wires fit snugly into the cap. Proceed to "Ignition Timing Adjustment."

DWELL ANGLE SETTING

The dwell angle is the number of degrees of distributor cam rotation through which the breaker points remain fully closed (conducting electricity). Increasing the point gap decreases dwell, while decreasing the point gap increases dwell.

Using a dwell meter of known accuracy, connect the red lead (positive) wire of the meter to the distributor primary wire connection on the positive (+) side of the coil, and the black ground (negative) wire of the meter to a good ground on the engine (e.g. thermostat housing nut).

The dwell angle may be checked either

with the distributor cap and rotor installed and the engine running, or with the cap and rotor removed and the engine cranking at starter speed. The meter gives a constant reading with the engine running. With the engine cranking, the reading will fluctuate between zero degrees dwell and the maximum figure for that angle. While cranking, the maximum figure is the correct one for that setting. Never attempt to change dwell angle while the ignition is on. Touching the point contacts or primary wire connection with a metal screwdriver may result in a 12 volt shock.

To change the dwell angle, loosen the point retaining screw slightly and make the approximate correction. Tighten the retaining screw and test the dwell with the engine cranking. If the dwell appears to be correct, install the breaker point protective cover, if so equipped, the rotor and distributor cap, and test the dwell with the engine running. Take the engine through its entire rpm range and observe the dwell meter. The dwell should remain within specifications at all times. Great fluctuation of dwell at different engine speeds indicates worn distributor parts.

Following the dwell angle adjustment, the ignition timing must be checked. A 1° increase in dwell results in the ignition timing being retarded 2° and vice versa.

IGNITION TIMING ADJUSTMENT

Volvo recommends that the ignition timing be checked every six months or 6,000 miles. The timing adjustment should always follow a breaker point gap and/or dwell angle adjustment, and be made with the engine at operating temperature.

Clean the crankshaft damper and pointer on the water pump housing with a solvent-soaked rag so that the marks can be seen. Connect a stroboscopic timing light to the no. 1 cylinder spark plug and to the battery, according to the manufacturer's instructions. Scribe a mark on the crankshaft damper and on the marker with chalk or luminescent (day-glo) paint to highlight the correct timing setting. On carbureted models, disconnect the vacuum advance line from the intake manifold at the distributor and plug it with a pencil, golf tee, or some other suitably small object. On fuel-injected models, disconnect and plug the above-mentioned vacuum line and also disconnect the hose between

Ignition timing marks

the air cleaner and the inlet duct at the duct. On 1973 models with exhaust gas recirculation, disconnect and plug the vacuum hose at the EGR valve.

Attach a tachometer to the engine and set the idle speed to specifications. With the engine running, aim the timing light at the pointer and the marks on the damper. If the marks made with the chalk or paint coincide when the timing light flashes, the engine is timed correctly. If the marks do not coincide, stop the engine, loosen the distributor attaching bolt, and start the engine again. While observing the timing light flashes on the markers, grasp the distributor vacuum regulator—not the distributor cap—and rotate the distributor until the marks do coincide. Stop the engine and tighten the distributor attaching bolt, taking care not to disturb the setting. As a final check, start the engine once more to make sure that the timing marks align.

Reconnect all disconnected hoses and remove the timing light and tachometer from the engine.

VALVE LASH ADJUSTMENT

The recommended maintenance interval for valve clearance adjustment is 12 months or 12,000 miles. Valve clearance should be checked at every tune-up or whenever excessive valve train noise is noticed. The clearance may be checked with the engine hot or cold.

Remove the valve cover and crank the engine until number one cylinder is at Top Dead Center (TDC). TDC is the point at which both intake and exhaust valves are fully closed and the piston is on its compression stroke. To find TDC, crank the engine, preferably with a remote starter switch, until the pushrods for both valves on the subject cylinder stop falling. Stop cranking the engine. At this point, it will be easier to find TDC by turning the engine over manually. To accomplish this, remove all of the spark plugs so the compression and resistance to cranking are diminished, and remove the distributor cap so the position of the rotor may be observed. To crank the engine manually, position a socket or closed-end wrench—with a long handle for greater leverage—on the crankshaft damper bolt and turn the crankshaft in the required direction. Do not attempt to crank the engine by grasping the viscous drive fan; damage to the fan may result. At TDC, the piston for the subject cylinder should be at its highest point of travel. Make a visual check or insert a screwdriver through the spark plug hole to make sure that the piston is no longer traveling upward. As an additional check, the distributor rotor should be pointed to the spark plug wire for the subject cylinder at TDC.

Number one cylinder is at TDC when the 0 degree mark on the crankshaft damper aligns with the pointer on the water pump housing. On four-cylinder models, with number one cylinder at TDC, valves (counting from the front) 1, 2, 3, and 5 may be adjusted. On six-cylinder models, with number one cylinder at TDC, valves 1, 2, 3, 6, 7, and 10 may be adjusted.

Insert a step-type (go and no-go) feeler gauge of the specified thickness between the rocker arm and the valve stem. Adjust each rocker arm so that the thinner gauge slides in easily but the thicker gauge cannot be inserted. Adjustment is accomplished by loosening the locknut and turning the adjusting screw and then, without disturbing the adjustment, retightening the locknut.

The remainder of the valves may be adjusted in the following manner. On four-cylinder models, with no. 4 cylinder at TDC, valves (counting from the front) 4, 6, 7, and 8 may be adjusted. On six-cylinder models, with no. 6 cylinder at TDC, valves 4, 5, 8, 9, 11, and 12 may be adjusted.

Make sure that the feeler gauge of the minimum thickness may pass between the

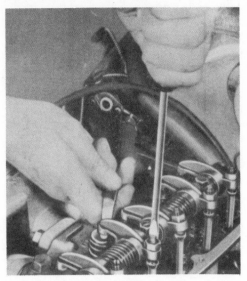

Adjusting valve clearance

rocker arm and the valve stem easily. Excessive clearance may cause greater valve train noise but insufficient clearance may burn a valve. When in doubt, be generous with the clearance adjustment to avoid costly valve work.

After adjusting the valves, replace the valve cover with a new gasket, if needed, and install the spark plugs and distributor cap if they were removed. Start the engine. Listen for excessive valve train noise and check for oil leaks.

CARBURETOR ADJUSTMENTS

Idle Speed and Mixture

ZENITH-STROMBERG 175 CD 2SE

NOTE: *Consult local law enforcement agency for regulations regarding adjustment of emission control equipment.*

1. Check the oil level in the damper cylinders. Top up as necessary as outlined in chapter one.

2. Run the engine until it has reached full operating temperature. A good way to check this is to feel the upper radiator hose. When the engine reaches operating temperature, the thermostat opens, filling the upper radiator hose with 180° coolant.

3. Adjust the idling speed of the engine to the specifications on the tune-up chart by turning the throttle stopscrews. Turn the screws on both carburetors equally. Check to make sure that both carburetors have the same air valve lift by visually

Stromberg 175 CD 2SE carburetor—left side

1. Lever for throttle control
2. Clamp for choke wire
3. Suction chamber
4. Hydraulic damper
5. Vent drilling from floatchamber
6. Drilling for air supply under diaphragm
7. Drilling for air supply to temp. compensator and idle trimming screw
8. Cold start device
9. Cam disc for fast idle
10. Connection for choke control
11. Fast idle stop screw
12. Throttle stop screw

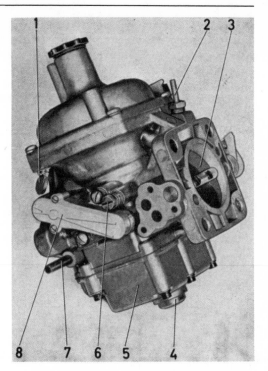

Stromberg 175 CD 2SE carburetor—right side

1. Sealed plug
2. Connection for vacuum hose to distributor
3. Primary throttle
4. Floatchamber plug
5. Floatchamber
6. Idle trimming screw
7. Connection for fuel hose
8. Temperature compensator

comparing the distance between the carburetor housing bridge and the air valve.

4. Adjust the idle mixture of the engine with the idle trimming screws until the highest engine speed is attained. The basic setting is two turns counterclockwise from lock. Again, turn the screws on both carburetors equally.

5. Adjust the idling speed of the engine to specifications with the throttle stop-screws.

SU HIF 6

1. Check the oil level in the damper cylinders. Top up as necessary as outlined in chapter one.

2. Remove the air cleaner.

3. Adjust the fuel jets to their basic setting by lifting the air valve and turning the adjusting screw until the upper edge of the fuel jet is level with the bridge. The jet is then lowered two and one-half turns clockwise. This basic jet setting is correct for a carburetor temperature of approximately 70° F. Turning the adjusting screw a quarter turn in either direction compensates for a temperature difference of approximately 70° F. Turn the adjusting screw less than the two and one-half turns for temperatures above 70° F, and more than two and one-half turns for lower temperatures.

4. Run the engine until it has reached full operating temperature. The upper radiator hose should be very warm at this point.

5. Adjust the idling speed of the engine to the specifications on the tune-up chart

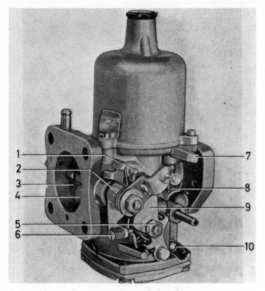

SU HIF 6 carburetor—front, left side

1. Throttle stop screw
2. Return spring
3. Throttle
4. Overrev valve
5. Cold-start device
6. Fast-idle stop screw
7. Attachment for choke control
8. Lift pin
9. Cam disc for fast idle
10. Screw head for float shaft

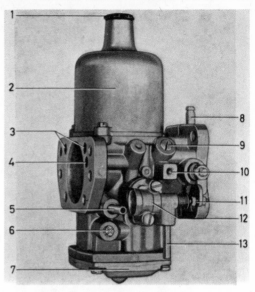

SU HIF 6 carburetor—front, right side

1. Hydraulic damper
2. Suction chamber
3. Drilling for air supply under air valve
4. Vent hole from floatchamber
5. Connection for fuel line
6. Jet adjusting screw
7. Floatchamber cover
8. Connection (positive) for hose to venting filter
9. Plug for outlet for speed compensator (air condition)
10. Boss for guard
11. Hot start valve adjusting screw
12. Hot start valve
13. Outlet from floatchamber (connection for hose to venting filter)

by turning the throttle stopscrews. Turn the screws on both carburetors equally. Check to make sure that both carburetors have the same air valve lift by visually comparing the distance between the carburetor housing bridge and the air valve.

6. Remove the plastic caps over the mixture adjusting screws. Turn both adjusting screws equally until maximum rpm is achieved. Turn both adjusting screws equally in the opposite direction until the engine just starts to falter. Remember that, in this case, the proper setting is not when maximum rpm is reached but when the engine just starts to falter. As a further check, unscrew the adjusting screws 1/4–1/2 of a turn. The speed should then drop a further 20–40 rpm. Turn back the screws equally to the point where the engine just starts to falter and install the plastic caps over the screws.

7. Adjust the idling speed of the engine to specifications with the throttle stopscrews.

BOSCH ELECTRONIC FUEL INJECTION ADJUSTMENTS

Idle Speed and Mixture

The idle mixture adjustment or CO value may be set only with the use of a CO meter. This adjustment is made by attaching a CO meter to the exhaust pipe of a vehicle with a warm (176° F) engine, and turning the adjusting screw of the Bosch control unit (beneath the passenger seat) until the correct CO value is obtained. The correct value is 1–1.5 percent for cars with manual transmissions and 0.5–1.0 percent for cars with automatic transmissions. Because this operation requires highly technical skills and expensive equipment, it is best referred to a Volvo or Bosch agency. In other words, don't mess with the control unit.

The idle speed adjustment may, on the other hand, be set with a tachometer and

Idle speed adjusting screw location—B20E, B20F

Idle speed adjusting screw location—B30F

an average amount of expertise. The check should be made with the engine idling at operating temperature (176° F). On 140 and 1800 series Volvos, remove the air cleaner-to-inlet duct hose. Check to see that the auxiliary air regulator is closed properly by removing the inlet duct-to-regulator hose and covering the opening with your hand. If the idle speed differs greatly, the engine is not fully warm or the regulator is faulty. Fit the hose again and adjust the idle speed to specifications with the idle adjusting screw. The idle adjusting screw is located on the inlet duct below the air cleaner hose opening on four-cylinder models, and inline in the auxiliary air pipe on six-cylinder models. (See illustrations.) On 140 and 1800 series Volvos, install the air cleaner hose.

Engine Tune-Up

Engine tune-up is a procedure performed to restore engine performance, deteriorated due to normal wear and loss of adjustment. The three major areas considered in a routine tune-up are compression, ignition, and carburetion, although valve adjustment may be included.

A tune-up is performed in three steps: *analysis*, in which it is determined whether normal wear is responsible for performance loss, and which parts require replacement or service; *parts replacement or service*; and *adjustment*, in which engine adjustments are returned to original specifications. Since the advent of emission control equipment, precision adjustment has become increasingly critical, in order to maintain pollutant emission levels.

Analysis

The procedures below are used to indicate where adjustments, parts service or replacement are necessary within the realm of a normal tune-up. If, following these tests, all systems appear to be functioning properly, proceed to the Troubleshooting Section for further diagnosis.

—Remove all spark plugs, noting the cylinder in which they were installed. Remove the air cleaner, and position the throttle and choke in the full open position. Disconnect the coil high tension lead from the coil and the distributor cap. Insert a compression gauge into the spark plug port of each cylinder, in succession, and crank the engine with

Maxi. Press. Lbs. Sq. In.	Min. Press. Lbs. Sq. In.	Max. Press. Lbs. Sq. In.	Min. Press. Lbs. Sq. In.
134	101	188	141
136	102	190	142
138	104	192	144
140	105	194	145
142	107	196	147
146	110	198	148
148	111	200	150
150	113	202	151
152	114	204	153
154	115	206	154
156	117	208	156
158	118	210	157
160	120	212	158
162	121	214	160
164	123	216	162
166	124	218	163
168	126	220	165
170	127	222	166
172	129	224	168
174	131	226	169
176	132	228	171
178	133	230	172
180	135	232	174
182	136	234	175
184	138	236	177
186	140	238	178

Compression pressure limits
© Buick Div. G.M. Corp.)

the starter to obtain the highest possible reading. Record the readings, and compare the highest to the lowest on the compression pressure limit chart. If the difference exceeds the limits on the chart, or if all readings are excessively low, proceed to a wet compression check (see Troubleshooting Section).

—Evaluate the spark plugs according to the spark plug chart

in the Troubleshooting Section, and proceed as indicated in the chart.

—Remove the distributor cap, and inspect it inside and out for cracks and/or carbon tracks, and inside for excessive wear or burning of the rotor contacts. If any of these faults are evident, the cap must be replaced.

—Check the breaker points for burning, pitting or wear, and the contact heel resting on the distributor cam for excessive wear. If defects are noted, replace the entire breaker point set.

—Remove and inspect the rotor. If the contacts are burned or worn, or if the rotor is excessively loose on the distributor shaft (where applicable), the rotor must be replaced.

—Inspect the spark plug leads and the coil high tension lead for cracks or brittleness. If any of the wires appear defective, the entire set should be replaced.

—Check the air filter to ensure that it is functioning properly.

Parts Replacement and Service

The determination of whether to replace or service parts is at the mechanic's discretion; however, it is suggested that any parts in questionable condition be replaced rather than reused.

—Clean and regap, or replace, the spark plugs as needed. Lightly coat the threads with engine oil and install the plugs. CAUTION: *Do not over-torque taper-seat spark plugs, or plugs being installed in aluminum cylinder heads.*

23

SPARK PLUG TORQUE

Thread size	Cast-Iron Heads	Aluminum Heads
10 mm.	14	11
14 mm.	30	27
18 mm.	34*	32
7/8 in.—18	37	35

* 17 ft. lbs. for tapered plugs using no gaskets.

—If the distributor cap is to be reused, clean the inside with a dry rag, and remove corrosion from the rotor contact points with fine emery cloth. Remove the spark plug wires one by one, and clean the wire ends and the inside of the towers. If the boots are loose, they should be replaced. If the cap is to be replaced, transfer the wires one by one, cleaning the wire ends and replacing the boots if necessary.

—If the original points are to remain in service, clean them lightly with emery cloth, lubricate the contact heel with grease specifically designed for this purpose. Rotate the crankshaft until the heel rests on a high point of the distributor cam, and adjust the point gap to specifications.

When replacing the points, remove the original points and condenser, and wipe out the inside of the distributor housing with a clean, dry rag. Lightly lubricate the contact heel and pivot point, and install the points and condenser. Rotate the crankshaft until the heel rests on a high point of the distributor cam, and adjust the point gap to specifications. NOTE: *Always replace the condenser when changing the points.*

—If the rotor is to be reused, clean the contacts with solvent. Do not alter the spring tension of the rotor center contact. Install the rotor and the distributor cap.

—Replace the coil high tension

lead and/or the spark plug leads as necessary.

—Clean the carburetor using a spray solvent (e.g., Gumout Spray). Remove the varnish from the throttle bores, and clean the linkage. Disconnect and plug the fuel line, and run the engine until it runs out of fuel. Partially fill the float chamber with solvent, and reconnect the fuel line. In extreme cases, the jets can be pressure flushed by inserting a rubber plug into the float vent, running the spray nozzle through it, and spraying the solvent until it squirts out of the venturi fuel dump.

—Clean and tighten all wiring connections in the primary electrical circuit.

Additional Services

The following services *should* be performed in conjunction with a routine tune-up to ensure efficient performance.

—Inspect the battery and fill to the proper level with distilled water. Remove the cable clamps, clean clamps and posts thoroughly, coat the posts lightly with petroleum jelly, reinstall and tighten.

—Inspect all belts, replace and/or adjust as necessary.

—Test the PCV valve (if so equipped), and clean or replace as indicated. Clean all crankcase ventilation hoses, or replace if cracked or hardened.

—Adjust the valves (if necessary) to manufacturer's specifications.

Adjustments

—Connect a dwell-tachometer between the distributor primary lead and ground. Remove the distributor cap and rotor (unless equipped with Delco externally adjustable distributor). With the ignition off, crank the engine with a remote starter switch and

measure the point dwell angle. Adjust the dwell angle to specifications. NOTE: *Increasing the gap decreases the dwell angle and vice-versa.* Install the rotor and distributor cap.

—Connect a timing light according to the manufacturer's specifications. Identify the proper timing marks with chalk or paint. NOTE: *Luminescent (day-glo) paint is excellent for this purpose.* Start the engine, and run it until it reaches operating temperature. Disconnect and plug any distributor vacuum lines, and adjust idle to the speed required to adjust timing, according to specifications. Loosen the distributor clamp and adjust timing to specifications by rotating the distributor in the engine. NOTE: *To advance timing, rotate distributor opposite normal direction of rotor rotation, and vice-versa.*

—Synchronize the throttles and mixture of multiple carburetors (if so equipped) according to procedures given in the individual car sections.

—Adjust the idle speed, mixture, and idle quality, as specified in the car sections. Final idle adjustments should be made with the air cleaner installed. CAUTION: *Due to strict emission control requirements on 1969 and later models, special test equipment (CO meter, SUN Tester) may be necessary to properly adjust idle mixture to specifications.*

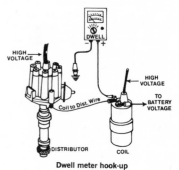

Dwell meter hook-up

Trouble-shooting

The following section is designed to aid in the rapid diagnosis of engine problems. The systematic format is used to diagnose problems ranging from engine starting difficulties to the need for engine overhaul. It is assumed that the user is equipped with basic hand tools and test equipment (tach-dwell meter, timing light, voltmeter, and ohmmeter).

Troubleshooting is divided into two sections. The first, *General Diagnosis*, is used to locate the problem area. In the second, *Specific Diagnosis*, the problem is systematically evaluated.

General Diagnosis

PROBLEM: *Symptom*	Begin diagnosis at Section Two, Number ———
Engine won't start:	
Starter doesn't turn	1.1, 2.1
Starter turns, engine doesn't	2.1
Starter turns engine very slowly	1.1, 2.4
Starter turns engine normally	3.1, 4.1
Starter turns engine very quickly	6.1
Engine fires intermittently	4.1
Engine fires consistently	5.1, 6.1
Engine runs poorly:	
Hard starting	3.1, 4.1, 5.1, 8.1
Rough idle	4.1, 5.1, 8.1
Stalling	3.1, 4.1, 5.1, 8.1
Engine dies at high speeds	4.1, 5.1
Hesitation (on acceleration from standing stop)	5.1, 8.1
Poor pickup	4.1, 5.1, 8.1
Lack of power	3.1, 4.1, 5.1, 8.1
Backfire through the carburetor	4.1, 8.1, 9.1
Backfire through the exhaust	4.1, 8.1, 9.1
Blue exhaust gases	6.1, 7.1
Black exhaust gases	5.1
Running on (after the ignition is shut off)	3.1, 8.1
Susceptible to moisture	4.1
Engine misfires under load	4.1, 7.1, 8.4, 9.1
Engine misfires at speed	4.1, 8.4
Engine misfires at idle	3.1, 4.1, 5.1, 7.1, 8.4

PROBLEM: *Symptom*	Probable Cause
Engine noises: ①	
Metallic grind while starting	Starter drive not engaging completely
Constant grind or rumble	*Starter drive not releasing, worn main bearings
Constant knock	Worn connecting rod bearings
Knock under load	Fuel octane too low, worn connecting rod bearings
Double knock	Loose piston pin
Metallic tap	*Collapsed or sticky valve lifter, excessive valve clearance, excessive end play in a rotating shaft
Scrape	*Fan belt contacting a stationary surface
Tick while starting	S.U. electric fuel pump (normal), starter brushes
Constant tick	*Generator brushes, shreaded fan belt
Squeal	*Improperly tensioned fan belt
Hiss or roar	*Steam escaping through a leak in the cooling system or the radiator overflow vent
Whistle	*Vacuum leak
Wheeze	Loose or cracked spark plug

①—It is extremely difficult to evaluate vehicle noises. While the above are general definitions of engine noises, those starred (*) should be considered as possibly originating elsewhere in the car. To aid diagnosis, the following list considers other potential sources of these sounds.

Metallic grind:
Throwout bearing; transmission gears, bearings, or synchronizers; differential bearings, gears; something metallic in contact with brake drum or disc.

Metallic tap:
U-joints; fan-to-radiator (or shroud) contact.

Scrape:
Brake shoe or pad dragging; tire to body contact; suspension contacting undercarriage or exhaust; something non-metallic contacting brake shoe or drum.

Tick:
Transmission gears; differential gears; lack of radio suppression; resonant vibration of body panels; windshield wiper motor or transmission; heater motor and blower.

Squeal:
Brake shoe or pad not fully releasing; tires (excessive wear, uneven wear, improper inflation); front or rear wheel alignment (most commonly due to improper toe-in).

Hiss or whistle:
Wind leaks (body or window); heater motor and blower fan.

Roar:
Wheel bearings; wind leaks (body and window).

Specific Diagnosis

This section is arranged so that following each test, instructions are given to proceed to another, until a problem is diagnosed.

INDEX

Group		Topic
1	*	Battery
2	*	Cranking system
3	*	Primary electrical system
4	*	Secondary electrical system
5	*	Fuel system
6	*	Engine compression
7	**	Engine vacuum
8	**	Secondary electrical system
9	**	Valve train
10	**	Exhaust system
11	**	Cooling system
12	**	Engine lubrication

*—The engine need not be running.
**—The engine must be running.

SAMPLE SECTION

Test and Procedure	Results and Indications	Proceed to
4.1—Check for spark: Hold each spark plug wire approximately ¼″ from ground with gloves or a heavy, dry rag. Crank the engine and observe the spark.	→ If no spark is evident: ———————	→ 4.2
	→ If spark is good in some cases: ——	→ 4.3
	→ If spark is good in all cases: ———	→ 4.6

DIAGNOSIS

1.1—Inspect the battery visually for case condition (corrosion, cracks) and water level.	If case is cracked, replace battery:	1.4
	If the case is intact, remove corrosion with a solution of baking soda and water (CAUTION: *do not get the solution into the battery*), and fill with water:	1.2
1.2—Check the battery cable connections: Insert a screwdriver between the battery post and the cable clamp. Turn the headlights on high beam, and observe them as the screwdriver is gently twisted to ensure good metal to metal contact.	If the lights brighten, remove and clean the clamp and post; coat the post with petroleum jelly, install and tighten the clamp:	1.4
	If no improvement is noted:	1.3

Testing battery cable connections using a screwdriver

1.3—Test the state of charge of the battery using an individual cell tester or hydrometer.	If indicated, charge the battery. NOTE: *If no obvious reason exists for the low state of charge (i.e., battery age, prolonged storage), the charging system should be tested:*	1.4

Spec. Grav. Reading	Charged Condition
1.260-1.280	Fully Charged
1.230-1.250	Three Quarter Charged
1.200-1.220	One Half Charged
1.170-1.190	One Quarter Charged
1.140-1.160	Just About Flat
1.110-1.130	All The Way Down

State of battery charge

Electrolyte temperature (°F)	Specific gravity correction	
+120	+.016	
+100	+.012	ADD to reading
	+.008	
+80	+.004	
	no correction	
	—.004	
+60	—.008	
	—.012	
+40	—.016	
	—.020	
+20	—.024	SUBTRACT from reading
	—.028	
0	—.032	
	—.036	
—20	—.040	

The effect of temperature on the specific gravity of battery electrolyte

Test and Procedure	Results and Indications	Proceed to
1.4—Visually inspect battery cables for cracking, bad connection to ground, or bad connection to starter.	If necessary, tighten connections or replace the cables:	2.1

Tests in Group 2 are performed with coil high tension lead disconnected to prevent accidental starting.

Test and Procedure	Results and Indications	Proceed to
2.1—Test the starter motor and sole-noid: Connect a jumper from the battery post of the solenoid (or relay) to the starter post of the solenoid (or relay).	If starter turns the engine normally:	2.2
	If the starter buzzes, or turns the engine very slowly:	2.4
	If no response, replace the solenoid (or relay). If the starter turns, but the engine doesn't, ensure that the flywheel ring gear is intact. If the gear is undamaged, replace the starter drive.	3.1 3.1
2.2—Determine whether ignition override switches are functioning properly (clutch start switch, neutral safety switch), by connecting a jumper across the switch(es), and turning the ignition switch to "start".	If starter operates, adjust or replace switch:	3.1
	If the starter doesn't operate:	2.3
2.3—Check the ignition switch "start" position: Connect a 12V test lamp between the starter post of the solenoid (or relay) and ground. Turn the ignition switch to the "start" position, and jiggle the key.	If the lamp doesn't light when the switch is turned, check the ignition switch for loose connections, cracked insulation, or broken wires. Repair or replace as necessary:	3.1
	If the lamp flickers when the key is jiggled, replace the ignition switch.	3.3

Checking the ignition switch "start" position

Test and Procedure	Results and Indications	Proceed to
2.4—Remove and bench test the starter, according to specifications in the car section.	If the starter does not meet specifications, repair or replace as needed:	3.1
	If the starter is operating properly:	2.5
2.5—Determine whether the engine can turn freely: Remove the spark plugs, and check for water in the cylinders. Check for water on the dipstick, or oil in the radiator. Attempt to turn the engine using an 18″ flex drive and socket on the crankshaft pulley nut or bolt.	If the engine will turn freely only with the spark plugs out, and hydrostatic lock (water in the cylinders) is ruled out, check valve timing:	9.2
	If engine will not turn freely, and it is known that the clutch and transmission are free, the engine must be disassembled for further evaluation:	Next Chapter

Tests and Procedures	*Results and Indications*	*Proceed to*
3.1—Check the ignition switch "on" position: Connect a jumper wire between the distributor side of the coil and ground, and a 12V test lamp between the switch side of the coil and ground. Remove the high tension lead from the coil. Turn the ignition switch on and jiggle the key.	If the lamp lights:	3.2
	If the lamp flickers when the key is jiggled, replace the ignition switch:	3.3
	If the lamp doesn't light, check for loose or open connections. If none are found, remove the ignition switch and check for continuity. If the switch is faulty, replace it:	3.3

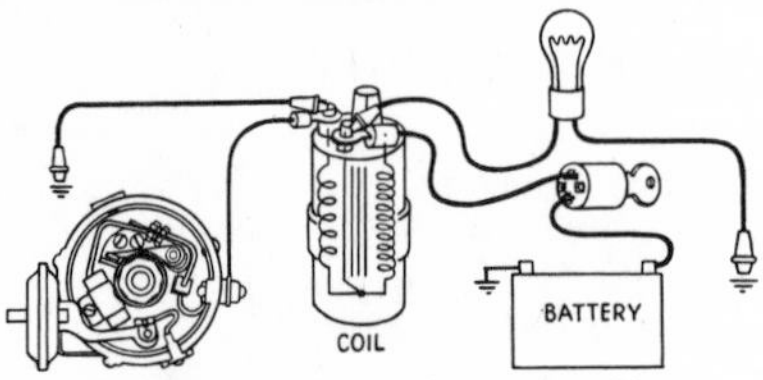

Checking the ignition switch "on" position

3.2—Check the ballast resistor or resistance wire for an open circuit, using an ohmmeter.	Replace the resistor or the resistance wire if the resistance is zero.	3.3

3.3—Visually inspect the breaker points for burning, pitting, or excessive wear. Gray coloring of the point contact surfaces is normal. Rotate the crankshaft until the contact heel rests on a high point of the distributor cam, and adjust the point gap to specifications.	If the breaker points are intact, clean the contact surfaces with fine emery cloth, and adjust the point gap to specifications. If pitted or worn, replace the points and condenser, and adjust the gap to specifications: NOTE: *Always lubricate the distributor cam according to manufacturer's recommendations when servicing the breaker points.*	3.4

3.4—Connect a dwell meter between the distributor primary lead and ground. Crank the engine and observe the point dwell angle.	If necessary, adjust the point dwell angle: NOTE: *Increasing the point gap decreases the dwell angle, and vice-versa.*	3.6
	If dwell meter shows little or no reading:	3.5

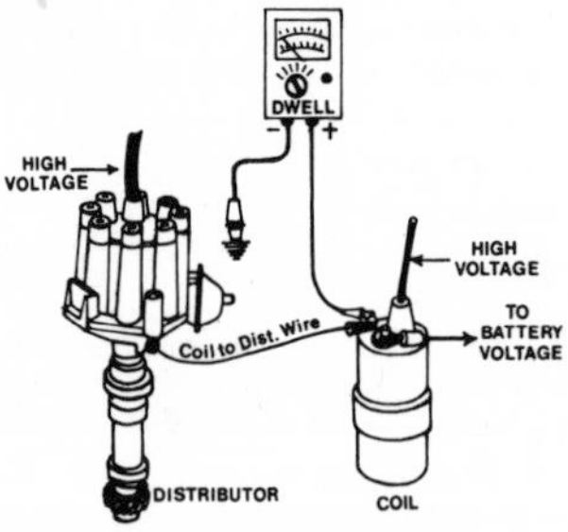

Dwell meter hook-up

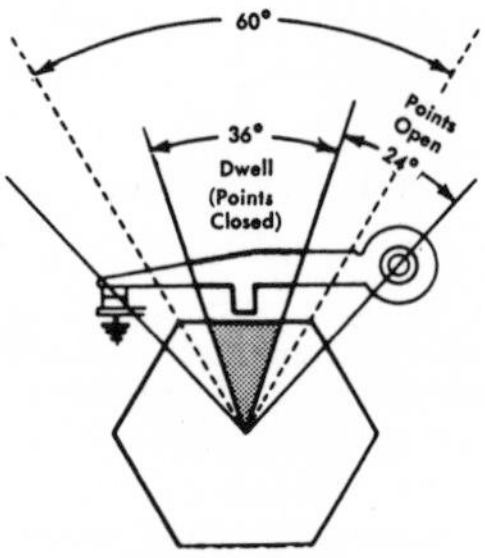

Dwell angle

3.5—Check the condenser for short: Connect an ohmmeter across the condenser body and the pigtail lead.	If any reading other than infinite resistance is noted, replace the condenser:	3.6

Checking the condenser for short

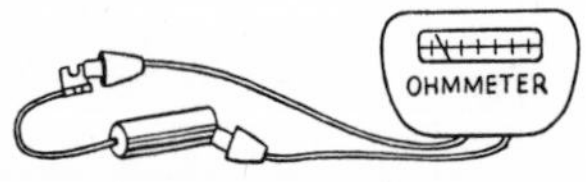

Test and Procedure	Results and Indications	Proceed to
3.6—Test the coil primary resistance: Connect an ohmmeter across the coil primary terminals, and read the resistance on the low scale. Note whether an external ballast resistor or resistance wire is utilized.	Coils utilizing ballast resistors or resistance wires should have approximately 1.0Ω resistance; coils with internal resistors should have approximately 4.0Ω resistance. If values far from the above are noted, replace the coil:	4.1

Testing the coil primary resistance

Test and Procedure	Results and Indications	Proceed to
4.1—Check for spark: Hold each spark plug wire approximately $\frac{1}{4}''$ from ground with gloves or a heavy, dry rag. Crank the engine, and observe the spark.	If no spark is evident:	4.2
	If spark is good in some cylinders:	4.3
	If spark is good in all cylinders:	4.6
4.2—Check for spark at the coil high tension lead: Remove the coil high tension lead from the distributor and position it approximately $\frac{1}{4}''$ from ground. Crank the engine and observe spark. CAUTION: *This test should not be performed on cars equipped with transistorized ignition.*	If the spark is good and consistent:	4.3
	If the spark is good but intermittent, test the primary electrical system starting at 3.3:	3.3
	If the spark is weak or non-existent, replace the coil high tension lead, clean and tighten all connections and retest. If no improvement is noted:	4.4
4.3—Visually inspect the distributor cap and rotor for burned or corroded contacts, cracks, carbon tracks, or moisture. Also check the fit of the rotor on the distributor shaft (where applicable).	If moisture is present, dry thoroughly, and retest per 4.1:	4.1
	If burned or excessively corroded contacts, cracks, or carbon tracks are noted, replace the defective part(s) and retest per 4.1:	4.1
	If the rotor and cap appear intact, or are only slightly corroded, clean the contacts thoroughly (including the cap towers and spark plug wire ends) and retest per 4.1:	
	If the spark is good in all cases:	4.6
	If the spark is poor in all cases:	4.5
4.4—Check the coil secondary resistance: Connect an ohmmeter across the distributor side of the coil and the coil tower. Read the resistance on the high scale of the ohmmeter.	The resistance of a satisfactory coil should be between $4K\Omega$ and $10K\Omega$. If the resistance is considerably higher (i.e., $40K\Omega$) replace the coil, and retest per 4.1: NOTE: *This does not apply to high performance coils.*	4.1

Testing the coil secondary resistance

Test and Procedure	Results and Indications	Proceed to
4.5—Visually inspect the spark plug wires for cracking or brittleness. Ensure that no two wires are positioned so as to cause induction firing (adjacent and parallel). Remove each wire, one by one, and check resistance with an ohmmeter.	Replace any cracked or brittle wires. If any of the wires are defective, replace the entire set. Replace any wires with excessive resistance (over 8000Ω per foot for suppression wire), and separate any wires that might cause induction firing.	4.6
4.6—Remove the spark plugs, noting the cylinders from which they were removed, and evaluate according to the chart below.	See below.	See below.

	Condition	Cause	Remedy	Proceed to
	Electrodes eroded, light brown deposits.	Normal wear. Normal wear is indicated by approximately .001″ wear per 1000 miles.	Clean and regap the spark plug if wear is not excessive: Replace the spark plug if excessively worn:	4.7
	Carbon fouling (black, dry, fluffy deposits).	If present on one or two plugs:		
		Faulty high tension lead(s).	Test the high tension leads:	4.5
		Burnt or sticking valve(s).	Check the valve train: (Clean and regap the plugs in either case.)	9.1
		If present on most or all plugs: Overly rich fuel mixture, due to restricted air filter, improper carburetor adjustment, improper choke or heat riser adjustment or operation.	Check the fuel system:	5.1
	Oil fouling (wet black deposits)	Worn engine components. NOTE: *Oil fouling may occur in new or recently rebuilt engines until broken in.*	Check engine vacuum and compression: Replace with new spark plug	6.1
	Lead fouling (gray, black, tan, or yellow deposits, which appear glazed or cinder-like).	Combustion by-products.	Clean and regap the plugs: (Use plugs of a different heat range if the problem recurs.)	4.7

Condition	Cause	Remedy	Proceed to
Gap bridging (deposits lodged between the electrodes).	Incomplete combustion, or transfer of deposits from the combustion chamber.	Replace the spark plugs:	4.7
Overheating (burnt electrodes, and extremely white insulator with small black spots).	Ignition timing advanced too far.	Adjust timing to specifications:	8.2
	Overly lean fuel mixture.	Check the fuel system:	5.1
	Spark plugs not seated properly.	Clean spark plug seat and install a new gasket washer: (Replace the spark plugs in all cases.)	4.7
Fused spot deposits on the insulator.	Combustion chamber blow-by.	Clean and regap the spark plugs:	4.7
Pre-ignition (melted or severely burned electrodes, blistered or cracked insulators, or metallic deposits on the insulator).	Incorrect spark plug heat range.	Replace with plugs of the proper heat range:	4.7
	Ignition timing advanced too far.	Adjust timing to specifications:	8.2
	Spark plugs not being cooled efficiently.	Clean the spark plug seat, and check the cooling system:	11.1
	Fuel mixture too lean.	Check the fuel system:	5.1
	Poor compression.	Check compression:	6.1
	Fuel grade too low.	Use higher octane fuel:	4.7

Test and Procedure	Results and Indications	Proceed to
4.7—Determine the static ignition timing: Using the flywheel or crankshaft pulley timing marks as a guide, locate top dead center on the *compression* stroke of the No. 1 cylinder. Remove the distributor cap.	Adjust the distributor so that the rotor points toward the No. 1 tower in the distributor cap, and the points are just opening:	4.8
4.8—Check coil polarity: Connect a voltmeter negative lead to the coil high tension lead, and the positive lead to ground (NOTE: *reverse the hook-up for positive ground cars*). Crank the engine momentarily. **Checking coil polarity**	If the voltmeter reads up-scale, the polarity is correct:	5.1
	If the voltmeter reads down-scale, reverse the coil polarity (switch the primary leads):	5.1

Test and Procedure	*Results and Indications*	*Proceed to*
5.1—Determine that the air filter is functioning efficiently: Hold paper elements up to a strong light, and attempt to see light through the filter.	Clean permanent air filters in gasoline (or manufacturer's recommendation), and allow to dry. Replace paper elements through which light cannot be seen:	5.2

5.2—Determine whether a flooding condition exists: Flooding is identified by a strong gasoline odor, and excessive gasoline present in the throttle bore(s) of the carburetor.	If flooding is not evident:
	
	 If flooding is evident, permit the gasoline to dry for a few moments and restart.
	     If flooding doesn't recur:
	     If flooding is persistant:
		5.3
		
		 5.6
		 5.5

5.3—Check that fuel is reaching the carburetor: Detach the fuel line at the carburetor inlet. Hold the end of the line in a cup (not styrofoam), and crank the engine.	If fuel flows smoothly: If fuel doesn't flow (NOTE: *Make sure that there is fuel in the tank*), or flows erratically:	5.6 5.4
5.4—Test the fuel pump: Disconnect all fuel lines from the fuel pump. Hold a finger over the input fitting, crank the engine (with electric pump, turn the ignition or pump on); and feel for suction.	If suction is evident, blow out the fuel line to the tank with low pressure compressed air until bubbling is heard from the fuel filler neck. Also blow out the carburetor fuel line (both ends disconnected): If no suction is evident, replace or repair the fuel pump: NOTE: *Repeated oil fouling of the spark plugs, or a no-start condition, could be the result of a ruptured vacuum booster pump diaphragm, through which oil or gasoline is being drawn into the intake manifold (where applicable).*	5.6 5.6
5.5—Check the needle and seat: Tap the carburetor in the area of the needle and seat.	If flooding stops, a gasoline additive (e.g., Gumout) will often cure the problem: If flooding continues, check the fuel pump for excessive pressure at the carburetor (according to specifications). If the pressure is normal, the needle and seat must be removed and checked, and/or the float level adjusted:	5.6 5.6
5.6—Test the accelerator pump by looking into the throttle bores while operating the throttle.	If the accelerator pump appears to be operating normally: If the accelerator pump is not operating, the pump must be reconditioned. Where possible, service the pump with the carburetor(s) installed on the engine. If necessary, remove the carburetor. Prior to removal:	5.7 5.7
5.7—Determine whether the carburetor main fuel system is functioning: Spray a commercial starting fluid into the carburetor while attempting to start the engine.	If the engine starts, runs for a few seconds, and dies: If the engine doesn't start:	5.8 6.1

Test and Procedures	Results and Indications	Proceed to
5.8—Uncommon fuel system malfunctions: See below:	If the problem is solved: If the problem remains, remove and recondition the carburetor.	6.1

Condition	Indication	Test	Usual Weather Conditions	Remedy
Vapor lock	Car will not restart shortly after running.	Cool the components of the fuel system until the engine starts.	Hot to very hot	Ensure that the exhaust manifold heat control valve is operating. Check with the vehicle manufacturer for the recommended solution to vapor lock on the model in question.
Carburetor icing	Car will not idle, stalls at low speeds.	Visually inspect the throttle plate area of the throttle bores for frost.	High humidity, 32-40° F.	Ensure that the exhaust manifold heat control valve is operating, and that the intake manifold heat riser is not blocked.
Water in the fuel	Engine sputters and stalls; may not start.	Pump a small amount of fuel into a glass jar. Allow to stand, and inspect for droplets or a layer of water.	High humidity, extreme temperature changes.	For droplets, use one or two cans of commercial gas dryer (Dry Gas) For a layer of water, the tank must be drained, and the fuel lines blown out with compressed air.

Test and Procedure	Results and Indications	Proceed to
6.1—Test engine compression: Remove all spark plugs. Insert a compression gauge into a spark plug port, crank the engine to obtain the maximum reading, and record.	If compression is within limits on all cylinders:	7.1
	If gauge reading is extremely low on all cylinders:	6.2
	If gauge reading is low on one or two cylinders: (If gauge readings are identical and low on two or more adjacent cylinders, the head gasket must be replaced.)	6.2

Testing compression
(© Chevrolet Div. G.M. Corp.)

Maxi. Press. Lbs. Sq. In.	Min. Press. Lbs. Sq. In.	Maxi. Press. Lbs. Sq. In.	Min. Press. Lbs. Sq. In.	Max. Press. Lbs. Sq. In.	Min. Press. Lbs. Sq. In.	Max. Press. Lbs. Sq. In.	Min. Press. Lbs. Sq. In.
134	101	162	121	188	141	214	160
136	102	164	123	190	142	216	162
138	104	166	124	192	144	218	163
140	105	168	126	194	145	220	165
142	107	170	127	196	147	222	166
146	110	172	129	198	148	224	168
148	111	174	131	200	150	226	169
150	113	176	132	202	151	228	171
152	114	178	133	204	153	230	172
154	115	180	135	206	154	232	174
156	117	182	136	208	156	234	175
158	118	184	138	210	157	236	177
160	120	186	140	212	158	238	178

Compression pressure limits
(© Buick Div. G.M. Corp.)

Test and Procedure	Results and Indications	Proceed to
6.2—Test engine compression (wet): Squirt approximately 30 cc. of engine oil into each cylinder, and retest per 6.1.	If the readings improve, worn or cracked rings or broken pistons are indicated:	Next Chapter
	If the readings do not improve, burned or excessively carboned valves or a jumped timing chain are indicated: NOTE: *A jumped timing chain is often indicated by difficult cranking.*	7.1
7.1—Perform a vacuum check of the engine: Attach a vacuum gauge to the intake manifold beyond the throttle plate. Start the engine, and observe the action of the needle over the range of engine speeds.	See below.	See below

	Reading	Indications	Proceed to
	Steady, from 17-22 in. Hg.	Normal.	8.1
	Low and steady.	Late ignition or valve timing, or low compression:	6.1
	Very low	Vacuum leak:	7.2
	Needle fluctuates as engine speed increases.	Ignition miss, blown cylinder head gasket, leaking valve or weak valve spring:	6.1, 8.3
	Gradual drop in reading at idle.	Excessive back pressure in the exhaust system:	10.1
	Intermittent fluctuation at idle.	Ignition miss, sticking valve:	8.3, 9.1
	Drifting needle.	Improper idle mixture adjustment, carburetors not synchronized (where applicable), or minor intake leak. Synchronize the carburetors, adjust the idle, and retest. If the condition persists:	7.2
	High and steady.	Early ignition timing:	8.2

Test and Procedure	Results and Indications	Proceed to
7.2—Attach a vacuum gauge per 7.1, and test for an intake manifold leak. Squirt a small amount of oil around the intake manifold gaskets, carburetor gaskets, plugs and fittings. Observe the action of the vacuum gauge.	If the reading improves, replace the indicated gasket, or seal the indicated fitting or plug: If the reading remains low:	8.1 7.3
7.3—Test all vacuum hoses and accessories for leaks as described in 7.2. Also check the carburetor body (dashpots, automatic choke mechanism, throttle shafts) for leaks in the same manner.	If the reading improves, service or replace the offending part(s): If the reading remains low:	8.1 6.1
8.1—Check the point dwell angle: Connect a dwell meter between the distributor primary wire and ground. Start the engine, and observe the dwell angle from idle to 3000 rpm.	If necessary, adjust the dwell angle. NOTE: *Increasing the point gap reduces the dwell angle and vice-versa.* If the dwell angle moves outside specifications as engine speed increases, the distributor should be removed and checked for cam accuracy, shaft end-play and concentricity, bushing wear, and adequate point arm tension (NOTE: *Most of these items may be checked with the distributor installed in the engine, using an oscilloscope*):	8.2
8.2—Connect a timing light (per manufacturer's recommendation) and check the dynamic ignition timing. Disconnect and plug the vacuum hose(s) to the distributor if specified, start the engine, and observe the timing marks at the specified engine speed.	If the timing is not correct, adjust to specifications by rotating the distributor in the engine: (Advance timing by rotating distributor opposite normal direction of rotor rotation, retard timing by rotating distributor in same direction as rotor rotation.)	8.3
8.3—Check the operation of the distributor advance mechanism(s): To test the mechanical advance, disconnect all but the mechanical advance, and observe the timing marks with a timing light as the engine speed is increased from idle. If the mark moves smoothly, without hesitation, it may be assumed that the mechanical advance is functioning properly. To test vacuum advance and/or retard systems, alternately crimp and release the vacuum line, and observe the timing mark for movement. If movement is noted, the system is operating.	If the systems are functioning: If the systems are not functioning, remove the distributor, and test on a distributor tester:	8.4 8.4
8.4—Locate an ignition miss: With the engine running, remove each spark plug wire, one by one, until one is found that doesn't cause the engine to roughen and slow down.	When the missing cylinder is identified:	4.1

Test and Procedure	Results and Indications	Proceed to
9.1—Evaluate the valve train: Remove the valve cover, and ensure that the valves are adjusted to specifications. A mechanic's stethoscope may be used to aid in the diagnosis of the valve train. By pushing the probe on or near push rods or rockers, valve noise often can be isolated. A timing light also may be used to diagnose valve problems. Connect the light according to manufacturer's recommendations, and start the engine. Vary the firing moment of the light by increasing the engine speed (and therefore the ignition advance), and moving the trigger from cylinder to cylinder. Observe the movement of each valve.	See below	See below

Observation	Probable Cause	Remedy	Proceed to
Metallic tap heard through the stethoscope.	Sticking hydraulic lifter or excessive valve clearance.	Adjust valve. If tap persists, remove and replace the lifter:	10.1
Metallic tap through the stethoscope, able to push the rocker arm (lifter side) down by hand.	Collapsed valve lifter.	Remove and replace the lifter:	10.1
Erratic, irregular motion of the valve stem.*	Sticking valve, burned valve.	Recondition the valve and/or valve guide:	Next Chapter
Eccentric motion of the pushrod at the rocker arm.*	Bent pushrod.	Replace the pushrod:	10.1
Valve retainer bounces as the valve closes.*	Weak valve spring or damper.	Remove and test the spring and damper. Replace if necessary:	10.1

*—When observed with a timing light.

Test and Procedure	Results and Indications	Proceed to
9.2—Check the valve timing: Locate top dead center of the No. 1 piston, and install a degree wheel or tape on the crankshaft pulley or damper with zero corresponding to an index mark on the engine. Rotate the crankshaft in its direction of rotation, and observe the opening of the No. 1 cylinder intake valve. The opening should correspond with the correct mark on the degree wheel according to specifications.	If the timing is not correct, the timing cover must be removed for further investigation:	

Test and Procedure	Results and Indications	Proceed to
10.1—Determine whether the exhaust manifold heat control valve is operating: Operate the valve by hand to determine whether it is free to move. If the valve is free, run the engine to operating temperature and observe the action of the valve, to ensure that it is opening.	If the valve sticks, spray it with a suitable solvent, open and close the valve to free it, and retest.	
	If the valve functions properly:	10.2
	If the valve does not free, or does not operate, replace the valve:	10.2
10.2—Ensure that there are no exhaust restrictions: Visually inspect the exhaust system for kinks, dents, or crushing. Also note that gasses are flowing freely from the tailpipe at all engine speeds, indicating no restriction in the muffler or resonator.	Replace any damaged portion of the system:	11.1
11.1—Visually inspect the fan belt for glazing, cracks, and fraying, and replace if necessary. Tighten the belt so that the longest span has approximately ½″ play at its midpoint under thumb pressure.	Replace or tighten the fan belt as necessary:	11.2

Checking the fan belt tension
(© Nissan Motor Co. Ltd.)

Test and Procedure	Results and Indications	Proceed to
11.2—Check the fluid level of the cooling system.	If full or slightly low, fill as necessary:	11.5
	If extremely low:	11.3
11.3—Visually inspect the external portions of the cooling system (radiator, radiator hoses, thermostat elbow, water pump seals, heater hoses, etc.) for leaks. If none are found, pressurize the cooling system to 14-15 psi.	If cooling system holds the pressure:	11.5
	If cooling system loses pressure rapidly, reinspect external parts of the system for leaks under pressure. If none are found, check dipstick for coolant in crankcase. If no coolant is present, but pressure loss continues:	11.4
	If coolant is evident in crankcase, remove cylinder head(s), and check gasket(s). If gaskets are intact, block and cylinder head(s) should be checked for cracks or holes. If the gasket(s) is blown, replace, and purge the crankcase of coolant:	12.6
	NOTE: *Occasionally, due to atmospheric and driving conditions, condensation of water can occur in the crankcase. This causes the oil to appear milky white. To remedy, run the engine until hot, and change the oil and oil filter.*	

Test and Procedure	*Results and Indication*	*Proceed to*
11.4—Check for combustion leaks into the cooling system: Pressurize the cooling system as above. Start the engine, and observe the pressure gauge. If the needle fluctuates, remove each spark plug wire, one by one, noting which cylinder(s) reduce or eliminate the fluctuation. **Radiator pressure tester** (© American Motors Corp.)	Cylinders which reduce or eliminate the fluctuation, when the spark plug wire is removed, are leaking into the cooling system. Replace the head gasket on the affected cylinder bank(s).	
11.5—Check the radiator pressure cap: Attach a radiator pressure tester to the radiator cap (wet the seal prior to installation). Quickly pump up the pressure, noting the point at which the cap releases. **Testing the radiator pressure cap** (© American Motors Corp.)	If the cap releases within ± 1 psi of the specified rating, it is operating properly: If the cap releases at more than ± 1 psi of the specified rating, it should be replaced:	11.6 11.6
11.6—Test the thermostat: Start the engine cold, remove the radiator cap, and insert a thermometer into the radiator. Allow the engine to idle. After a short while, there will be a sudden, rapid increase in coolant temperature. The temperature at which this sharp rise stops is the thermostat opening temperature.	If the thermostat opens at or about the specified temperature: If the temperature doesn't increase: (If the temperature increases slowly and gradually, replace the thermostat.)	11.7 11.7
11.7—Check the water pump: Remove the thermostat elbow and the thermostat, disconnect the coil high tension lead (to prevent starting), and crank the engine momentarily.	If coolant flows, replace the thermostat and retest per 11.6: If coolant doesn't flow, reverse flush the cooling system to alleviate any blockage that might exist. If system is not blocked, and coolant will not flow, recondition the water pump.	11.6 —
12.1—Check the oil pressure gauge or warning light: If the gauge shows low pressure, or the light is on, for no obvious reason, remove the oil pressure sender. Install an accurate oil pressure gauge and run the engine momentarily.	If oil pressure builds normally, run engine for a few moments to determine that it is functioning normally, and replace the sender. If the pressure remains low: If the pressure surges: If the oil pressure is zero:	— 12.2 12.3 12.3

Test and Procedure	Results and Indications	Proceed to
12.2—Visually inspect the oil: If the oil is watery or very thin, milky, or foamy, replace the oil and oil filter.	If the oil is normal:	12.3
	If after replacing oil the pressure remains low:	12.3
	If after replacing oil the pressure becomes normal:	—
12.3—Inspect the oil pressure relief valve and spring, to ensure that it is not sticking or stuck. Remove and thoroughly clean the valve, spring, and the valve body.	If the oil pressure improves:	—
	If no improvement is noted:	12.4

Oil pressure relief valve
(© British Leyland Motors)

12.4—Check to ensure that the oil pump is not cavitating (sucking air instead of oil): See that the crankcase is neither over nor underfull, and that the pickup in the sump is in the proper position and free from sludge.	Fill or drain the crankcase to the proper capacity, and clean the pickup screen in solvent if necessary. If no improvement is noted:	12.5
12.5—Inspect the oil pump drive and the oil pump:	If the pump drive or the oil pump appear to be defective, service as necessary and retest per 12.1:	12.1
	If the pump drive and pump appear to be operating normally, the engine should be disassembled to determine where blockage exists:	Next Chapter
12.6—Purge the engine of ethylene glycol coolant: Completely drain the crankcase and the oil filter. Obtain a commercial butyl cellosolve base solvent, designated for this purpose, and follow the instructions precisely. Following this, install a new oil filter and refill the crankcase with the proper weight oil. The next oil and filter change should follow shortly thereafter (1000 miles).		

Chapter Three

Engine and Engine Rebuilding

Engine Electrical

All Volvos with B 20 and B 30 engines are equipped with a 12 V, negative ground electrical system which consists of a battery, alternator and voltage regulator, starter motor, ignition system, lighting system, accessories, and signaling and instrumentation components.

All Volvos bearing the suffix "E" also employ the Bosch electronic fuel injection system. This is an assembly of sensitive electronic parts including an electric fuel pump, a highly sophisticated control unit, and various electronic engine sensors. Because of the complexity of this fuel injection system, the Volvos using it require special precautions when fast-charging the battery, jump starting, arc welding, or oven baking (after painting). Consult chapter 4 ("Fuel Systems and Emission Control System") for details.

Distributor

The distributor performs two functions: within the ignition system: its breaker points time (with changing engine speed) the collapse of the magnetic field in the ignition coil, converting primary voltage (12 V) to secondary (high) voltage; and its rotor and cap then distribute the high volt-

Distributor installation—B30F shown

1. Primary connection with condenser
2. Attaching bolt
3. Plug contact for triggering contacts
4. Vacuum regulator

age spark to the correct spark plug. In order to prevent arcing between the points, and subsequent burning when they are open (not making contact), a distribu-

1. Distributor cap
2. Distributor arm
3. Contact breaker
4. Lubricating felt
5. Circlip
6. Washer
7. Vacuum regulator
8. Cap clasp
9. Fiber washer
10. Steel washer
11. Driving collar

19. Centrifugal weight
20. Breaker camshaft
21. Breaker cam
22. Breaker plate
23. Lock screw for breaker contacts
24. Rod brush (carbon)

12. Lock pin
13. Resilient ring
14. Rubber seal
15. Lubricator
16. Primary connection
17. Distributor housing
18. Centrifugal governor spring

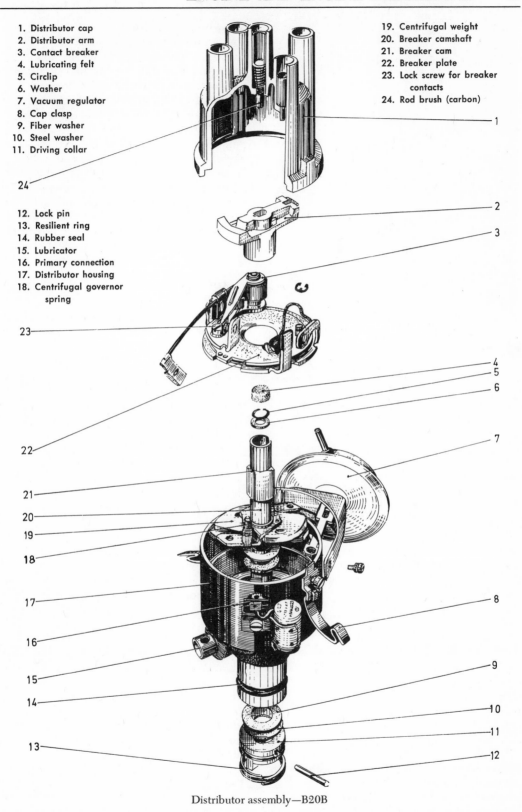

Distributor assembly—B20B

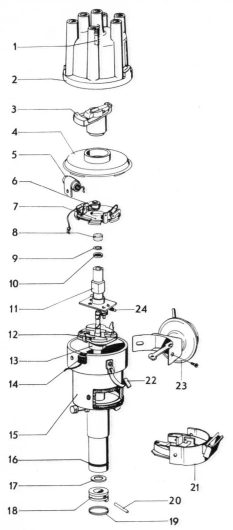

Distributor assembly—B30F

1. Rod brush (carbon)
2. Distributor cap
3. Distributor arm
4. Protective cover
5. Condenser
6. Ignition contact breaker
7. Breaker plate
8. Lubricating felt
9. Circlip
10. Washer
11. Breaker cam
12. Centrifugal weight
13. Cam for triggering contacts
14. Primary terminal
15. Distributor body
16. Rubber seal
17. Washers
18. Driving collar
19. Resilient ring
20. Lock pin
21. Contact device
22. Lock clamp for distr. cap
23. Vacuum regulator
24. Centrifugal governor spring

according to engine speed. A vacuum regulator outside the distributor controls advance in relation to engine load. All six-cylinder models have a dual-diaphragm vacuum regulator. The regulator retards the basic ignition timing adjustment during engine idling. On some early production B 20 B models with automatic transmissions, a plastic holder (vacuum delay valve) is fitted inline between the carburetor and the vacuum regulator. Its function is to delay the resetting of the vacuum regulator to the idle advance setting for approximately six seconds. There are two triggering contacts beneath the centrifugal governor on fuel-injected models.

Distributor Removal and Installation

1. Unsnap the distributor cap clasps and remove the cap.

2. Crank the engine until no. 1 cylinder is at Top Dead Center (TDC). At this point, the rotor should point to the spark plug wire socket for no. 1 cylinder, and the 0° timing mark on the crankshaft damper should be aligned with the pointer. For ease of assembly, scribe a chalk mark on the distributor housing to note the position of the rotor.

3. Disconnect the primary lead from the coil at its terminal on the distributor housing. On fuel-injected models, disconnect the plug for the triggering contacts.

4. Remove the vacuum hose(s) from the regulator. Take care not to damage the bakelite connection during removal.

5. Slacken the distributor attaching screw and hold-down clamp enough to slide the distributor up and out of position.

6. When ready to install the distributor, if the engine has been disturbed (cranked), find TDC for no. 1 cylinder as outlined under "Valve Lash Adjustment" in chapter 2. If the engine has not been disturbed, install the distributor with the rotor pointing to the no. 1 cylinder spark plug wire socket, or the chalk mark made prior to removal. To approximate ignition timing, position the vacuum regulator to the rear of the distributor (firewall side). If the distributor is installed incorrectly, the rotor will be 180° (of distributor rotation) out of place; incorrectly pointing at no. 4 spark plug wire on four-cylinder engines

tor condenser is arranged in parallel with the breaker point circuit.

All Volvos have Bosch distributors on the left side of the engine which are driven by a camshaft. A centrifugal governor beneath the breaker plate regulates advance, and incorrectly pointing at no. 6 spark plug wire on six-cylinder engines. Do not tighten the distributor attaching screw at this time.

7. Connect the primary lead to its terminal on the distributor housing. On fuel-injected models, connect the plug for the triggering contacts.

8. Connect the vacuum hose(s) to the bakelite connection(s) on the vacuum regulator.

9. If the distributor was disassembled, or if the contact point setting was disturbed, proceed to set the point gap and/or dwell angle as outlined in chapter 2.

10. Install the distributor cap and secure the clasps. Proceed to set the ignition timing as outlined in chapter 2. Tighten the distributor attaching screw.

Firing Order

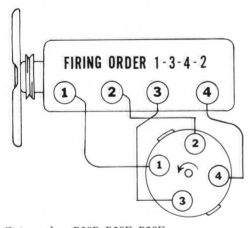

Firing order—B20B, B20E, B20F

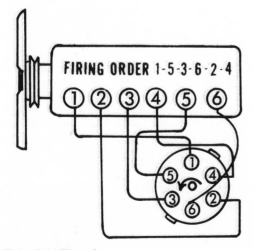

Firing Order Illustration

ALTERNATOR

The alternator converts the mechanical energy which is supplied by the drive belt into electrical energy by electromagnetic induction. When the ignition switch is turned on, current flows from the battery, through the charging system light or ammeter, to the voltage regulator, and finally to the alternator. When the engine is started, the drive belt turns the rotating field (rotor) in the stationary windings (stator), inducing alternating current. This alternating current is converted into usable direct current by the diode rectifier. Most of this current is used to charge the battery and power the electrical components of the vehicle. A small part is returned to the field windings of the alternator enabling it to increase its output. When the current in the field windings reaches a predetermined control voltage, the voltage regulator grounds the circuit, preventing any further increase. The cycle is continued so that the voltage remains constant.

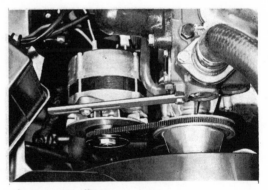

Alternator installation

Volvo has used five different alternators in its 1970–73 models. Three Motorola (two 35 and one 55 amp) and two Bosch (one 35 and one 55 amp) have been utilized. Removal and replacement procedures are the same for all.

Alternator Precautions

Several precautions must be observed when performing work on alternator equipment.

1. If the battery is removed for any reason, make sure that it is reconnected with the correct polarity. Reversing the battery connections may result in damage to the one-way rectifiers.

Alternator and Regulator Specifications

		Alternator			Regulator	
Year	Vehicle Model	Part No. and Manufacturer	Output (amps)	Min. Brush Length (in.)	Part No. and Manufacturer	Volts @ Alternator rpm (cold)
1970	140	S.E.V. Motorola 14V 26641	35	0.20	S.E.V. Motorola 14V 33525	13.1–14.4 @ 4000
1970–71	140, 1800	Bosch K1 14V 35A20	35	0.31	Bosch AD 14V	14.0–15.0 @ 4000
1970–72	164	S.E.V. Motorola 14V 34833	55	0.20	S.E.V. Motorola 14V 33544	13.1–14.4 @ 4000
1972	140, 1800					
1971	1800	S.E.V. Motorola 14V 71270202	35	0.20	S.E.V. Motorola 14V 33525	13.1–14.4 @ 4000
1971–72	140					
1972	1800	Bosch K1 14V 55A20	55	0.53	Bosch AD 14V	13.9–14.8 @ 4000

2. Never operate the alternator with the main circuit broken. Make sure that the battery, alternator, and regulator leads are not disconnected while the engine is running.

3. Never attempt to polarize an alternator.

4. When charging a battery that is installed in the vehicle, disconnect the negative battery cable.

5. When utilizing a booster battery as a starting aid, always connect it in parallel; negative to negative, and positive to positive.

6. When arc welding is to be performed on any part of the vehicle, disconnect the negative battery cable, disconnect the alternator leads, and unplug the voltage regulator.

Alternator Removal and Installation

1. Disconnect the negative battery cable.

2. Disconnect the electrical leads to the alternator.

3. Remove the adjusting arm-to-alternator bolt and adjusting arm-to-engine bolt.

4. Remove the alternator-to-engine mounting bolt.

5. Remove the fan belt and lift the alternator forward and out.

6. Reverse the above procedure to install, taking care to properly tension the fan (drive) belt as outlined in the "Routine Maintenance" section of chapter 1.

VOLTAGE REGULATOR

The voltage regulator, as previously mentioned, controls the amount of current fed to the field windings of the alternator.

When the control voltage value is reached, the regulator forces the current to pass through a resistance. If the voltage rises further, the circuit is grounded by the regulator, thereby lowering the voltage to a safe level. Temperature compensation is accomplished by a bimetal spring which adjusts the spring tension in the regulator to receive less voltage at higher operating temperatures, and more voltage at lower temperatures.

Volvo uses Bosch and Motorola voltage regulators. The regulator and alternator are a matched pair. On 1970 140 series Volvos, the regulator is located to the right of the radiator. On all other Volvos, except the 1800 series, the regulator is located on the right wheel well in the engine compartment. The regulators on Volvo 1800s are located on the left wheel well in the engine compartment.

Voltage Regulator Removal and Installation

1. Disconnect the negative battery cable.

2. Disconnect the leads or plug socket from the old regulator taking note of their (its) location.

3. Remove the hold-down screws from the old regulator and install the new one.

4. Connect the leads or plug socket and reconnect the negative battery cable.

Voltage Adjustment

MOTOROLA REGULATOR

If the Motorola regulator is found to be defective, it must be replaced. No adjustments can be made on this unit.

The following test may be performed on

Motorola regulator installed

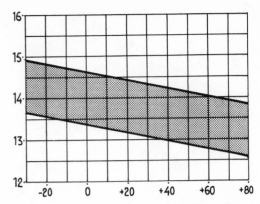

Voltage-temperature diagram for cold regulator—
Motorola

the Motorola regulator to see if it is functioning properly. An ammeter, tachometer, and voltmeter are required.

1. Connect the alternator and regulator as shown in the illustration.

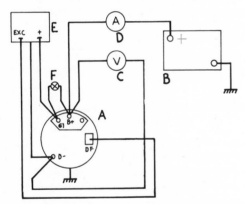

Wiring diagram for testing Motorola regulator

A. Alternator
B. Battery 60 Ah
C. Voltmeter 0–20 amps.
D. Ammeter 0–50 amps.

E. Voltage regulator
F. Warning lamp 12 volts,
   2 watts

2. Run the engine at 2500 rpm (5000 alternator rpm) for 15 seconds. With no load on the alternator, and the regulator ambient temperature at 77° F, the reading on the voltmeter should be 13.1–14.4 V. For regulator ambient temperatures other than 77° F, consult the voltage-temperature diagram for cold regulator.

3. Load the alternator with 10–15 amps (high-beam headlights) while the engine is running at 2500 rpm. The voltmeter reading should again be 13.1–14.4 V. Replace the regulator if it does not fall within these limits.

4. For a more accurate indication of the regulator's performance, drive the vehicle for about 45 minutes at a minimum speed of 30 mph. The regulator will be at the correct working temperature immediately after this drive.

5. With the engine running at 2500 rpm, and the regulator ambient temperature at 77° F, the voltmeter reading should be 13.85–14.25 V. For regulator ambient temperatures other than 77° F, consult the voltage-temperature diagram for warm regulator.

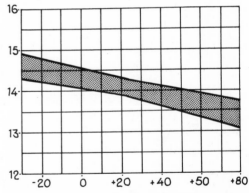

Voltage-temperature diagram for warm regulator
—Motorola

Bosch Regulator

The Bosch regulator is fully adjustable. To determine which adjustments are necessary—if any—perform the following test. (An ammeter, 12 V control lamp, tachometer, and voltmeter are required for this test.)

NOTE: *Where the numerical values differ for the 35 amp voltage regulator and the 55 amp unit, the figures for the 55*

Bosch regulator installed

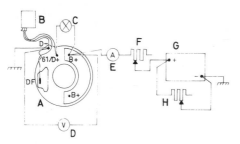

Wiring diagram for testing Bosch regulator

A. Alternator
B. Voltage lamp 12 volts
C. Control lamp 12 volts,
   2 watts
D. Voltmeter 0–20 volts

F. Regulator resistance
G. Battery 60 amperehours
H. Load resistance
E. Ammeter 0–50 amps

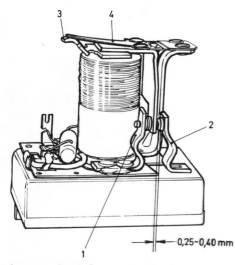

Voltage regulator adjustments—Bosch

1. Regulator contact for
   lower control range
   (lower contact)
2. Regulator contact for
   upper control range
   (upper contact)

3. Spring tensioner
4. Spring upper section:
   Steel spring
   Lower section:
   Bimetal spring

amp regulator will be given in parentheses.

1. Connect the alternator and regulator as shown in the illustration.

NOTE: *The first reading must be taken within 30 seconds of beginning of test.*

2. While running the engine at 2000 rpm, load the alternator with 28–30 amps (44–46 for 55 amp alternator).

3. Rapidly lower the engine to idle speed or 500 rpm, and then return it to 2000 rpm. With a load of 28–30 amps (44–46 for 55 amp alternator), the voltmeter reading should be 14.0–15.0 V (13.9–14.8 V for 55 amp alternator). The regulator should be regulated on the left (lower) contact.

4. Reduce the alternator load to 3–8 amps. The voltmeter reading should not decrease more than 0.3 V (0.4 for 55 amp alternator). The regulator should be regulated on the right (upper) contact.

5. Adjustment is made by bending the stop bracket for the bimetal spring. Bending the stop bracket down lowers the regulating voltage; bending it up raises the voltage. If the voltmeter reading for the low amp alternator load decreased more than 0.3 V (0.4 for 55 amp alternator), compared to the reading for the high amp alternator load, adjust the regulator by bending the holder for the left (lower) contact and simultaneously adjust the gap between the right (upper) contact and the movable contact. The gap should be adjusted to 0.010–0.015 in. (0.25–0.40 mm). If the holder is bent toward the right (upper) contact, the regulating voltage under high amp alternator load will be lowered.

To avoid faulty adjustments due to residual magnetism in the regulator core, it may be necessary to rapidly lower the engine rpm to idle after each adjustment, and then raise it to 2000 rpm to take a new reading.

NOTE: *Warm regulators may be cooled to ambient temperature by directing a stream of compressed air on them. Final readings should be made with the regulator at ambient temperature.*

STARTER

The starter motor on all Volvos is on the flywheel housing at the left-hand side of the engine. It is a four-pole series-wound unit to which an outboard solenoid is mounted. When the ignition is turned to

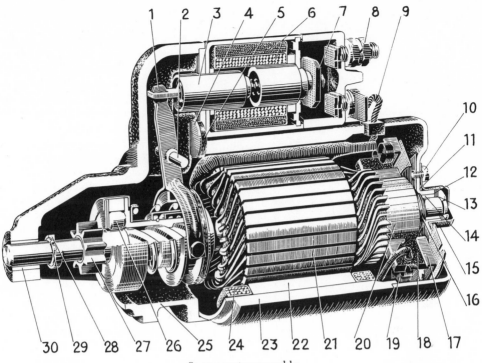

Starter motor assembly

1. Shift lever	9. Connection lead to field	17. Brush holder	26. Roller bearing
2. Pivot pin	10. Screw	18. Brush	27. Pinion
3. Plunger	11. Rubber gasket	19. Bush spring	28. Stop ring
4. Steel washer	12. Shims	20. Commutator	29. Snap ring
5. Rubber washer	13. Lock washer	21. Armature	30. Bushing
6. Winding	14. Bushing	22. Pole shoe	
7. Contact plate	15. Commutator end frame	23. Stator	
8. Terminal for battery lead	16. Adjusting washers	24. Field winding	
		25. Drive end frame	

the starting position, the solenoid armature is drawn in, engaging the starter pinion with the flywheel. When the starter pinion and flywheel are fully engaged, the solenoid armature closes the main contacts for the starter, causing the starter to crank the engine. When the engine starts, the increased speed of the flywheel causes the gear to overrun the starter clutch and rotor. The gear continues in full mesh until the ignition is switched from the "start" to the "on" position, interrupting the starter current. The shift lever spring then returns the gear to its neutral position.

Starter Removal and Installation

1. Disconnect the negative battery cable at the battery.

2. Disconnect the leads from the starter motor.

3. Remove the bolts retaining the starter

Starter motor installed

Battery and Starter Specifications

Year	Engine Displacement (cu in.)	Battery			Lock Test			Starters		No-Load Test		Brush Spring Tension
		Ampere Hour Capacity	Volts	Terminal Grounded	Amps	Volts	Torque (ft lbs)	Amps	Volts	@ rpm		
1970–73	All Models	60	12	Negative	300–350	6	——	40–50	12	6900–8100		2.53–2.86 lbs

motor to the flywheel housing and lift it off.

4. Position the starter motor to the flywheel housing and install the retaining bolts finger-tight. Torque the bolts to approximately 25 ft lbs, and apply locking compound to the threads.

5. Connect the starter motor leads and the negative battery cable.

Starter Drive Replacement

In order to remove the starter pinion drive, it is necessary to disassemble the starter. The procedure for disassembling the starter is as follows.

1. Remove the starter from the car as outlined in "Starter Removal and Installation."

2. Unscrew the two screws and remove the small cover from the front end of the starter shaft.

3. Unsnap the lockwasher and remove the adjusting washers from the front end of the shaft.

4. Unscrew the two screws retaining the commutator bearing shield and remove the shield.

5. Lift up the brushes and retainers and remove the brush bridge from the rotor shaft. The negative brushes are removed with the bridge while the positive brushes remain in the field winding. Do not remove the steel washer and the fiber washer at this time.

Starter with brush bridge removed

1. Steel washer   2. Fiber washer

6. Unscrew the nut retaining the field terminal connection to the control solenoid.

7. Unscrew the two solenoid-to-starter housing retaining screws and remove the solenoid.

8. Remove the drive end shield and rotor from the stator.

9. Remove the rubber and metal sealing washers from the housing.

10. Unscrew the nut and remove the screw on which the engaging arm pivots.

11. Remove the rotor, with the pinion and engaging arm attached, from the drive end shield.

12. Push back the stop washer and remove the snap-ring from the rotor shaft.

13. Remove the stop washer and pull off the starter pinion with a gear puller.

While the starter is disassembled, a few quick checks may be performed. Check the rotor shaft, commutator, and windings. If the rotor shaft is bent or worn, it must be replaced. Maximum rotor shaft radial throw is 0.003 in. If the commutator is scored or worn unevenly, it should be turned. Minimum commutator diameter is 1.3 in. Check the end shield, which houses the brushes, for excessive wear. Maximum bearing clearance is 0.005 in.

14. Lubricate the starter as shown in the illustration.

Starter motor lubrication

Use Bosch lubricant (or equivalent) in accordance with the following directions:

1. Ft 2 V 3. Place a thin layer of grease on the insulation washers, the shaft end, the adjusting washers and lock washer.

2. Ol 1 V 13. Place the bush in oil for 1 hour before fitting.

3. Ft 2 V 3. Apply plenty of grease in the rotor thread and the engaging lever groove.

4. Ft 2 V 3. Place a thin layer of grease on the armature shaft.

5. Ol 1 V 13. Place the bushes in oil for 1 hour before fitting.

6. Ft 2 V 3. Lubricate the engaging lever joints and the iron core of the solenoid with a thin layer of grease.

15. Press the starter pinion onto the rotor shaft. Install the stop washer and secure it with a new snap-ring.

16. Position the engaging arm on the pinion. Install the rotor into the drive end frame.

17. Install the screw and nut for the engaging arm pivot.

18. Install the rubber and metal sealing washers into the drive end housing.

19. Install the stator onto the rotor and drive end shield.

20. Position the solenoid so that the eyelet on the end of the solenoid plunger fits onto the engaging arm (shift lever). Tighten the solenoid retaining screws.

21. Place the metal and fiber washers on the rotor shaft.

22. Install the brush bridge on the rotor shaft and replace the brushes.

23. Fit the commutator bearing shield into position and install the retaining screws.

24. Install the adjusting washers and snap a new lockwasher into position on the end of the shaft. Make sure that the rotor axial clearance does not exceed 0.12 in. If necessary, adjust the clearance with washers, maintaining a minimum clearance of 0.002 in.

25. Replace the small cover over the front end of the shaft and install the two retaining screws.

26. Install the starter in the car as outlined in "Starter Removal and Installation."

Solenoid Replacement

Before replacing the solenoid when the starter will not crank, see if the battery has sufficient charge. If the no-crank condition persists when the battery is known to be good, connect a jumper wire between the positive terminal of the battery and the contact screw for the solenoid lead. If the solenoid engages the starter pinion, the starter switch or leads are at fault. If the starter still does not crank, replace the solenoid. To remove the solenoid, remove the starter from the car. The solenoid may be removed from the starter while installed in the car, but then aligning the solenoid plunger eyelet with the engaging arm during installation can be difficult. The procedure for replacement of the solenoid is as follows.

1. Remove the starter from the car as outlined in "Starter Removal and Installation."

2. Unscrew the two solenoid-to-starter housing retaining screws and remove the solenoid.

3. As a final test, wipe the solenoid clean and press in the armature. Test its operation by connecting it to a battery. If the solenoid still does not function, replace it with a new unit.

4. Position the new solenoid so that the eyelet on the end of the plunger fits into the engaging arm. Tighten the retaining screws.

5. Replace the starter in the car as outlined in "Starter Removal and Installation."

BATTERY

The battery is located in the engine compartment of all Volvos, and is mounted on a shelf to the left of the radiator on 140 series models; to the right of the radiator on 164 models; and on the firewall to the left of the engine on 1800 series models. The battery on all models is a 12 V, 60 ampere hour, lead-acid, negative ground unit.

Consult chapter 1 for routine maintenance procedures such as checking electrolyte level and state of charge. Never run fuel-injected Volvo engines with the battery removed, and never use a fast charger as a starting aid. If a fast charger is used to recharge a dead battery, isolate the battery from the injection system by disconnecting the battery cables.

Battery Removal and Installation

1. Remove the positive and negative cables from their terminals on the top of the battery. If the cables remain stuck to the terminals after loosening the cable clamps, use a puller to free them. Do not try to pry the cables off the terminals; damage to the battery case and/or the terminals may result.

2. Remove the battery hold-down bar and lift out the battery. Keep the battery upright to avoid spilling acidic electrolyte.

3. Clean the battery case and support shelf with a brush and rinse with clean, lukewarm water. Remove any deposits from the terminals and cable ends with a wire brush.

4. Replace the battery on its support shelf and install the hold-down bar.

5. Install the cables on their proper terminals and tighten the clamps. Coat the exposed metal of the cables and terminals with petroleum jelly to prevent corrosion.

General Engine Specifications

Year	Engine Designation	Engine Displacement Cu in. (cc)	Carburetor Type	Horsepower @ rpm (gross)	Torque @ rpm (ft lbs) (gross)	Bore x Stroke (in.)	Compression Ratio	Oil Pressure @ rpm (psi)
1970	B 20 B	122 (1990)	2 sidedraft Zenith-Stromberg 175 CD 2SE	118 @ 5800	123@ 3500	3.5000 x 3.150	9.3 : 1	36–85 @ 2000
1971–72	B 20 B	122 (1990)	2 sidedraft SU HIF 6	118 @ 5800	123@ 3500	3.5004 x 3.150	9.3 : 1	36–85 @ 2000
1970–71	B 20 E	122 (1990)	Bosch electronic fuel injection	130 @ 6000	130 @ 3500	3.5008 x 3.150	10.5 : 1	36–85 @ 2000
1972–73	B 20 F	122 (1990)	Bosch electronic fuel injection	125 @ 6000	123@ 3500	3.5008 x 3.150	8.7 : 1	36–85 @ 2000
1970–72	B 30 A	183 (2978)	2 sidedraft Zenith-Stromberg 175 CD 2SE	145 @ 5500	163 @ 3000	3.5000 x 3.150	9.3 : 1	36–85 @ 2000
1972–73	B 30 F	183 (2978)	Bosch electronic fuel injection	160 @ 5800	167 @2500	3.5010 x 3.150	8.7 : 1	36–85 @ 2000

Valve Specifications

Year	Engine Type	Seat Angle (deg)	Face Angle (deg)	Seat Width (in.)	Spring Test Pressure (lbs @ in.)	Spring Installed Height (in.)	Stem to Guide Clearance (in.) Intake	Stem to Guide Clearance (in.) Exhaust	Stem Diameter (in.) Intake	Stem Diameter (in.) Exhaust
1970–72 1970–71 1972–73	B 20 B B 20 E 122 (1990) B 20 F	44.5	45	0.08	181.5 @ 1.18	1.81	0.0012–0.0026	0.0024–0.0038	0.3132–0.3138	0.3120–0.3126
1970–72	B 30 A	44.5	45	0.08	145.0 @ 1.20	1.77	0.0012–0.0026	0.0024–0.0038	0.3132–0.3138	0.3120–0.3126
1972–73	B 30 F	44.5	45	0.08	181.5 @ 1.18	1.81	0.0012–0.0026	0.0024–0.0038	0.3132–0.3138	0.3120–0.3126

Crankshaft and Connecting Rod Specifications

All measurements are given in inches.

Year	Engine Type	Crankshaft Main Brg Journal Dia	Crankshaft Main Brg Oil Clearance	Crankshaft Shaft End-Play	Crankshaft Thrust on No.	Connecting Rod Journal Diameter	Connecting Rod Oil Clearance	Connecting Rod Side Clearance
1970–71	B 20	2.4981–2.4986	0.0011–0.0031	0.0018–0.0054	5	2.1299–2.1304	0.0012–0.0028	0.006–0.014
1972–73	B 20	2.4981–2.4986	0.0011–0.0033	0.0018–0.0054	5	2.1299–2.1304	0.0012–0.0028	0.006–0.014
1970–71	B 30	2.4981–2.4986	0.0011–0.0031	0.0018–0.0054	7	2.1299–2.1304	0.0012–0.0028	0.006–0.014
1972–73	B 30	2.4981–2.4986	0.0011–0.0033	0.0018–0.0054	7	2.1299–2.1304	0.0012–0.0028	0.006–0.014

Piston and Ring Specifications
(All measurements in inches)

Year	Engine Type	Piston Clearance	Ring Gap			Ring Side Clearance		
			Top Compression	Bottom Compression	Oil Control	Top Compression	Bottom Compression	Oil Control
1970	B 20 B	0.0008–0.0016	0.016–0.022	0.016–0.022	0.016–0.022	0.0017–0.0028	0.0017–0.0028	0.0017–0.0028
1970	B 30 A	0.0008–0.0016	0.016–0.022	0.016–0.022	0.016–0.022	0.0017–0.0028	0.0017–0.0028	0.0017–0.0028
1971	B 20 B	0.0014–0.0020	0.016–0.022	0.016–0.022	0.016–0.022	0.0017–0.0028	0.0017–0.0028	0.0017–0.0028
1971	B 20 E	0.0016–0.0024	0.016–0.022	0.016–0.022	0.016–0.022	0.0017–0.0028	0.0017–0.0028	0.0017–0.0028
1971	B 30 A	0.0016–0.0024	0.016–0.022	0.016–0.022	0.016–0.022	0.0017–0.0028	0.0017–0.0028	0.0017–0.0028
1972	B 20 B	0.0014–0.0020	0.016–0.022	0.016–0.022	0.016–0.022	0.0016–0.0028	0.0016–0.0028	0.0016–0.0028
1972–73	B 20 F	0.0016–0.0024	0.016–0.022	0.016–0.022	0.016–0.022	0.0016–0.0028	0.0016–0.0028	0.0016–0.0028
1972	B 30 A	0.0016–0.0024	0.016–0.022	0.016–0.022	0.016–0.022	0.0016–0.0028	0.0016–0.0028	0.0016–0.0028
1972–73	B 30 F	0.0016–0.0024	0.016–0.022	0.016–0.022	0.016–0.022	0.0016–0.0028	0.0016–0.0028	0.0016–0.0028

Torque Specifications
(All readings in ft lbs)

Year	Engine	Cylinder Head Bolts	Rod Bearing Bolts	Main Bearing Bolts	Crankshaft Pulley Bolt	Flywheel-To-Crankshaft Bolts	Manifold Bolts		Camshaft Nut	Spark Plug	Oil Pan	Alternator Bolt (½ in.)
							Intake	Exhaust				
1970–73	All	65①	38–42	87–94	50–58	36–40	13–16	13–16	94–108	25–29	6–8	50–60

① Torque head bolts in three stages; first, torque in sequence 29 ft lbs, then to 58 ft lbs, and finally after driving the car for 10 minutes, torque to the final figure of 65 ft lbs.

Engine Mechanical

DESIGN

All post-1969 Volvos are equipped with either the B 20 or B 30 engine. Both of these engines have evolved from those seemingly indestructible cast-iron, water-cooled, push rod, inline fours of yesteryear. The B 20, introduced in 1968, is a two liter (1990 cc) four-cylinder powerplant. The B 30, introduced in 1969, is a three liter (2978 cc) six-cylinder powerplant. The six-cylinder B 30 is, in effect, a stretched four-cylinder B 20. Both engines share the same basic design.

The B 20 engine has been manufactured in four variations, the B 20 A, B 20 B, B 20 E, and the B 20 F. The B 20 A, with its relatively low-compression head (8.7:1) and single sidedraft Zenith-Stromberg carburetor, is not imported into the U.S. The B 20 B, with its 9.3:1 compression ratio and dual sidedraft carburetors (Stromberg 175 CD2 SE in 1970, and SU HIF in 1971–72), has been standard equipment in the 140 series Volvos of 1970–72 vintage, but will not be imported for 1973. The B 20 E, with its high-compression head (10.5:1) and Bosch electronic fuel injection, has been standard equipment in all 1970–71 1800 E series, and optional in

the 1971 142S (known as the 142E). Due to the decision to convert to low-lead fuels in this country, which makes high-compression engines unfeasible, the B 20 F engine was introduced in 1972. This engine incorporates the Bosch electronic fuel injection with the low-compression head (8.7:1). The B 20 F was optional on 1972 140 series models, and is standard on all 1972–73 1800 series, and all 1973 140 series models.

The B 30 engine has been manufactured in three variations, the B 30 A, B 30 E, and the B 30 F. The B 30 A has a 9.3:1 compression ratio and is equipped with dual sidedraft Stromberg 175 CD2 SE carburetors. This engine is standard equipment on all 1970–72 164 models. The B 20 E, with its high-compression (10:1) head and Bosch electronic fuel injection, has not been imported into this country since 1971 due to its reliance on high-octane, leaded fuel. The B 30 F is the same engine with a lower compression ratio (8.7:1) and is optional on 1972 164 models, and standard for 1973.

The cylinder block is a single unit made of cast-iron alloy. The machined cylinder bores are surrounded by cooling jackets. Oil openings are arranged so that the full-flow oil filter (with the oil cooler in B 20 E engines) is attached directly to the right side of the block.

The cylinder head is bolted to the block.

1. Cold air hose
2. Hot air hose
3. Flap, constant air temperature device
4. Fuel line
5. Thermostat
6. Valve tappet
7. Valve spring
8. Washer
9. Valve collet
10. Exhaust valve
11. Connection for crankcase hose
12. Va've tappet seal
13. Intake valve
14. Oil filler cap
15. Carburetor
16. Damping device
17. Air cleaner
18. Hose for crankcase gases
19. Vacuum hose for distributor
20. Choke wire
21. Rocker arm
22. Rocker arm shaft
23. Spring
24. Push rod
25. Bearing bracket
26. Rocker arm casing
27. Rubber seal
28. Rubber terminal
29. Rubber seal
30. Cylinder head
31. Vacuum hose
32. Vacuum governor
33. Distributor
34. Condenser
35. Valve tappet
36. Retainer
37. Flywheel casing
38. Gear wheel
40. Pilot bearing
41. Flywheel
42. Flange bearing shell
43. Sealing flange
44. Reinforcing bracket
45. Bushing
46. Seal
47. Oil pump
48. Main bearing cap
49. Delivery pipe
50. Main bearing shell
51. Crankshaft
52. Sump
53. Piston rings
54. Connecting rod cap
55. Connecting rod
56. Camshaft
57. Piston
58. Bushing
59. Big-end bearing shell
60. Wrist pin
61. Washer
62. Spacing ring
63. Camshaft gear
64. Nut
65. Crankshaft gear
66. Hub
67. Washer
68. Bolt
69. Pulley
70. Key
71. Seal
72. Fan
73. Oil nozzle
74. Key
75. Timing gear cover
76. Coolant inlet
77. Gasket
78. Water pump
79. Gasket
80. Pulley
81. Alternator
82. Sealing ring
83. Cylinder head gasket
84. Tensioner
85. Water distributing pipe
86. Thermostat
87. Coolant outlet
88. Guard for throttle spindle
89. Air cleaner
90. Carburetor
91. Manifold
92. Connection for servo brake hose
93. Connection for crankcase hose
94. Hose for crankcase gases
95. Clamp

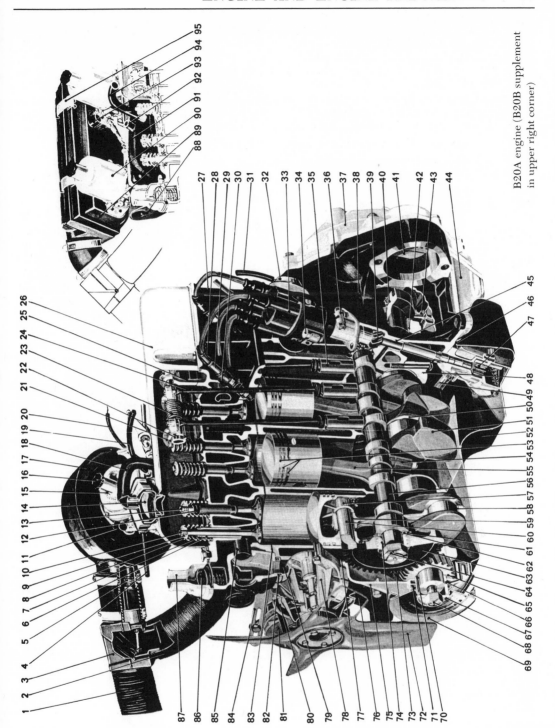

B20A engine (B20B supplement in upper right corner)

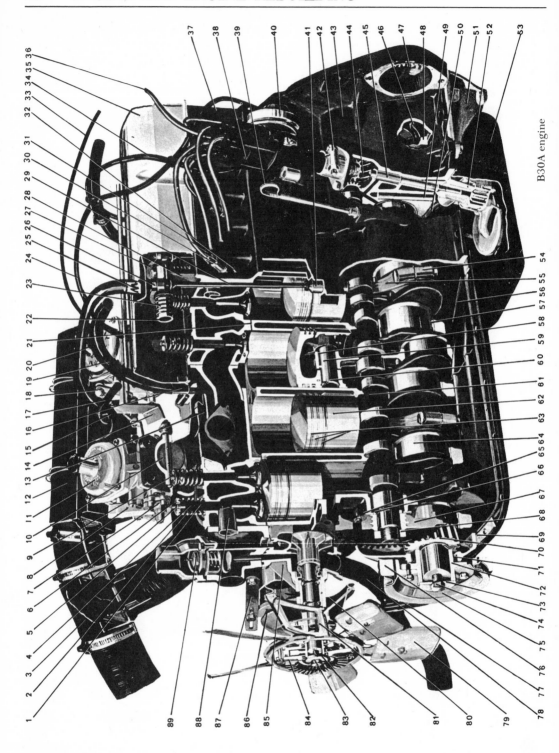

B30A engine

1. Valve guide	22. Rocker arm shaft	42. Retainer	66. Spacer ring
2. Valve spring	23. Spring	43. Cylinder block	67. Camshaft gear
3. Air preheating flap	24. Vacuum hose for ignition distributor	44. Gear wheel	68. Nut
4. Valve guide seal		45. Bushing	69. Seal
5. Valve collet	25. Flame protector	46. Rubber lip seal	70. Crankshaft gear
6. Intake valve	26. Adjusting device	47. Flywheel	71. Rubber lip seal
7. By-pass valve	27. Rocker arm	48. Sealing flange	72. Polygon hub
8. Temperature compensator	28. Bearing bracket	49. Main bearing bolt	73. Washer
	29. Push rod	50. Delivery pipe	74. Pulley
9. Exhaust valve	30. Cable terminal	51. Cover plate	76. Flywheel damper
10. Secondary throttle	31. Rubber seal	52. Oil pump	77. Fan belt
11. Front carburetor	32. Rubber seal	53. Sump	78. Coolant pipe
12. Air cleaner	33. Choke wire	54. Cap	79. Fan blade
13. Manifold pipe	34. Vacuum hose for negative vacuum adjustment	55. Connecting rod	80. Pulley
14. Bracket		56. Splash plate	81. Flange
15. Hose for fresh air supply		57. Main bearing	82. Washer
	35. Rocker arm casing	58. Bushing	83. Center bolt
16. Nipple	36. Ignition cable to ignition coil	59. Wrist pin	84. Fan coupling
17. Fuel hose		60. Circlip	85. Water pump
18. Carburetor control	37. Cylinder head	61. Camshaft	86. Alternator
19. Hose for crankcase gases	38. Distributor	62. Piston	87. Tensioner
	39. Oil dipstick	63. Piston rings	88. Water distribution pipe
20. Rear carburetor	40. Vacuum governor	64. Crankshaft	89. Thermostat
21. Cylinder head gasket	41. Valve tappet	65. Thrust washer	

All combustion chambers are machined with intake and exhaust ports. Cooling jackets surround each cylinder and spark plug, providing good heat-dissipating qualities. The overhead valves are made of special steel with chrome stems and are mounted in replaceable guides.

The crankshaft is constructed of drop-forged steel with drilled oilways and case-hardened crankpins. There are five main bearings on the B 20 and seven on the B 30, since the rear bearing also functions as a thrust bearing. The main bearings and bearing inserts are steel-backed, indium-plated bronze. Bearing inserts can be replaced without removing the engine.

A camshaft of special alloy cast-iron with case-hardened lobes is driven from the crankshaft through a gear train which has a reduction ratio of 2:1. The camshaft is guided axially by a thrust washer at the front end. A shim behind the camshaft gear determines the clearance. Valve lifters are actuated directly by the camshaft. There are no inspection covers for the valve lifters since they are accessible from above when the cylinder head is removed.

The drop-forged steel connecting rods are fitted with precision machined bushings which provide a bearing surface for the wrist pins. Bearing inserts are replaceable. Pistons are made of aluminum alloy and have two compression rings and one

oil ring. The upper compression ring is chrome, thereby reducing cylinder wear. The wrist pins have a floating fit in both the piston and connecting rod. Axial movement of the wrist pin is limited by circlips in the wrist pin hole.

ENGINE REMOVAL

All Volvo engines and transmissions are removed as a unit. Volvo recommends special SVO tools for this operation, but, in most cases, a good chain hoist will suffice. Do not attempt to lift the engine with the chain wrapped around either the oil filter or the distributor. The SVO tool part numbers appear in the illustrations. Lifting

Front engine lifting lug installation—B20

Front engine lifting lug installation—B30

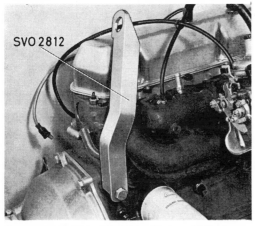

Rear engine lifting lug installation—B30 shown, B20 similar

eyes may be fabricated from heavy gauge steel or angle iron.

1. Scribe the outline of the hinges on the hood and remove the hood.

2. Drain the oil from the crankcase. Open the drain plug on the right-hand side of the engine block, disconnect the lower radiator hose at the radiator, and drain the cooling system. On Volvos with automatic transmissions, disconnect and plug the transmission oil cooler lines.

3. Remove the expansion tank, radiator cover plate, upper radiator hose, radiator, and fan shroud, if so equipped.

4. Remove the positive lead from the battery.

5. Remove the electric cables for the starter, the coil high-tension wire, the distributor lead, alternator wires, water and oil temperature sensors, and the lead for the oil pressure sensor, if so equipped.

6. Remove the vacuum hoses for the distributor advance, and the power brake booster, if so equipped. Remove the positive crankcase ventilation (PCV) hoses, and the oil pressure gauge hose at the pipe connection, if so equipped.

7. On carbureted models, remove the air cleaner, air intake hoses, and preheating plate. Also disconnect and plug the inlet hose to the fuel pump, disconnect the choke linkage, and remove the throttle control shaft from the pedal shaft, intermediate shaft, and bracket.

8. On fuel-injected models, remove the: air cleaner and intake hoses; pressure sensor hose from the inlet duct; the plug contacts for the temperature sensor, cold start valve, throttle valve switch, fuel injectors, and distributor impulse. In addition, remove the ground wire from the inlet duct, the throttle cable bracket from the inlet duct, the throttle cable from the throttle valve switch, the cold start valve fuel hose from the distribution pipe, the fuel return line from the pressure regulator, and the fuel inlet line from the distribution pipe. Remove the injectors by turning the lockrings counterclockwise and lifting them out of their bayonet fittings. The injectors should then be fitted with protective covers and plugs to prevent dirt from entering.

9. Disconnect the heater pipes from all models. Remove the exhaust pipe flange nuts and disconnect the exhaust pipe from the manifold. On models equipped with power steering, remove the steering pump bolts and place the pump and reservoir to one side.

10. On Volvos with manual transmissions, place the gearshift in neutral and remove the shifter lever. On Volvos with automatic transmissions, disconnect the control rod from the selector lever, and the ground cable from the start inhibitor switch.

11. Disconnect the wires for the back-up lights and overdrive, if so equipped. Remove the speedometer drive cable from the transmission. Remove the clamp for the exhaust manifold and the clamp for the automatic transmission filler tube, if so equipped.

12. Jack up the vehicle and place two jackstands under the front jack attachments and two more in front of the rear jack attachments.

13. Place a hydraulic jack under the

transmission. On manual transmission cars, remove the return spring from the throwout fork, and disconnect the clutch cable.

14. Separate the transmission (or overdrive) from the front universal joint by unbolting the flange. Unbolt the rear crossmember.

15. Disconnect the negative ground cable from the engine.

16. Remove the rear crossmember and rear engine mounts. Remove the lower nuts for the front engine mounts.

17. Install the lifting eyes and lifting crossbar. The lifting eyes are attached by $3/8$ x $1 3/4$ x 1 in. bolts. Lift out the engine and set it on an engine stand or rack. The engine is removed by raising its front and lowering its back while pulling forward until it clears the front crossmember, then leveling it and raising the complete unit.

ENGINE INSTALLATION

1. Install the lifting apparatus to the engine. Make sure that the jackstands are located beneath the front jack attachments and in front of the rear jack attachments. Place the hydraulic jack beneath the transmission tunnel.

2. Carefully lower the engine into the engine compartment. Place the hydraulic jack under the transmission and guide the unit into place. Be careful not to damage the oil filter, or oil pressure sending unit against the exhaust pipe. Be careful not to damage the distributor against the steering column.

3. Tighten the nuts for the front engine mounts.

4. Connect the wires for the back-up lights, start inhibitor switch (automatic transmission), and overdrive, if so equipped.

5. Install the brackets for the exhaust manifold and the automatic transmission filler tube. Install the rear engine mounts and rear crossmember, then tighten the nuts.

6. Remove the hydraulic jack from the transmission and the lifting apparatus from the engine. Connect the negative ground cable to the engine.

7. Connect the front universal joint to the transmission (or overdrive) flange. Connect the speedometer drive cable.

8. On manual transmission cars, connect the clutch cable and install the return spring. Adjust clutch free-play. On automatic transmission cars, connect the control rod to the selector lever, and the ground cable to the start inhibitor switch.

9. Connect the exhaust pipe to the exhaust manifold with new gaskets and tighten the nuts.

10. Remove the jackstands from the jack attachments and lower the vehicle.

11. Connect the heater pipes. On models with power steering, install the pump and reservoir to the engine block and adjust the drive belt tension.

12. On fuel-injected models, place the injectors in their bayonet fittings with new rubber seals, and turn them clockwise to install. In addition, connect the fuel inlet line and the cold start valve hose to the distribution pipe, and the return line from the pressure regulator. Install the ground wire and the throttle cable bracket to the inlet duct, and connect the throttle cable. Connect the plug contacts for the temperature sensor, cold start valve, throttle valve switch, fuel injectors, and distributor impulse. Install the pressure sensor vacuum hose, air cleaner, and intake hoses.

13. On carburetted models, connect the fuel pump inlet hose, choke linkage, and throttle linkage. Install the preheating plate, intake hoses, and air cleaner.

14. On all models, connect the positive crankcase ventilation hoses, and the distributor vacuum advance hose. Connect the vacuum hose for the power brake booster, and the oil pressure gauge hose at the pipe connection, if so equipped.

15. Install the electric cables for the starter, the coil high-tension wire, the distributor lead, alternator wires, water and oil temperature sensors, and the lead for the oil pressure sensor, if so equipped.

16. Connect the positive lead to the battery.

17. Install the radiator and fan shroud, if so equipped, and the radiator cover plate. Install the expansion tank, the upper and lower radiator hoses, and, on automatic transmission cars, the transmission oil cooler lines.

18. Fill the crankcase to the proper level with oil. Fill the cooling system with a 50 percent ethylene glycol, 50 percent water solution.

19. Install the hood. Install the gearshift lever.

20. Start the engine and check for leaks.

Cylinder Head Removal and Installation

NOTE: *To prevent warpage of the head, removal should be attempted only on a cold engine.*

B 20 B AND B 30 A

1. Drain the cooling system by opening the drain plug on the right-hand side of the engine and disconnecting the lower radiator hose at the radiator.

2. Disconnect the choke control cables at the carburetors. Remove the positive crankcase ventilation hoses from the air cleaner and intake manifold. Remove the vacuum hoses for the distributor advance and the power brake booster, if so equipped.

3. Remove the throttle control shaft from the pedal shaft, link rods, and bracket. (Disconnect the downshift linkage on cars with automatic transmissions.)

4. Remove the air cleaner, inlet hose, and heat control valve hose from the engine.

5. Remove the upper radiator hose. Remove the heater hose clamp from the head.

6. Remove and plug the fuel line at the carburetors.

7. Label the spark plug wires and disconnect them from the plugs. Disconnect the coolant temperature sensor.

8. Remove the exhaust manifold preheating plate. Remove the nuts and disconnect the exhaust pipe from the exhaust manifold.

9. Unbolt the alternator adjusting arm from the head.

10. Remove the valve cover. Remove the rocker shaft and arm assembly as a unit and draw out the push rods, keeping them in order.

11. Loosen the head bolts gradually, in the same order as their tightening sequence. Remove the head bolts, noting their locations, and lift off the head. Do not attempt to pry off the head. The head may be tapped lightly with a rubber mallet to break the gasket seal. If any residual water in the cooling passages of the head falls into the combustion chambers during removal, remove it immediately and coat the cylinder walls with oil.

12. Remove the integrally cast intake and exhaust manifold from the cylinder head.

13. Remove the old head gasket, flange gasket, and rubber sealing rings for the water pump.

14. Inspect the condition of the valves in the combustion chambers, and the intake and exhaust ports in the head. Small deposits may be removed with rotating brushes. If large deposits are present, however, proceed to "Cylinder Head Reconditioning" in the "Engine Rebuilding" section of this chapter. Make sure that no foreign matter has fallen into the cylinders or onto the tops of the pistons. Thoroughly clean the mating surfaces of the cylinder head and block and remove any traces of the old head gasket. Check the mating surfaces for warpage. There is an oil feed hole for the rocker arm assembly on the tappet side, in the middle of the head. (See illustration.) Make sure it is clean. A clogged oil feed hole may be opened with a length of thin gauge metal wire and some kerosine to dissolve some of the deposits.

Oil feed hole in cylinder head

Clean the top of the cylinder head and the oil return holes to remove any gum or foreign deposits. Clean and oil the head bolts.

15. Install the combination intake and exhaust manifold on the head with new gaskets.

16. Install new sealing rings for the water pump.

17. Use a pair of guide studs for proper alignment of the cylinder head, head gasket, and block. Guide studs can be easily made by cutting the heads off a pair of spare head bolts. The tops of the bolts are

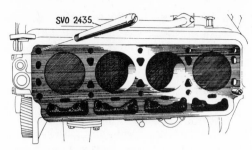

Guide stud installation

then filed to a tapered edge and slotted so that they may be installed and removed with a screwdriver. The guide studs should be installed in the cylinder block; one in the front right-hand head bolt hole, and the other in the rear left-hand head bolt hole.

18. Fit a new head gasket on the cylinder block with the lettering "TOP" (wide edge) facing up. Slide the gasket down over the two guide studs.

19. Carefully lower the cylinder head over the guide studs onto the block. Install, but do not tighten, two head bolts at opposite ends to secure the gasket, and remove the guide studs. Install the remaining head bolts finger-tight. Torque the head bolts in proper sequence first to 29 ft lbs, and then to 58 ft lbs.

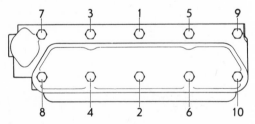

Cylinder head bolt tightening sequence—B20

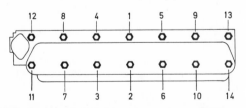

Cylinder head bolt tightening sequence—B30

20. Roll the pushrods on a level surface to inspect them for straightness. Replace any bent pushrods. Install the pushrods in their original positions and install the rocker shaft and arm assembly. Torque the bolts to approximately 20 ft lbs.

21. Adjust the valve clearance to a *preliminary* setting of 0.018–0.020 for the B 30 A, and 0.022–0.024 for the B 20 B. Use the procedure outlined under "Valve Lash Adjustment" in chapter 2. Install the valve cover with a new gasket.

22. Install the alternator adjusting arm and adjust the drive (fan) belt tension as outlined in the "Routine Maintenance" section of chapter 1.

23. Install the following: exhaust manifold preheating plate, exhaust pipe and flange nuts (with new gaskets), spark plug wires, coolant temperature sensor, heater hose clamp, upper and lower radiator hoses, fuel line, air cleaner, inlet hose, heat control valve hose, choke and throttle linkage (downshift linkage on cars with automatic transmissions), vacuum hoses for the distributor and power brake (if so equipped), and the positive crankcase ventilation hoses.

24. Close the drain plug and fill the cooling system with a 50 percent antifreeze, 50 percent water solution.

25. Run the engine for 10 minutes so that it reaches operating temperature. Stop the engine.

26. Remove the valve cover and torque the head bolts in proper sequence to the final figure of 65 ft lbs. Adjust the valve clearance to the final setting of 0.020–0.022 as outlined in chapter 1. Install the valve cover.

B 20 E, B 20 F, AND B 30 F

NOTE: *To prevent warpage of the head, removal should only be attempted on a cold engine.*

The procedure for removal and installation of the cylinder head for the previously mentioned fuel-injected engines differs from the carburetted engines only in the type of fuel system equipment that must be moved to gain access to the head.

1. Drain the cooling system by opening the drain plug on the right-hand side of the engine and disconnecting the lower radiator hose at the radiator.

2. Disconnect the positive battery cable from the engine.

3. On the B 30 F engine, remove the air cleaner.

4. Remove the following hoses from the inlet duct: pressure sensor, power brake (if so equipped), distributor advance, and crankcase ventilation.

5. Remove the electrical contacts for the throttle valve switch, cold start valve, thermal timer, temperature sensor, and injectors.

6. Remove the ground cable from the inlet duct and remove the cable harness.

7. Disconnect the sensor for the coolant temperature gauge. Remove the spark plug wires from the plugs.

8. On the B 20 E and B 20 F engines, remove the inlet hose.

9. Disconnect the throttle control cable from the throttle valve and inlet duct.

10. Remove and pinch the fuel hoses from the distributing pipe.

11. Remove the upper radiator hose, the heater control valve hose, and the clamp for the heater pipe.

12. Unbolt the alternator adjusting arm from the head.

13. Remove the bolts for the inlet duct stay. Remove the inlet duct-to-cylinder head retaining nuts and disconnect the inlet duct.

14. If any cleaning or machine work is to be performed on the cylinder head, remove the fuel injectors beforehand. Turn the lockrings on the injectors counterclockwise and lift out the injectors and distributing pipe as a unit. Remove the injector holders from the head.

15. Remove the exhaust manifold-to-exhaust pipe flange nuts and disconnect the pipe.

16. Refer to steps 10 and 11 under "Cylinder Head Removal and Installation" for the B 20 B and B 30 A.

17. Remove the exhaust manifold from the head.

18. Refer to steps 13 and 14 under "Cylinder Head Removal and Installation" for the B 20 B and B 30 A.

19. Install the exhaust manifold on the head with a new gasket.

20. Refer to steps 16–20 under "Cylinder Head Removal and Installation" for the B 20 B and B 30 A engines.

21. Adjust the valve clearance to a *preliminary* setting of 0.018–0.020 for the B 20 E and B 20 F, and 0.022–0.024 for the B 30 F. Use the procedure outlined under "Valve Lash Adjustment" in chapter 2. Install the valve cover with a new gasket.

22. If the injectors were removed, install the holders with new sealing rings. Install the injectors and distributing pipe as a unit.

23. Install the alternator adjusting arm and adjust the drive (fan) belt tension as outlined in the "Routine Maintenance" section of chapter 1.

24. Install the inlet duct with a new gasket. Install the inlet duct retaining nuts and the bolts for the inlet duct stay. On B 20 engines, install the inlet hose.

25. Install the following: upper and lower radiator hoses, heater hose, heater hose clamp, exhaust pipe flange nuts, fuel line, throttle linkage, temperature gauge sensor, ground cable to inlet duct, cable harness, electrical contacts for the throttle valve switch, cold start valve, thermal timer, temperature sensor and injectors, pressure sensor hose, power brake hose, distributor advance line, crankcase ventilation hoses, and the positive battery cable.

26. On the B 30 F engine, install the air cleaner.

27. Close the drain plug and fill the cooling system with a 50 percent antifreeze, 50 percent water solution.

28. Run the engine for 10 minutes so that it reaches operating temperature and then stop it.

29. Remove the valve cover and torque the head bolts in proper sequence to the final figure of 65 ft lbs. Adjust the valve clearance to the final setting of 0.016–0.018 for the B 20 E and B 20 F, and 0.020–0.022 for the B 30 F as outlined under "Valve Lash Adjustment" in chapter 2. Install the valve cover.

Cylinder Head Overhaul

Refer to "Cylinder Head Reconditioning" in the "Engine Rebuilding" section of this chapter.

Rocker Shaft and Arm Assembly Removal and Installation

1. Remove the four retaining screws and the valve cover and gasket.

2. Remove the rocker shaft-to-cylinder head bolts and lift out the shaft and rocker arms as a unit.

3. Lift out the pushrods, keeping them in order, and check them for straightness by rolling them on a flat surface. Replace any bent pushrods.

4. Inspect the rocker shaft and arms. If the shaft and rockers are coated with baked-on sludge, oil may not be reaching them. Clean out the oil feed holes in the rocker shaft with 0.020 in. wire (piano

wire). If the clearance between the rocker arms and shaft exceeds 0.004 in., the rocker arm needs to be rebushed. The rocker arm bushings are press fitted, and are removed with a drift. When pressing in a new bushing, make sure that the oil hole in the bushing aligns with the hole in the arm.

5. Position the pushrods on their respective lifters. Install the rocker shaft and arm assembly on the head, and install the retaining bolts. Step-tighten the bolts, moving front to rear, until a torque of approximately 20 ft lbs is reached.

6. Check to see that valve lash has remained within specifications. Adjust valve lash, if necessary, as outlined in chapter 1.

7. Install the valve cover and gasket, and snugly tighten the valve cover retaining screws.

INTAKE AND EXHAUST MANIFOLDS

On all carbureted Volvos, the intake and exhaust manifolds are cast integrally. A preheating chamber is located within the combination manifold. The chamber's function is to transfer the heat from the exhaust ports to the fuel-air mixture in the intake manifold for improved cold-weather operation.

On all fuel-injected Volvos, the intake manifold (inlet duct) and exhaust manifold are separate units. The inlet duct is constructed of a light aluminum alloy, while the exhaust manifold is cast iron.

Intake and/or Exhaust Manifold Removal and Installation

1. Remove the exhaust manifold preheating plate. Remove the nuts and disconnect the exhaust pipe from the exhaust manifold.

2. Remove the air cleaner. Disconnect the throttle, choke, and downshift linkage, if so equipped. Disconnect the positive crankcase ventilation hoses, and the vacuum hoses for the distributor advance, and power brake, if so equipped.

3. Remove the nuts and slide the combination intake and exhaust manifold off the studs. Remove and discard the old manifold gasket.

4. To install, reverse the above procedure. Remember to use a new manifold gasket and exhaust pipe flange gasket in

assembly. Torque the manifold retaining nuts to 13–16 ft lbs.

Inlet Duct Removal and Installation

1. On B 30 F engines, remove the air cleaner. On B 20 E and B 20 F engines, remove the inlet duct-to-air cleaner hose at the inlet duct.

2. Disconnect the positive battery cable.

3. Disconnect the throttle and downshift linkage. Remove from the inlet duct, the positive crankcase ventilation, distributor advance, pressure sensor, and power brake hoses.

4. Disconnect the contact for the throttle valve switch, and remove the ground cable for the inlet duct.

5. Remove the bolts for the inlet duct stay. Remove the inlet duct-to-cylinder head retaining nuts and slide the inlet duct off the studs.

6. Discard the old gasket. To install, reverse the above procedure. Use a new inlet duct gasket. Torque the nuts to 13–16 ft lbs.

Timing Gear Cover Removal and Installation

B 20 ENGINE

1. Loosen the fan (drive) belt. Remove the fan and water pump pulley. Disconnect the stabilizer attachment from the frame.

2. Remove the crankshaft pulley and bolt.

3. Remove the retaining bolts and the timing gear cover. Loosen a few oil pan bolts, being careful not to damage the pan gasket.

4. Remove the circlip, washer, and felt ring from the cover. Replace any gasket in questionable condition. Make sure that the oil drain hole is open and clean.

5. Place the cover in position and install the retaining bolts finger-tight.

6. Center the cover with a sleeve. Turn the sleeve while tightening and adjust the position of the cover so that the sleeve may be easily rotated without jamming.

7. Install a new felt ring, washer, and circlip. Push them into their positions with the engaging sleeve. Check to make sure that the circlip has seated in its groove.

8. Tighten the cover bolts. Install the pulleys and fan. Tension the accessory

drive belts. Tighten the stabilizer attachment firmly to the frame.

Timing Gear Cover Oil Seal Replacement

B 20 ENGINE

1. Remove the fan belt. Loosen the stabilizer attachment at the frame.

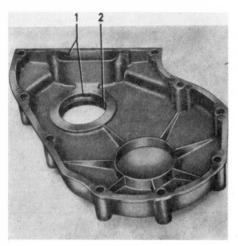

Timing gear cover—B20

1. Drain holes   2. Sealing ring

2. Remove the crankshaft pulley and bolt.

3. Remove the circlip for the washer retaining the felt ring. Check to make sure that the cover is correctly installed by inserting a 0.004 in. feeler gauge between the casing and the crankshaft hub. If the feeler gauge jams at any point, the cover must be centered.

4. Install a new felt ring. Place the washer in position and install the circlip in its groove.

5. Install the crankshaft pulley and fan. Tension the fan (drive) belt. Tighten the stabilizer attachment at the frame.

B 30 ENGINE

1. Drain the cooling system by opening the engine drain plug and disconnecting the lower radiator hose. On automatic transmission cars, disconnect and plug the transmission oil cooler lines at the radiator. Remove the radiator, fan shroud, and grille.

2. Remove the fan (drive) belt. Remove the bolts for the pulley and crankshaft damper.

3. Remove the center bolt and pull off

Removing hub—B30

the hub by hand or, if necessary, with a puller.

4. Remove the oil seal. Lubricate the sealing lip on the new seal and install the seal with a drift. The seal may be installed in one of three positions, depending on the amount of wear on the hub. With a new hub, the seal will be installed in its outer position (position 1). With a wear mark on the hub, install the seal in position 2. With two wear marks on the hub, install the seal in position 3. With three wear marks on the hub, you either have a very old engine or you have gone through more than a normal share of oil seals, and it is time to think about replacing that old hub with a new one.

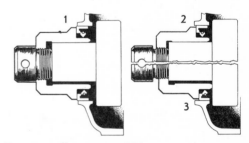

Center spindle position—B30

5. Grease the sliding surfaces of the hub and install the hub. Note the center punch marks on the crankshaft end and hub. Install the center bolt and torque it to 50–57 ft lbs.

6. Install the crankshaft damper and pulley.

7. Install and properly tension the fan (drive) belt. Install the radiator, fan

shroud, and grille. Install the lower radiator hose, close the drain plug, and fill the cooling system. On cars with automatic transmissions, connect the oil cooler lines at the radiator.

Timing Gear and Camshaft Replacement

1. Disconnect the lower radiator hose, open the engine drain plug, and drain the cooling system. On cars with automatic transmissions, disconnect and plug the transmission oil cooler lines at the radiator. Remove the fan shroud (if so equipped) and the radiator.

2. Remove the fan and the pulley on the water pump. Remove the crankshaft bolt and remove the pulley using a puller.

Removing camshaft gear—B20

Removing crankshaft gear—B30

3. Remove the timing gear cover. Loosen a few oil pan bolts, being careful not to damage the pan gasket.

4. Measure the tooth flank clearance. Maximum permissible gear backlash is 0.005 in. Check to make sure that the end-play of the camshaft does not exceed 0.002 in. Camshaft end-play is determined by the shim behind the camshaft timing gear.

5. Try to align the marks on the timing gears dot to dot (or line to dot) prior to removing the gears. If this is not possible, note the correct relative position of the timing gear marks. Remove the hub from the crankshaft with a puller. Remove the crankshaft gear and the camshaft gear with a puller. Remove the oil jet, blow it clean, and reposition it. Oil fed through this jet lubricates the timing gears.

6. If the camshaft is being replaced, it is necessary to remove the distributor (noting its position), fuel pump, valve cover, rocker shaft and arm assembly, pushrods, cylinder head, valve lifters, and the thrust flange. The camshaft may then be pulled out the front.

Timing gear alignment—B20 shown, B30 similar

1. Oil nozzle   2. Markings

7. Reverse the above procedure to install. Replace the camshaft if the lobes exhibit excessive or uneven wear. Install the crankshaft and camshaft timing gears, making sure that they align in the correct relative positions. Do not push the camshaft backward, or the seal washer on the rear end may be forced out. Recheck the tooth flank clearance and the camshaft end-play.

8. When installing the timing case cover, make sure that the drain holes are open. Center the cover with a sleeve.

9. Install the pulleys and fan. Install the fan (drive) belt and adjust the tension. Refit the radiator hose, close the drain plug, and fill the cooling system.

Pistons and Connecting Rods Removal

This procedure is more easily accomplished with the engine removed from the vehicle and placed in an engine stand.

1. Remove the cylinder head. Remove any ridge and/or carbon deposits from the upper end of the cylinder bores with a ridge reamer.

2. Remove the oil pan. Check connecting rods and pistons for identification numbers and, if necessary, number them.

3. Remove the connecting rod cap nuts and caps from the crankshaft. Push the rods away from the crankshaft and install the bearing shells, caps, and nuts on the rods to avoid possible interchange of parts.

4. Push the piston and rod assemblies up and out of the cylinders. Remove the rings.

Piston and Connecting Rod Inspection

1. Inspect the cylinder walls for scoring, roughness, or ridges formed from excessive wear. With an accurate cylinder gauge or inside micrometer, check for cylinder taper and out-of-round at the top, middle, and bottom of the bore, both parallel and at right angles to the center line of the engine. Wear is indicated by the difference between the highest and lowest readings. The cylinder is in need of reboring when wear reaches 0.010 in., or if scoring is evident. Hone or rebore the cylinder for fitting of smallest possible oversized piston and rings. Clearance between the piston and cylinder wall, with the rings removed, should be 0.0008–0.0016 in.

2. Measure the outside diameter of the pistons with a micrometer at right angles to the wrist pin hole approximately 0.098 in. from the bottom of the piston.

3. Check the piston ring gap by pressing the rings, one after another, into the bore and inserting a feeler gauge into the gap. The gap should be 0.016–0.022 in. The gap may be widened by filing the ring ends with a thin, flat file. Remember that when

Measuring piston ring gap

you are checking ring gap in a worn cylinder, the rings should be positioned at the bottom of the bore where the diameter is the smallest.

4. Clean the ring grooves on the sides of the pistons. With the rings installed in their respective grooves, measure the side clearance at several points around the piston, and check the reading against the specifications. Inspect the ring grooves for wear, especially the upper edge of the chromed top compression ring.

Measuring piston ring side clearance

5. If the wrist pin hole in the piston exhibits excessive wear, an oversized wrist pin should be installed in the connecting rod. Ream out the hole to the oversized wrist pin specification. This is correct when the wrist pin can be pushed through the hole with light resistance.

6. Inspect the connecting rods for straightness. Check the bushings for excessive wear. When installing a new bushing, make sure that the oil holes align with the holes in the connecting rod. Ream the

bushing to the correct fit. When the wrist pin slides through the hole with light thumb pressure, but without noticeable looseness, the bushing is fitted correctly.

Piston and Connecting Rod Installation

1. Lightly coat the pistons, rings, wrist pins, and cylinder walls with light engine oil.

2. Install the wrist pin and fit the circlip into position.

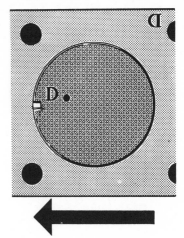

Piston marking

tive bore from the top, using a piston installation ring as shown. A hardwood hammer handle may be used to lightly tap the piston into position. Guide the rod

Wrist pin fit

Piston installation ring

3. Use a piston ring expander tool to install the rings on the piston. Position the rings so that their gaps do not come directly under one another, or directly opposite one another. Remember that the top compression ring is chromed and its upper side is marked "TOP."

4. Prior to installation, make sure that the pistons will be positioned in the cylinders with the slot facing forward, and that the numbers on the side of the connecting rods will be facing away from the camshaft side. Install each piston in its respec-

bearings into place on the crankshaft journal.

5. Install the lower half of the bearing and cap. Torque the bolts to 38–42 ft lbs. Check the clearances against specifications.

6. Install the oil pan with a new gasket.

7. Install the cylinder head as outlined in "Cylinder Head Removal and Installation" in this chapter.

Engine Lubrication

All Volvos use a forced-feed lubricating system. Oil pressure is provided by a camshaft-driven pump fitted beneath the crankshaft in the oil pan. The pump forces oil past the relief valve on the pump, through the oil filter and oil cooler, if so equipped, through the oil passages to the various lubricating points. Therefore, all oil reaching the lubricating points has first passed through the oil filter.

Oil Pan Removal and Installation

The oil pan may be removed from the engine while the engine is still in the chassis.

1. Place the supports on the frame side members as shown. Insert a lifting hook into the lifting plate bolted to the front of the engine. Using the lifting apparatus, raise the engine until there is no weight on the front engine mounts. Remove the oil dipstick.

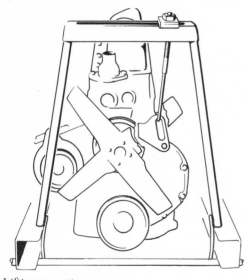

Lifting apparatus

2. Jack up the vehicle and place jackstands under the front jacking points. Drain the crankcase oil.

3. Remove the lower nuts for the engine mounts. On 140 series models, remove the steering rods from the pitman arm and relay arm with a puller.

4. Place a hydraulic floor jack beneath the front axle member. Remove the rear

bolts of the front axle member and replace them with two longer auxiliary bolts (UNC ½–13 x 114). Remove the front bolts for the front axle member and lower the hydraulic jack, allowing the axle member to hang on the auxiliary bolts.

5. Remove the plug for the oil temperature gauge, if so equipped, and the reinforcing bracket at the flywheel.

6. Unscrew the oil pan bolts and lower the pan. Remove the old gasket and clean the surfaces of the cylinder block and oil pan. Remove any sludge or foreign matter that has accumulated at the bottom of the pan.

7. Using a new gasket, position the pan to the cylinder block and install the oil pan bolts. Torque the bolts to 6–8 ft lbs.

8. Install the plug for the oil temperature gauge, if so equipped. Position the reinforcing bracket to the cylinder block and flywheel casing and install the bolts finger-tight. Snugly tighten the bolts for the flywheel casing and then those for the cylinder block.

9. Raise the hydraulic jack, raising the front axle member, and tighten the front bolts. Remove the auxiliary bolts and install the original rear bolts of the front axle member.

10. Install the lower nuts for the front engine mounts. On 140 series models, connect the steering rods at the pitman arm and relay arm, and fit the nuts.

11. Remove the jackstands and hydraulic jack. Lower the vehicle. Remove the lifting apparatus.

12. Insert the dipstick. Fill the crankcase with the proper amount and grade of oil.

13. Start the engine and check for leaks.

Rear Main Oil Seal Replacement

1. Remove the transmission, clutch (if so equipped), and flywheel from the engine. Remove the two oil pan bolts from the bottom of the sealing flange, and loosen two more on each side so that the pressure on the sealing flange is reduced.

2. Remove the sealing flange retaining bolts and pull off the sealing flange and old gasket. Press out the sealing ring in the flange with a drift.

3. Make sure that the sealing surfaces of the flange are clean. Also make sure that

Rear end of engine

1. Dowel pin
2. Core plug
3. Sealing flange
4. Circlip
5. Pilot bearing
6. Sealing ring
7. Crankshaft
8. Plug
9. Dowel pin

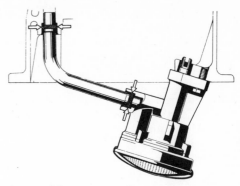

Oil pump delivery pipe sealing rings

the oil drain hole is not blocked by the oil pan gasket.

4. Oil the sealing ring. Install the sealing ring, sealing flange, and new gasket to the block, but do not tighten the bolts.

5. Center the flange with special SVO 2439 (for B 20), or 2817 (for B 30). Rotate the sleeve while tightening the flange bolts. Adjust the position of the flange if the sleeve jams. After tightening, the sleeve should rotate easily if the flange is properly positioned. Make sure that the sealing flange is seated against the underside of the block.

6. Install a new felt ring and replace the washer and circlip. Install the sealing ring into its groove with the centering sleeve.

7. Install and tighten the oil pan bolts. Install the flywheel, clutch (if so equipped), and transmission.

Oil Pump Replacement

The oil pump must be removed with the engine removed from the car.

1. Crank the engine to TDC at no. 1 cylinder. Remove the distributor.

2. Drain the crankcase and remove the oil pan. Remove the oil pump retaining bolts.

3. Disconnect the oil pump from the delivery tube by unscrewing the connecting flange. Be careful not to discard the rubber sealing rings from the sealing flange.

4. Unscrew the connecting flange and remove the delivery tube from the block.

5. To install, fit the delivery tube with sealing rings to the oil pump, and then to

the block. If the tube does not seat properly in the block, it may be tapped lightly with a soft mallet. Tightly screw the connecting flanges.

6. With no. 1 cylinder at TDC, install the oil pump drive and distributor. Make sure that the shaft goes down into its groove in the pump shaft. Tighten the oil pump retaining bolts.

7. Install the oil pan with a new gasket and fill the crankcase.

Oil Cooler Replacement

1. Remove the plug in the oil cooler and drain the coolant.

2. Disconnect the coolant connection at the oil cooler. Remove the oil filter.

3. Unscrew the oil cooler nipple nut and remove the cooler. Remove and discard

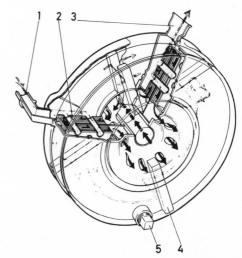

Oil cooler

1. Coolant inlet
2. Discs
3. Cooling outlet
4. Rubber seal
5. Coolant drain plug

the rubber sealing ring at the cylinder block connection.

4. Install a new O-ring into the groove in the oil cooler and apply a thin layer of oil-resistant (up to 280° F) adhesive, such as Pliobond 20, to the groove. Position the cooler and new rubber sealing ring to the block and tighten the nipple nut to 23–25 ft lbs. Make sure that the cooler is flush against the block.

5. Install the oil filter and connect the coolant pipe. Install the cooler plug.

6. Replace the coolant, and, if necessary, the engine oil. Run the engine and check for leaks.

Engine Cooling

All Volvos are equipped with a sealed cooling system. Radiator overflow and trapped air in the system are conveyed to the expansion tank where they are stored. Therefore, loss of coolant is prevented, reducing the chances of corrosion forming in the system or of the antifreeze being diluted. The air cushion developed in the expansion tank forces the coolant back into the radiator until it is full, ensuring that the radiator is always topped up.

The fan is of the viscous type, with a slip coupling that limits the maximum fan speed to approximately 3500 rpm. This arrangement reduces fan noise and lowers the load on the engine at high engine rpm, but provides a good cooling air current at low rpm where it is needed.

The water pump is belt-driven by the engine pulleys and provides coolant circulation in direct proportion to engine speed. When the engine is cold, the thermostat is closed, directing the coolant through the engine passages and to the car heater. At approximately 190° F, the thermostat is open, allowing the coolant to flow through the radiator.

Radiator Removal and Installation

1. Remove the radiator and expansion tank caps, disconnect the lower radiator hose, and drain the cooling system.

2. Remove the expansion tank and hose, and drain the coolant. Remove the upper radiator hose. On cars with automatic transmissions, disconnect and plug the transmission oil cooler lines at the radiator.

3. Remove the retaining bolts for the radiator and fan shroud, if so equipped, and lift out the radiator.

4. To install, place the radiator and fan shroud in position and install the retaining bolts.

5. On automatic transmission cars, connect the oil cooler lines.

6. Install the lower and upper radiator hoses.

7. Install the expansion tank with its hose. Make sure that the overflow hose is clear of the fan and is free of any sharp bends.

8. Fill the cooling system with a 50 percent ethylene glycol, 50 percent water solution. Replace the caps.

9. Start the engine and check for leaks. After the engine has reached operating temperature, make sure that the coolant level in the expansion tank is between the maximum and minimum marks.

Water Pump Removal and Installation

1. Drain the cooling system and remove the radiator as previously described.

2. Loosen the fan belt by slackening the alternator adjusting bolt. Remove the fan.

3. Remove the housing bolts from the water pump. Carefully remove the aluminum housing from the engine along with all the old gasket material.

4. Pull the water pump assembly from the block and remove the sealing rings.

5. To install, position the water pump assembly to the block, making sure that the sealing rings on the upper side of the pump are seated fully. Press the pump upward against the cylinder head extension to seat the rings.

6. Install the housing and new gasket. Hand-tighten the housing bolts until snug. Do not tighten the bolts more than ½ turn further to avoid cracking the housing or breaking the bolts.

7. Install the fan and adjust the fan (drive) belt tension.

8. Install the radiator as previously described. Fill the cooling system.

9. Start the engine and check for leaks.

Thermostat Removal and Installation

1. Disconnect the lower radiator hose and drain the cooling system.

2. Remove the two bolts securing the thermostat housing to the cylinder head and carefully lift the housing free.

3. Remove all old gasket material from the mating surfaces and remove the thermostat.

4. Test the operation of the thermostat by immersing it in a container of heated water. Two types of thermostats are used on 1970–73 Volvos. Type one is a 170° unit which bears a 170 marking. It begins to open at 168–172° F and is fully open at 194° F. Type two is a 180° unit which bears an 85° marking (85° Centigrade). It begins to open at 177–181° F and is fully open at 195° F. Replace any thermostat that does not open at the correct temperatures.

5. Place the thermostat, with a new gasket, in the cylinder head. Fit the thermostat housing to the head and hand-tighten the two bolts until snug. Do not tighten the bolts more than 1/4 turn past snug.

6. Connect the lower radiator hose and replace the coolant.

Engine Rebuilding

This section describes, in detail, the procedures involved in rebuilding a typical engine. The procedures specifically refer to an inline engine, however, they are basically identical to those used in rebuilding engines of nearly all design and configurations. Procedures for servicing atypical engines (i.e., horizontally opposed) are described in the appropriate section, although in most cases, cylinder head reconditioning procedures described in this chapter will apply.

The section is divided into two sections. The first, Cylinder Head Reconditioning, assumes that the cylinder head is removed from the engine, all manifolds are removed, and the cylinder head is on a workbench. The camshaft should be removed from overhead cam cylinder heads. The second section, Cylinder Block Reconditioning, covers the block, pistons, connecting rods and crankshaft. It is assumed that the engine is mounted on a work stand, and the cylinder head and all accessories are removed.

Procedures are identified as follows:

Unmarked—Basic procedures that must be performed in order to successfully complete the rebuilding process.

Starred (*)—Procedures that should be performed to ensure maximum performance and engine life.

Double starred (**)—Procedures that may be performed to increase engine performance and reliability. These procedures are usually reserved for extremely heavy-duty or competition usage.

In many cases, a choice of methods is also provided. Methods are identified in the same manner as procedures. The choice of method for a procedure is at the discretion of the user.

The tools required for the basic rebuilding procedure should, with minor exceptions, be those

TORQUE (ft. lbs.) *

U.S.

| Bolt Diameter (inches) | Bolt Grade (SAE) | | | | Wrench Size (inches) | |
	⬡ 1 and 2	⬡ 5	⬡ 6	⬡ 8	Bolt	Nut
1/4	5	7	10	10.5	3/8	7/16
5/16	9	14	19	22	1/2	9/16
3/8	15	25	34	37	9/16	5/8
7/16	24	40	55	60	5/8	3/4
1/2	37	60	85	92	3/4	13/16
9/16	53	88	120	132	7/8	7/8
5/8	74	120	167	180	15/16	1
3/4	120	200	280	296	1-1/8	1-1/8
7/8	190	302	440	473	1-5/16	1-5/16
1	282	466	660	714	1-1/2	1-1/2

Metric

| Bolt Diameter (mm) | Bolt Grade | | | | Wrench Size (mm) |
	5D	8G	10K	12K	Bolt and Nut
6	5	6	8	10	10
8	10	16	22	27	14
10	19	31	40	49	17
12	34	54	70	86	19
14	55	89	117	137	22
16	83	132	175	208	24
18	111	182	236	283	27
22	182	284	394	464	32
24	261	419	570	689	36

*—Torque values are for lightly oiled bolts. CAUTION: Bolts threaded into aluminum require much less torque.

General Torque Specifications

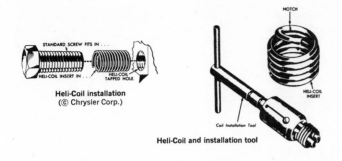

Heli-Coil installation
(© Chrysler Corp.)

Heli-Coil and installation tool

Heli-Coil Insert			Drill	Tap	Insert. Tool	Extract- ing Tool
Thread Size	Part No.	Insert Length (In.)	Size	Part No.	Part No.	Part No.
1/2 -20	1185-4	3/8	17/64 (.266)	4 CPB	528-4N	1227-6
5/16-18	1185-5	15/32	Q (.332)	5 CPB	528-5N	1227-6
3/8 -16	1185-6	9/16	X (.397)	6 CPB	528-6N	1227-6
7/16-14	1185-7	21/32	29/64 (.453)	7 CPB	528-7N	1227-16
1/2 -13	1185-8	3/4	33/64 (.516)	8 CPB	528-8N	1227-16

Heli-Coil Specifications

included in a mechanic's tool kit. An accurate torque wrench, and a dial indicator (reading in thousandths) mounted on a universal base should be available. Bolts and nuts with no torque specification should be tightened according to size (see chart). Special tools, where required, all are readily available from the major tool suppliers (i.e., Craftsman, Snap-On, K-D). The services of a competent automotive machine shop must also be readily available.

When assembling the engine, any parts that will be in frictional contact must be pre-lubricated, to provide protection on initial start-up. Vortex Pre-Lube, STP, or any product specifically formulated for this purpose may be used. NOTE: *Do not use engine oil.* Where semi-permanent (locked but removable) installation of bolts or nuts is desired, threads should be cleaned and coated with Loctite. Studs may be permanently installed using Loctite Stud and Bearing Mount.

Aluminum has become increasingly popular for use in engines, due to its low weight and excellent heat transfer characteristics. The following precautions must be observed when handling aluminum engine parts:

—Never hot-tank aluminum parts.

—Remove all aluminum parts (identification tags, etc.) from engine parts before hot-tanking (otherwise they will be removed during the process).

—Always coat threads lightly with engine oil or anti-seize compounds before installation, to prevent seizure.

—Never over-torque bolts or spark plugs in aluminum threads. Should stripping occur, threads can be restored according to the following procedure, using Heli-Coil thread inserts:

Tap drill the hole with the stripped threads to the specified size (see chart). Using the specified tap (NOTE: *Heli-Coil tap sizes refer to the size thread being replaced, rather than the actual tap size*), tap the hole for the Heli-Coil. Place the insert on the proper installation tool (see chart). Apply pressure on the insert while winding it clockwise into the hole, until the top of the insert is one turn below the surface. Remove the installation tool, and break the installation tang from the bottom of the in-

sert by moving it up and down. If the Heli-Coil must be removed, tap the removal tool firmly into the hole, so that it engages the top thread, and turn the tool counter-clockwise to extract the insert.

Snapped bolts or studs may be removed, using a stud extractor (unthreaded) or Vise-Grip pliers (threaded). Penetrating oil (e.g., Liquid Wrench) will often aid in breaking frozen threads. In cases where the stud or bolt is flush with, or below the surface, proceed as follows:

Drill a hole in the broken stud or bolt, approximately 1/2 its diameter. Select a screw extractor (e.g., Easy-Out) of the proper size, and tap it into the stud or bolt. Turn the extractor counter-clockwise to remove the stud or bolt.

Magnaflux and Zyglo are inspection techniques used to locate material flaws, such as stress cracks. Magnafluxing coats the part with fine magnetic particles, and subjects the part to a magnetic field. Cracks cause breaks

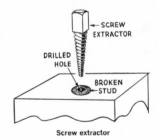

Screw extractor

in the magnetic field, which are outlined by the particles. Since Magnaflux is a magnetic process, it is applicable only to ferrous materials. The Zyglo process coats the material with a fluorescent dye penetrant, and then subjects it to blacklight inspection, under which cracks glow bright-

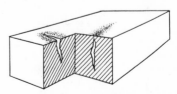

Magnaflux indication of cracks

ly. Parts made of any material may be tested using Zyglo. While Magnaflux and Zyglo are excellent for general inspection, and locating hidden defects, specific checks of suspected cracks may be made at lower cost and more readily using spot check dye. The dye is sprayed onto the suspected area, wiped off, and the area is then sprayed with a developer. Cracks then will show up bright-ly. Spot check dyes will only indicate surface cracks; therefore, structural cracks below the surface may escape detection. When questionable, the part should be tested using Magnaflux or Zyglo.

CYLINDER HEAD RECONDITIONING

Procedure	*Method*
Identify the valves:  **Valve identification** (© SAAB)	Invert the cylinder head, and number the valve faces front to rear, using a permanent felt-tip marker.
Remove the rocker arms:	Remove the rocker arms with shaft(s) or balls and nuts. Wire the sets of rockers, balls and nuts together, and identify according to the corresponding valve.
Remove the valves and springs:	Using an appropriate valve spring compressor (depending on the configuration of the cylinder head), compress the valve springs. Lift out the keepers with needlenose pliers, release the compressor, and remove the valve, spring, and spring retainer.
Check the valve stem-to-guide clearance:  **Checking the valve stem-to-guide clearance** (© American Motors Corp.)	Clean the valve stem with lacquer thinner or a similar solvent to remove all gum and varnish. Clean the valve guides using solvent and an expanding wire-type valve guide cleaner. Mount a dial indicator so that the stem is at 90° to the valve stem, as close to the valve guide as possible. Move the valve off its seat, and measure the valve guide-to-stem clearance by moving the stem back and forth to actuate the dial indicator. Measure the valve stems using a micrometer, and compare to specifications, to determine whether stem or guide wear is responsible for excessive clearance.
De-carbon the cylinder head and valves: 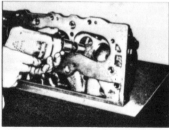 **Removing carbon from the cylinder head** (© Chevrolet Div. G.M. Corp.)	Chip carbon away from the valve heads, combustion chambers, and ports, using a chisel made of hardwood. Remove the remaining deposits with a stiff wire brush. NOTE: *Ensure that the deposits are actually removed, rather than burnished.*

Procedure	Method
Hot-tank the cylinder head:	Have the cylinder head hot-tanked to remove grease, corrosion, and scale from the water passages. NOTE: *In the case of overhead cam cylinder heads, consult the operator to determine whether the camshaft bearings will be damaged by the caustic solution.*
Degrease the remaining cylinder head parts:	Using solvent (i.e., Gunk), clean the rockers, rocker shaft(s) (where applicable), rocker balls and nuts, springs, spring retainers, and keepers. Do not remove the protective coating from the springs.
Check the cylinder head for warpage:  Checking the cylinder head for warpage (ⓒ Ford Motor Co.)	Place a straight-edge across the gasket surface of the cylinder head. Using feeler gauges, determine the clearance at the center of the straight-edge. Measure across both diagonals, along the longitudinal centerline, and across the cylinder head at several points. If warpage exceeds .003″ in a 6″ span, or .006″ over the total length, the cylinder head must be resurfaced. NOTE: *If warpage exceeds the manufacturers maximum tolerance for material removal, the cylinder head must be replaced.* When milling the cylinder heads of V-type engines, the intake manifold mounting position is altered, and must be corrected by milling the manifold flange a proportionate amount.
** Porting and gasket matching:  Marking the cylinder head for gasket matching (ⓒ Petersen Publishing Co.)  Port configuration before and after gasket matching (ⓒ Petersen Publishing Co.)	** Coat the manifold flanges of the cylinder head with Prussian blue dye. Glue intake and exhaust gaskets to the cylinder head in their installed position using rubber cement and scribe the outline of the ports on the manifold flanges. Remove the gaskets. Using a small cutter in a hand-held power tool (i.e., Dremel Moto-Tool), gradually taper the walls of the port out to the scribed outline of the gasket. Further enlargement of the ports should include the removal of sharp edges and radiusing of sharp corners. Do not alter the valve guides. NOTE: *The most efficient port configuration is determined only by extensive testing. Therefore, it is best to consult someone experienced with the head in question to determine the optimum alterations.*

Procedure	Method

** Polish the ports:

Relieved and polished ports
(© Petersen Publishing Co.)

Polished combustion chamber
(© Petersen Publishing Co.)

** Using a grinding stone with the above mentioned tool, polish the walls of the intake and exhaust ports, and combustion chamber. Use progressively finer stones until all surface imperfections are removed. NOTE: *Through testing, it has been determined that a smooth surface is more effective than a mirror polished surface in intake ports, and vice-versa in exhaust ports.*

* Knurling the valve guides:

Cut-away view of a knurled valve guide
(© Petersen Publishing Co.)

* Valve guides which are not excessively worn or distorted may, in some cases, be knurled rather than replaced. Knurling is a process in which metal is displaced and raised, thereby reducing clearance. Knurling also provides excellent oil control. The possibility of knurling rather than replacing valve guides should be discussed with a machinist.

Replacing the valve guides: NOTE: *Valve guides should only be replaced if damaged or if an oversize valve stem is not available.*

A-VALVE GUIDE I.D.
B-SLIGHTLY SMALLER THAN VALVE GUIDE O.D.

Valve guide removal tool

WASHERS

A-VALVE GUIDE I.D.
B-LARGER THAN THE VALVE GUIDE O.D.

Valve guide installation tool (with washers used during installation)

Depending on the type of cylinder head, valve guides may be pressed, hammered, or shrunk in. In cases where the guides are shrunk into the head, replacement should be left to an equipped machine shop. In other cases, the guides are replaced as follows: Press or tap the valve guides out of the head using a stepped drift (see illustration). Determine the height above the boss that the guide must extend, and obtain a stack of washers, their I.D. similar to the guide's O.D., of that height. Place the stack of washers on the guide, and insert the guide into the boss. NOTE: *Valve guides are often tapered or beveled for installation.* Using the stepped installation tool (see illustration), press or tap the guides into position. Ream the guides according to the size of the valve stem.

Procedure	Method
Replacing valve seat inserts:	Replacement of valve seat inserts which are worn beyond resurfacing or broken, if feasible, must be done by a machine shop.
Resurfacing (grinding) the valve face:  **Grinding a valve** (© Subaru) 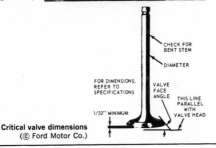 **Critical valve dimensions** (© Ford Motor Co.)	Using a valve grinder, resurface the valves according to specifications. CAUTION: *Valve face angle is not always identical to valve seat angle.* A minimum margin of 1/32″ should remain after grinding the valve. The valve stem tip should also be squared and resurfaced, by placing the stem in the V-block of the grinder, and turning it while pressing lightly against the grinding wheel.
Resurfacing the valve seats using reamers:  **Reaming the valve seat** (© S.p.A. Fiat) **Valve seat width and centering** (© Ford Motor Co.)	Select a reamer of the correct seat angle, slightly larger than the diameter of the valve seat, and assemble it with a pilot of the correct size. Install the pilot into the valve guide, and using steady pressure, turn the reamer clockwise. CAUTION: *Do not turn the reamer counter-clockwise.* Remove only as much material as necessary to clean the seat. Check the concentricity of the seat (see below). If the dye method is not used, coat the valve face with Prussian blue dye, install and rotate it on the valve seat. Using the dye marked area as a centering guide, center and narrow the valve seat to specifications with correction cutters. NOTE: *When no specifications are available, minimum seat width for exhaust valves should be 5/64″, intake valves 1/16″.* After making correction cuts, check the position of the valve seat on the valve face using Prussian blue dye.
* Resurfacing the valve seats using a grinder:  **Grinding a valve seat** (© Subaru)	Select a pilot of the correct size, and a coarse stone of the correct seat angle. Lubricate the pilot if necessary, and install the tool in the valve guide. Move the stone on and off the seat at approximately two cycles per second, until all flaws are removed from the seat. Install a fine stone, and finish the seat. Center and narrow the seat using correction stones, as described above.

In the figure: CHECK FOR BENT STEM / DIAMETER / FOR DIMENSIONS, REFER TO SPECIFICATIONS / VALVE FACE ANGLE / THIS LINE PARALLEL WITH VALVE HEAD / 1/32″ MINIMUM

45° / VALVE SEAT WIDTH / A 2897-A

Procedure	Method
Checking the valve seat concentricity: 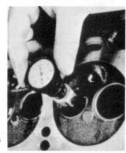 Checking the valve seat concentricity using a dial gauge (© American Motors Corp.)	Coat the valve face with Prussian blue dye, install the valve, and rotate it on the valve seat. If the entire seat becomes coated, and the valve is known to be concentric, the seat is concentric.
	* Install the dial gauge pilot into the guide, and rest the arm on the valve seat. Zero the gauge, and rotate the arm around the seat. Run-out should not exceed .002".
* Lapping the valves: NOTE: *Valve lapping is done to ensure efficient sealing of resurfaced valves and seats. Valve lapping alone is not recommended for use as a resurfacing procedure.*  Hand lapping the valves 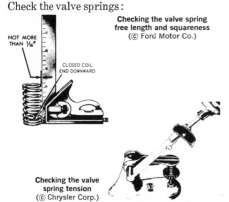 HAND DRILL ROD SUCTION CUP Home made mechanical valve lapping tool	* Invert the cylinder head, lightly lubricate the valve stems, and install the valves in the head as numbered. Coat valve seats with fine grinding compound, and attach the lapping tool suction cup to a valve head (NOTE: *Moisten the suction cup*). Rotate the tool between the palms, changing position and lifting the tool often to prevent grooving. Lap the valve until a smooth, polished seat is evident. Remove the valve and tool, and rinse away all traces of grinding compound.
	** Fasten a suction cup to a piece of drill rod, and mount the rod in a hand drill. Proceed as above, using the hand drill as a lapping tool. CAUTION: *Due to the higher speeds involved when using the hand drill, care must be exercised to avoid grooving the seat.* Lift the tool and change direction of rotation often.
Check the valve springs: NOT MORE THAN 1/16" CLOSED COIL END DOWNWARD Checking the valve spring free length and squareness (© Ford Motor Co.) Checking the valve spring tension (© Chrysler Corp.)	Place the spring on a flat surface next to a square. Measure the height of the spring, and rotate it against the edge of the square to measure distortion. If spring height varies (by comparison) by more than 1/16" or if distortion exceeds 1/16", replace the spring.
	** In addition to evaluating the spring as above, test the spring pressure at the installed and compressed (installed height minus valve lift) height using a valve spring tester. Springs used on small displacement engines (up to 3 liters) should be ± 1 lb. of all other springs in either position. A tolerance of ± 5 lbs. is permissible on larger engines.

Procedure	Method
* Install valve stem seals:  **Valve stem seal installation** (© Ford Motor Co.) SEAL	* Due to the pressure differential that exists at the ends of the intake valve guides (atmospheric pressure above, manifold vacuum below), oil is drawn through the valve guides into the intake port. This has been alleviated somewhat since the addition of positive crankcase ventilation, which lowers the pressure above the guides. Several types of valve stem seals are available to reduce blow-by. Certain seals simply slip over the stem and guide boss, while others require that the boss be machined. Recently, Teflon guide seals have become popular. Consult a parts supplier or machinist concerning availability and suggested usages. NOTE: *When installing seals, ensure that a small amount of oil is able to pass the seal to lubricate the valve guides; otherwise, excessive wear may result.*
Install the valves:	Lubricate the valve stems, and install the valves in the cylinder head as numbered. Lubricate and position the seals (if used, see above) and the valve springs. Install the spring retainers, compress the springs, and insert the keys using needlenose pliers or a tool designed for this purpose. NOTE: *Retain the keys with wheel bearing grease during installation.*
Checking valve spring installed height: 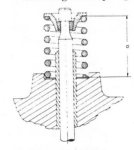  **Valve spring installed height dimension** (© Porsche) **Measuring valve spring installed height** (© Petersen Publishing Co.)	Measure the distance between the spring pad and the lower edge of the spring retainer, and compare to specifications. If the installed height is incorrect, add shim washers between the spring pad and the spring. CAUTION: *Use only washers designed for this purpose.*
** CC'ing the combustion chambers:	** Invert the cylinder head and place a bead of sealer around a combustion chamber. Install an apparatus designed for this purpose (burette mounted on a clear plate; see illustration) over the combustion chamber, and fill with the specified fluid to an even mark on the burette. Record the burette reading, and fill the combustion chamber with fluid. (NOTE: *A hole drilled in the plate will permit air to escape*). Subtract the burette reading, with the combustion chamber filled, from the previous reading, to determine combustion chamber volume in cc's. Duplicate this procedure in all combustion

Procedure	Method

CC'ing the combustion chamber
(© Petersen Publishing Co.)

chambers on the cylinder head, and compare the readings. The volume of all combustion chambers should be made equal to that of the largest. Combustion chamber volume may be increased in two ways. When only a small change is required (usually), a small cutter or coarse stone may be used to remove material from the combustion chamber. NOTE: *Check volume frequently.* Remove material over a wide area, so as not to change the configuration of the combustion chamber. When a larger change is required, the valve seat may be sunk (lowered into the head). NOTE: *When altering valve seat, remember to compensate for the change in spring installed height.*

Inspect the rocker arms, balls, studs, and nuts (where applicable):

Stress cracks in rocker nuts
(© Ford Motor Co.)

Visually inspect the rocker arms, balls, studs, and nuts for cracks, galling, burning, scoring, or wear. If all parts are intact, liberally lubricate the rocker arms and balls, and install them on the cylinder head. If wear is noted on a rocker arm at the point of valve contact, grind it smooth and square, removing as little material as possible. Replace the rocker arm if excessively worn. If a rocker stud shows signs of wear, it must be replaced (see below). If a rocker nut shows stress cracks, replace it. If an exhaust ball is galled or burned, substitute the intake ball from the same cylinder (if it is intact), and install a new intake ball. NOTE: *Avoid using new rocker balls on exhaust valves.*

Replacing rocker studs:

Reaming the stud bore for oversize rocker studs
(© Buick Div. G.M. Corp.)

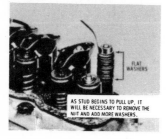

Extracting a pressed in rocker stud
(© Buick Div. G.M. Corp.)

In order to remove a threaded stud, lock two nuts on the stud, and unscrew the stud using the lower nut. Coat the lower threads of the new stud with Loctite, and install.

Two alternative methods are available for replacing pressed in studs. Remove the damaged stud using a stack of washers and a nut (see illustration). In the first, the boss is reamed .005-.006″ oversize, and an oversize stud pressed in. Control the stud extension over the boss using washers, in the same manner as valve guides. Before installing the stud, coat it with white lead and grease. To retain the stud more positively, drill a hole through the stud and boss, and install a roll pin. In the second method, the boss is tapped, and a threaded stud installed. Retain the stud using Loctite Stud and Bearing Mount.

Procedure	*Method*
Inspect the rocker shaft(s) and rocker arms (where applicable):  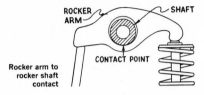 Disassembled rocker shaft parts arranged for inspection (© American Motors Corp.) ROCKER ARM — SHAFT — CONTACT POINT Rocker arm to rocker shaft contact	Remove rocker arms, springs and washers from rocker shaft. NOTE: *Lay out parts in the order they are removed.* Inspect rocker arms for pitting or wear on the valve contact point, or excessive bushing wear. Bushings need only be replaced if wear is excessive, because the rocker arm normally contacts the shaft at one point only. Grind the valve contact point of rocker arm smooth if necessary, removing as little material as possible. If excessive material must be removed to smooth and square the arm, it should be replaced. Clean out all oil holes and passages in rocker shaft. If shaft is grooved or worn, replace it. Lubricate and assemble the rocker shaft.
Inspect the camshaft bushings and the camshaft (overhead cam engines):	See next section.
Inspect the pushrods:	Remove the pushrods, and, if hollow, clean out the oil passages using fine wire. Roll each pushrod over a piece of clean glass. If a distinct clicking sound is heard as the pushrod rolls, the rod is bent, and must be replaced.
	* The length of all pushrods must be equal. Measure the length of the pushrods, compare to specifications, and replace as necessary.
Inspect the valve lifters: 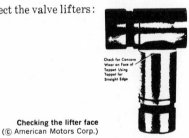 Check for Concave Wear on Face of Tappet Using Tappet for Straight Edge Checking the lifter face (© American Motors Corp.)	Remove lifters from their bores, and remove gum and varnish, using solvent. Clean walls of lifter bores. Check lifters for concave wear as illustrated. If face is worn concave, replace lifter, and carefully inspect the camshaft. Lightly lubricate lifter and insert it into its bore. If play is excessive, an oversize lifter must be installed (where possible). Consult a machinist concerning feasibility. If play is satisfactory, remove, lubricate, and reinstall the lifter.
* Testing hydraulic lifter leak down:  Lock Ring Plunger Cap Push Rod Socket Metering Disc Plunger Valve Seat Valve Valve Spring Valve Retainer Plunger Return Spring Tappet Body Exploded view of a typical hydraulic lifter (© American Motors Corp.)	Submerge lifter in a container of kerosene. Chuck a used pushrod or its equivalent into a drill press. Position container of kerosene so pushrod acts on the lifter plunger. Pump lifter with the drill press, until resistance increases. Pump several more times to bleed any air out of lifter. Apply very firm, constant pressure to the lifter, and observe rate at which fluid bleeds out of lifter. If the fluid bleeds very quickly (less than 15 seconds), lifter is defective. If the time exceeds 60 seconds, lifter is sticking. In either case, recondition or replace lifter. If lifter is operating properly (leak down time 15-60 seconds), lubricate and install it.

CYLINDER BLOCK RECONDITIONING

Procedure	*Method*
Checking the main bearing clearance:	Invert engine, and remove cap from the bearing to be checked. Using a clean, dry rag, thoroughly clean all oil from crankshaft journal and bearing insert. NOTE: *Plastigage is soluble in oil; therefore, oil on the journal or bearing could result in erroneous readings.* Place a piece of Plastigage along the full length of journal, reinstall cap, and torque to specifications. Remove bearing cap, and determine bearing clearance by comparing width of Plastigage to the scale on Plastigage envelope. Journal taper is determined by comparing width of the Plastigage strip near its ends. Rotate crankshaft 90° and retest, to determine journal eccentricity. NOTE: *Do not rotate crankshaft with Plastigage installed.* If bearing insert and journal appear intact, and are within tolerances, no further main bearing service is required. If bearing or journal appear defective, cause of failure should be determined before replacement.

Plastigage installed on main bearing journal
(© Chevrolet Div. G.M. Corp.)

Measuring Plastigage to determine
main bearing clearance
(© Chevrolet Div. G.M. Corp.)

Causes of bearing failure
(© Ford Motor Co.)

* Remove crankshaft from block (see below). Measure the main bearing journals at each end twice (90° apart) using a micrometer, to determine diameter, journal taper and eccentricity. If journals are within tolerances, reinstall bearing caps at their specified torque. Using a telescope gauge and micrometer, measure bearing I.D. parallel to piston axis and at 30° on each side of piston axis. Subtract journal O.D. from bearing I.D. to determine oil clearance. If crankshaft journals appear defective, or do not meet tolerances, there is no need to measure bearings; for the crankshaft will require grinding and/or undersize bearings will be required. If bearing appears defective, cause for failure should be determined prior to replacement.

Checking the connecting rod bearing clearance:	Connecting rod bearing clearance is checked in the same manner as main bearing clearance, using Plastigage. Before removing the crankshaft, connecting rod side clearance also should be measured and recorded.

Plastigage installed on connecting rod
bearing journal
(© Chevrolet Div. G.M. Corp.)

* Checking connecting rod bearing clearance, using a micrometer, is identical to checking main bearing clearance. If no other service

Procedure	Method

Measuring Plastigage to determine connecting rod bearing clearance
(© Chevrolet Div. G.M. Corp.)

is required, the piston and rod assemblies need not be removed.

Removing the crankshaft:

Connecting rod matching marks
(© Ford Motor Co.)

Using a punch, mark the corresponding main bearing caps and saddles according to position (i.e., one punch on the front main cap and saddle, two on the second, three on the third, etc.). Using number stamps, identify the corresponding connecting rods and caps, according to cylinder (if no numbers are present). Remove the main and connecting rod caps, and place sleeves of plastic tubing over the connecting rod bolts, to protect the journals as the crankshaft is removed. Lift the crankshaft out of the block.

Remove the ridge from the top of the cylinder:

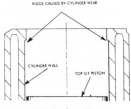

Cylinder bore ridge
(© Pontiac Div. G.M. Corp.)

In order to facilitate removal of the piston and connecting rod, the ridge at the top of the cylinder (unworn area; see illustration) must be removed. Place the piston at the bottom of the bore, and cover it with a rag. Cut the ridge away using a ridge reamer, exercising extreme care to avoid cutting too deeply. Remove the rag, and remove cuttings that remain on the piston. CAUTION: *If the ridge is not removed, and new rings are installed, damage to rings will result.*

Removing the piston and connecting rod:

Removing the piston
(© SAAB)

Invert the engine, and push the pistons and connecting rods out of the cylinders. If necessary, tap the connecting rod boss with a wooden hammer handle, to force the piston out. CAUTION: *Do not attempt to force the piston past the cylinder ridge* (see above).

Procedure	Method
Service the crankshaft:	Ensure that all oil holes and passages in the crankshaft are open and free of sludge. If necessary, have the crankshaft ground to the largest possible undersize.
	** Have the crankshaft Magnafluxed, to locate stress cracks. Consult a machinist concerning additional service procedures, such as surface hardening (e.g., nitriding, Tuftriding) to improve wear characteristics, cross drilling and chamfering the oil holes to improve lubrication, and balancing.
Removing freeze plugs:	Drill a hole in the center of the freeze plugs, and pry them out using a screwdriver or drift.
Remove the oil gallery plugs:	Threaded plugs should be removed using an appropriate (usually square) wrench. To remove soft, pressed in plugs, drill a hole in the plug, and thread in a sheet metal screw. Pull the plug out by the screw using pliers.
Hot-tank the block:	Have the block hot-tanked to remove grease, corrosion, and scale from the water jackets. NOTE: *Consult the operator to determine whether the camshaft bearings will be damaged during the hot-tank process.*
Check the block for cracks:	Visually inspect the block for cracks or chips. The most common locations are as follows: Adjacent to freeze plugs. Between the cylinders and water jackets. Adjacent to the main bearing saddles. At the extreme bottom of the cylinders. Check only suspected cracks using spot check dye (see introduction). If a crack is located, consult a machinist concerning possible repairs.
	** Magnaflux the block to locate hidden cracks. If cracks are located, consult a machinist about feasibility of repair.
Install the oil gallery plugs and freeze plugs:	Coat freeze plugs with sealer and tap into position using a piece of pipe, slightly smaller than the plug, as a driver. To ensure retention, stake the edges of the plugs. Coat threaded oil gallery plugs with sealer and install. Drive replacement soft plugs into block using a large drift as a driver.
	* Rather than reinstalling lead plugs, drill and tap the holes, and install threaded plugs.

Procedure	*Method*

Check the bore diameter and surface:

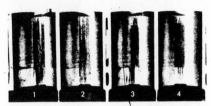

1, 2, 3 Piston skirt seizure resulted in this pattern. Engine must be rebored

4. Piston skirt and oil ring seizure caused this damage. Engine must be rebored

5, 6 Score marks caused by a split piston skirt. Damage is not serious enough to warrant reboring

7. Ring seized longitudinally, causing a score mark 1 3/16" wide, on the land side of the piston groove. The honing pattern is destroyed and the cylinder must be rebored

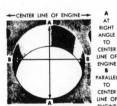

8. Result of oil ring seizure. Engine must be rebored

9. Oil ring seizure here was not serious enough to warrant reboring. The honing marks are still visible

Cylinder wall damage
(© Daimler-Benz A.G.)

Visually inspect the cylinder bores for roughness, scoring, or scuffing. If evident, the cylinder bore must be bored or honed oversize to eliminate imperfections, and the smallest possible oversize piston used. The new pistons should be given to the machinist with the block, so that the cylinders can be bored or honed exactly to the piston size (plus clearance). If no flaws are evident, measure the bore diameter using a telescope gauge and micrometer, or dial gauge, parallel and perpendicular to the engine centerline, at the top (below the ridge) and bottom of the bore. Subtract the bottom measurements from the top to determine taper, and the parallel to the centerline measurements from the perpendicular measurements to determine eccentricity. If the measurements are not within specifications, the cylinder must be bored or honed, and an oversize piston installed. If the measurements are within specifications the cylinder may be used as is, with only finish honing (see below). NOTE: *Prior to submitting the block for boring, perform the following operation(s).*

Cylinder bore measuring positions
(© Ford Motor Co.)

Measuring the cylinder bore with a telescope gauge
(© Buick Div. G.M. Corp.)

Determining the cylinder bore by measuring the telescope gauge with a micrometer
(© Buick Div. G.M. Corp.)

Measuring the cylinder bore with a dial gauge
(© Chevrolet Div. G.M. Corp.)

Procedure	Method
Check the block deck for warpage:	Using a straightedge and feeler gauges, check the block deck for warpage in the same manner that the cylinder head is checked (see Cylinder Head Reconditioning). If warpage exceeds specifications, have the deck resurfaced. NOTE: *In certain cases a specification for total material removal (Cylinder head and block deck) is provided. This specification must not be exceeded.*
* Check the deck height:	The deck height is the distance from the crankshaft centerline to the block deck. To measure, invert the engine, and install the crankshaft, retaining it with the center main cap. Measure the distance from the crankshaft journal to the block deck, parallel to the cylinder centerline. Measure the diameter of the end (front and rear) main journals, parallel to the centerline of the cylinders, divide the diameter in half, and subtract it from the previous measurement. The results of the front and rear measurements should be identical. If the difference exceeds .005″, the deck height should be corrected. NOTE: *Block deck height and warpage should be corrected concurrently.*
Check the cylinder block bearing alignment:  **Checking main bearing saddle alignment** (© Petersen Publishing Co.)	Remove the upper bearing inserts. Place a straightedge in the bearing saddles along the centerline of the crankshaft. If clearance exists between the straightedge and the center saddle, the block must be align-bored.
Clean and inspect the pistons and connecting rods:  **Removing the piston rings** (© Subaru)	Using a ring expander, remove the rings from the piston. Remove the retaining rings (if so equipped) and remove piston pin. NOTE: *If the piston pin must be pressed out, determine the proper method and use the proper tools; otherwise the piston will distort.* Clean the ring grooves using an appropriate tool, exercising care to avoid cutting too deeply. Thoroughly clean all carbon and varnish from the piston with solvent. CAUTION: *Do not use a wire brush or caustic solvent on pistons.* Inspect the pistons for scuffing, scoring, cracks, pitting, or excessive ring groove wear. If wear is evident, the piston must be replaced. Check the connecting rod length by measuring the rod from the inside of the large end to the inside of the small end using calipers (see

Procedure	Method

Ring Groove Cleaner

A1404-C

Cleaning the piston ring grooves
(© Ford Motor Co.)

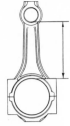

Connecting rod
length checking
dimension

illustration). All connecting rods should be equal length. Replace any rod that differs from the others in the engine.

* Have the connecting rod alignment checked in an alignment fixture by a machinist. Replace any twisted or bent rods.

* Magnaflux the connecting rods to locate stress cracks. If cracks are found, replace the connecting rod.

Fit the pistons to the cylinders:

90° FROM PISTON PIN

Measuring the cylinder
with a telescope gauge
for piston fitting
(© Buick Div.
G.M. Corp.)

60-91

Measuring the piston
for fitting
(© Buick Div.
G.M. Corp.)

90°

60-90

Using a telescope gauge and micrometer, or a dial gauge, measure the cylinder bore diameter perpendicular to the piston pin, 2½″ below the deck. Measure the piston perpendicular to its pin on the skirt. The difference between the two measurements is the piston clearance. If the clearance is within specifications or slightly below (after boring or honing), finish honing is all that is required. If the clearance is excessive, try to obtain a slightly larger piston to bring clearance within specifications. Where this is not possible, obtain the first oversize piston, and hone (or if necessary, bore) the cylinder to size.

Assemble the pistons and connecting rods:

Installing piston pin lock rings
(© Nissan Motor Co., Ltd.)

Inspect piston pin, connecting rod small end bushing, and piston bore for galling, scoring, or excessive wear. If evident, replace defective part(s). Measure the I.D. of the piston boss and connecting rod small end, and the O.D. of the piston pin. If within specifications, assemble piston pin and rod. CAUTION: *If piston pin must be pressed in, determine the proper method and use the proper tools; otherwise the piston will distort.* Install the lock rings; ensure that they seat properly. If the parts are not within specifications, determine the service method for the type of engine. In some cases, piston and pin are serviced as an assembly when either is defective. Others specify reaming the piston and connecting rods for an oversize pin. If the connecting rod bushing is worn, it may in many cases be replaced. Reaming the piston and replacing the rod bushing are machine shop operations.

Procedure	*Method*
Clean and inspect the camshaft:	Degrease the camshaft, using solvent, and clean out all oil holes. Visually inspect cam lobes and bearing journals for excessive wear. If a lobe is questionable, check all lobes as indicated below. If a journal or lobe is worn, the camshaft must be reground or replaced. NOTE: *If a journal is worn, there is a good chance that the bushings are worn.* If lobes and journals appear intact, place the front and rear journals in V-blocks, and rest a dial indicator on the center journal. Rotate the camshaft to check straightness. If deviation exceeds .001″, replace the camshaft.

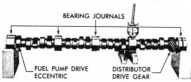

Checking the camshaft for straightness
(© Chevrolet Motor Div. G.M. Corp.)

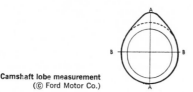

Camshaft lobe measurement
(© Ford Motor Co.)

* Check the camshaft lobes with a micrometer, by measuring the lobes from the nose to base and again at 90° (see illustration). The lift is determined by subtracting the second measurement from the first. If all exhaust lobes and all intake lobes are not identical, the camshaft must be reground or replaced.

Replace the camshaft bearings:

If excessive wear is indicated, or if the engine is being completely rebuilt, camshaft bearings should be replaced as follows: Drive the camshaft rear plug from the block. Assemble the removal puller with its shoulder on the bearing to be removed. Gradually tighten the puller nut until bearing is removed. Remove remaining bearings, leaving the front and rear for last. To remove front and rear bearings, reverse position of the tool, so as to pull the bearings in toward the center of the block. Leave the tool in this position, pilot the new front and rear bearings on the installer, and pull them into position. Return the tool to its original position and pull remaining bearings into position. NOTE: *Ensure that oil holes align when installing bearings.* Replace camshaft rear plug, and stake it into position to aid retention.

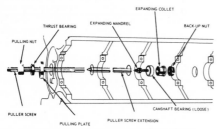

Camshaft removal and installation tool (typical)
(© Ford Motor Co.)

Finish hone the cylinders:

Chuck a flexible drive hone into a power drill, and insert it into the cylinder. Start the hone, and move it up and down in the cylinder at a rate which will produce approximately a 60° cross-hatch pattern (see illustration). NOTE: *Do not extend the hone below the cylinder bore.* After developing the pattern, remove the hone and recheck piston fit. Wash the cylinders with a detergent and water solution to remove abrasive dust, dry, and wipe several times with a rag soaked in engine oil.

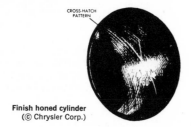

Finish honed cylinder
(© Chrysler Corp.)

Procedure	Method
Check piston ring end-gap:  **Checking ring end-gap** (© Chevrolet Motor Div. G.M. Corp.)	Compress the piston rings to be used in a cylinder, one at a time, into that cylinder, and press them approximately 1″ below the deck with an inverted piston. Using feeler gauges, measure the ring end-gap, and compare to specifications. Pull the ring out of the cylinder and file the ends with a fine file to obtain proper clearance. CAUTION: *If inadequate ring end-gap is utilized, ring breakage will result.*
Install the piston rings: 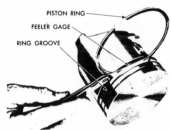 **Checking ring side clearance** (© Chrysler Corp.) 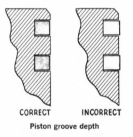 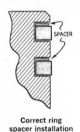 CORRECT INCORRECT Correct ring spacer installation **Piston groove depth**	Inspect the ring grooves in the piston for excessive wear or taper. If necessary, recut the groove(s) for use with an overwidth ring or a standard ring and spacer. If the groove is worn uniformly, overwidth rings, or standard rings and spacers may be installed without recutting. Roll the outside of the ring around the groove to check for burrs or deposits. If any are found, remove with a fine file. Hold the ring in the groove, and measure side clearance. If necessary, correct as indicated above. NOTE: *Always install any additional spacers above the piston ring.* The ring groove must be deep enough to allow the ring to seat below the lands (see illustration). In many cases, a "go-no-go" depth gauge will be provided with the piston rings. Shallow grooves may be corrected by recutting, while deep grooves require some type of filler or expander behind the piston. Consult the piston ring supplier concerning the suggested method. Install the rings on the piston, lowest ring first, using a ring expander. NOTE: *Position the ring markings as specified by the manufacturer (see car section).*
Install the camshaft:	Liberally lubricate the camshaft lobes and journals, and slide the camshaft into the block. CAUTION: *Exercise extreme care to avoid damaging the bearings when inserting the camshaft.* Install and tighten the camshaft thrust plate retaining bolts.
Check camshaft end-play:  **Checking camshaft end-play with a feeler gauge** (© Ford Motor Co.)	Using feeler gauges, determine whether the clearance between the camshaft boss (or gear) and backing plate is within specifications. Install shims behind the thrust plate, or reposition the camshaft gear and retest end-play.

Procedure	*Method*

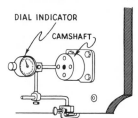

Checking camshaft end-play with a
dial indicator

* Mount a dial indicator stand so that the stem of the dial indicator rests on the nose of the camshaft, parallel to the camshaft axis. Push the camshaft as far in as possible and zero the gauge. Move the camshaft outward to determine the amount of camshaft end-play. If the end-play is not within tolerance, install shims behind the thrust plate, or reposition the camshaft gear and retest.

Install the rear main seal (where applicable):

Seating the rear
main seal
(© Buick Div. G.M. Corp.)

Position the block with the bearing saddles facing upward. Lay the rear main seal in its groove and press it lightly into its seat. Place a piece of pipe the same diameter as the crankshaft journal into the saddle, and firmly seat the seal. Hold the pipe in position, and trim the ends of the seal flush if required.

Install the crankshaft:

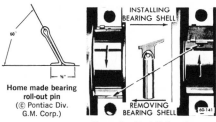

Home made bearing
roll-out pin
(© Pontiac Div.
G.M. Corp.)

Removal and installation of upper
bearing insert using a roll-out pin
(© Buick Div. G.M. Corp.)

Thoroughly clean the main bearing saddles and caps. Place the upper halves of the bearing inserts on the saddles and press into position. NOTE: *Ensure that the oil holes align.* Press the corresponding bearing inserts into the main bearing caps. Lubricate the upper main bearings, and lay the crankshaft in position. Place a strip of Plastigage on each of the crankshaft journals, install the main caps, and torque to specifications. Remove the main caps, and compare the Plastigage to the scale on the Plastigage envelope. If clearances are within tolerances, remove the Plastigage, turn the crankshaft 90°, wipe off all oil and retest. If all clearances are correct, remove all Plastigage, thoroughly

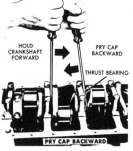

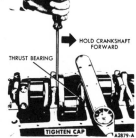

Aligning the thrust bearing
(© Ford Motor Co.)

Procedure	*Method*
	lubricate the main caps and bearing journals, and install the main caps. If clearances are not within tolerance, the upper bearing inserts may be removed, without removing the crankshaft, using a bearing roll out pin (see illustration). Roll in a bearing that will provide proper clearance, and retest. Torque all main caps, excluding the thrust bearing cap, to specifications. Tighten the thrust bearing cap finger tight. To properly align the thrust bearing, pry the crankshaft the extent of its axial travel several times, the last movement held toward the front of the engine, and torque the thrust bearing cap to specifications. Determine the crankshaft end-play (see below), and bring within tolerance with thrust washers.
Measure crankshaft end-play:  **Checking crankshaft end-play with a dial indicator** (© Ford Motor Co.) 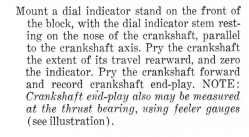  **Checking crankshaft end-play with a feeler gauge** (© Chevrolet Div. (G.M. Corp.)	Mount a dial indicator stand on the front of the block, with the dial indicator stem resting on the nose of the crankshaft, parallel to the crankshaft axis. Pry the crankshaft the extent of its travel rearward, and zero the indicator. Pry the crankshaft forward and record crankshaft end-play. NOTE: *Crankshaft end-play also may be measured at the thrust bearing, using feeler gauges* (see illustration).
Install the pistons:	Press the upper connecting rod bearing halves into the connecting rods, and the lower halves into the connecting rod caps. Position the piston ring gaps according to specifications (see car section), and lubricate the pistons. Install a ring compresser on a piston, and press two long (8″) pieces of plastic tubing over the rod bolts. Using the plastic tubes as a guide, press the pistons into the bores and onto the crankshaft with a wooden hammer handle. After seating the rod on the crankshaft journal, remove the tubes and install the cap finger tight. Install the remaining pistons in the same man-

Procedure	*Method*

Tubing used as guide when installing
a piston
(© Oldsmobile Div. G.M. Corp.)

ner. Invert the engine and check the bearing clearance at two points (90° apart) on each journal with Plastigage. NOTE: *Do not turn the crankshaft with Plastigage installed.* If clearance is within tolerances, remove *all* Plastigage, thoroughly lubricate the journals, and torque the rod caps to specifications. If clearance is not within specifications, install different thickness bearing inserts and recheck. CAUTION: *Never shim or file the connecting rods or caps.* Always install plastic tube sleeves over the rod bolts when the caps are not installed, to protect the crankshaft journals.

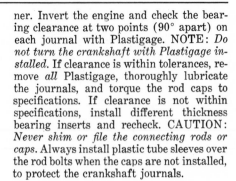

Installing a piston
(© Chevrolet Div. G.M. Corp.)

Check connecting rod side clearance:

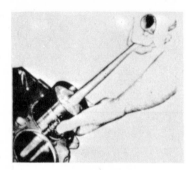

Checking connecting rod side clearance
(© Chevrolet Div. G.M. Corp.)

Determine the clearance between the sides of the connecting rods and the crankshaft, using feeler gauges. If clearance is below the minimum tolerance, the rod may be machined to provide adequate clearance. If clearance is excessive, substitute an unworn rod, and recheck. If clearance is still outside specifications, the crankshaft must be welded and reground, or replaced.

Inspect the timing chain:

Visually inspect the timing chain for broken or loose links, and replace the chain if any are found. If the chain will flex sideways, it must be replaced. Install the timing chain as specified. NOTE: *If the original timing chain is to be reused, install it in its original position.*

Procedure	Method
Check timing gear backlash and runout:  **Checking camshaft gear backlash** (© Chevrolet Div. G.M. Corp.)  **Checking camshaft gear runout** (© Chevrolet Div. G.M. Corp.)	Mount a dial indicator with its stem resting on a tooth of the camshaft gear (as illustrated). Rotate the gear until all slack is removed, and zero the indicator. Rotate the gear in the opposite direction until slack is removed, and record gear backlash. Mount the indicator with its stem resting on the edge of the camshaft gear, parallel to the axis of the camshaft. Zero the indicator, and turn the camshaft gear one full turn, recording the runout. If either backlash or runout exceed specifications, replace the worn gear(s).

Completing the Rebuilding Process

Following the above procedures, complete the rebuilding process as follows:

Fill the oil pump with oil, to prevent cavitating (sucking air) on initial engine start up. Install the oil pump and the pickup tube on the engine. Coat the oil pan gasket as necessary, and install the gasket and the oil pan. Mount the flywheel and the crankshaft vibrational damper or pulley on the crankshaft. NOTE: *Always use new bolts when installing the flywheel.* Inspect the clutch shaft pilot bushing in the crankshaft. If the bushing is excessively worn, remove it with an expanding puller and a slide hammer, and tap a new bushing into place.

Position the engine, cylinder head side up. Lubricate the lifters, and install them into their bores. Install the cylinder head, and torque it as specified in the car section. Insert the pushrods (where applicable), and install the rocker shaft(s) (if so equipped) or position the rocker arms on the pushrods. If solid lifters are utilized, adjust the valves to the "cold" specifications.

Mount the intake and exhaust manifolds, the carburetor(s), the distributor and spark plugs. Adjust the point gap and the static ignition timing. Mount all accessories and install the engine in the car. Fill the radiator with coolant, and the crankcase with high quality engine oil.

Break-in Procedure

Start the engine, and allow it to run at low speed for a few minutes, while checking for leaks. Stop the engine, check the oil level, and fill as necessary. Restart the engine, and fill the cooling system to capacity. Check the point dwell angle and adjust the ignition timing and the valves. Run the engine at low to medium speed (800-2500 rpm) for approximately $\frac{1}{2}$ hour, and retorque the cylinder head bolts. Road test the car, and check again for leaks.

Follow the manufacturer's recommended engine break-in procedure and maintenance schedule for new engines.

Chapter Four

Emission Controls and Fuel System

Emission Controls

There are three basic sources of automotive pollution in the modern internal combustion engine. They are the crankcase with its accompanying blow-by vapors, the fuel system with its evaporation of unburned gasoline, and, of course, the combustion chambers themselves. Pollution arising from the incomplete combustion of gasoline falls into three categories; hydrocarbons (HC), carbon monoxide (CO), and oxides of nitrogen (NO_x).

Volvos have been equipped with positive crankcase ventilation (PCV) systems to control crankcase vapors since the early 1960s. The present system is a closed one; it is sealed to the atmosphere. When the engine is idling or under a light load, fresh filtered air is supplied to the crankcase via a hose from the air cleaner. Intake manifold vacuum draws the crankcase vapors and fresh air through a hose into the intake manifold where they are combined with the air-fuel mixture and then fired in the combustion chambers. The ensuing circular flow is regulated by a nipple which is located in-line between the vacuum source (intake manifold) and the crankcase. Under heavy load or throttling conditions, the fresh air hose reverses its

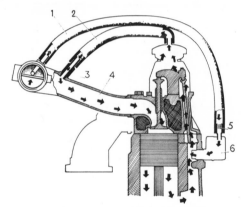

Positive crankcase ventilation system—B20E, B20F shown

1. Hose for fresh air supply
2. Hose for crankcase gases
3. Nipple
4. Inlet duct
5. Flame guard
6. Oil trap

direction of flow, permitting the crankcase vapors to be drawn into the carburetor (or, on fuel-injected models, the inlet duct), and hence into the combustion chambers, thus providing an additional mode of crankcase ventilation. A metal filter located inline between the fresh air source and the crankcase prevents engine backfire from reaching the crankcase and oil from being drawn into the induction system.

All post-1969 model Volvos have been equipped with an evaporative control sys-

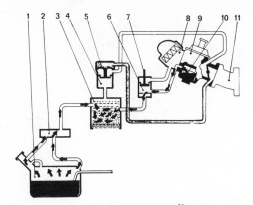

Fuel evaporative control system at idle

1. Fuel tank
2. Expansion tank
3. Venting filter
4. Air valve
5. Diaphragm
6. Valve (hot start valve)
7. Control rod (connected to throttle)
8. Air cleaner
9. Carburetor
10. Floatchamber
11. Intake manifold

Fuel evaporative control system at throttling

tem to prevent unburned fuel vapors in the fuel tank and, in carbureted models, the float chambers, from escaping into the atmosphere. An expansion tank above the fuel tank provides for thermal expansion of fuel vapors in warm weather. Those vapors which do not condense and return to the fuel tank are displaced and drawn into an activated charcoal canister in the engine compartment. The charcoal canister then absorbs and stores these fuel tank vapors, along with the float chamber vapors (on carbureted models) when the engine is shut off or is idling. Throttling the engine causes the vapors to be drawn out of the canister into the carburetor venturi (on fuel-injected models, the inlet duct) and then into the combustion chambers where they are burned. On carbureted models, the float chamber vapors are diverted from the canister to the air cleaner upon accel-

eration. As a result of these fumes being vented to the air cleaner, an overly rich fuel mixture may develop, leading to starting difficulties—especially in warm weather. A hot start valve is located in-line between the float chamber and the air cleaner which returns the vapors to the charcoal canister until the engine can handle the extra-rich mixture.

Various measures have been taken since 1968 to limit exhaust emissions of hydrocarbons, carbon monoxide, and more recently, oxides of nitrogen. Generally speaking, these measures have been designed to provide more efficient combustion of a "leaner" air-fuel mixture. Basic modifications include a distributor which retards the timing from its basic setting during idle, and the installation of a "hotter" 190° F thermostat in the cooling system. By far, the fuel system has received the most attention. Fuel injection, which is inherently cleaner due to its precise regulation of the air-fuel mixture under varying rpm, engine load, and ambient temperature conditions, has been available since 1970 and will be discussed later in this chapter. Carbureted engines have incorporated many modifications including such pullutant control devices as a temperature-regulated fuel jet, an air-fuel mixture preheating chamber, and a throttle bypass or overrev valve, and measures to improve the operation and driveability of emission-controlled engines such as a cold-start device, a constant intake air temperature device, and, as previously mentioned, a hot-start valve.

The temperature-regulated fuel mixture is accomplished differently on the Zenith-Stromberg carburetor than on the SU carburetor. On the Zenith-Stromberg carburetor, a temperature-sensitive bimetal spring in the temperature compensator actuates an air valve that varies the air supplied the venturi area to maintain the air-fuel ratio constant, despite changing fuel temperature. On the SU carburetor, a temperature-sensitive bimetal spring raises or lowers the adjustable jet to maintain the proper air-fuel ratio at changing fuel temperatures.

The air-fuel mixture preheating chamber used on pre-1972 models is located between the primary throttles in the carburetors and the secondary throttles in the intake manifold. The function of the cham-

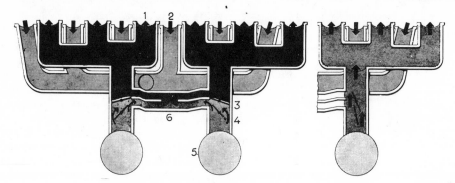

Preheating chamber—light load (left), heavy load (right)
(B30A shown—B20B similar)

1. Intake manifold   3. Secondary throttle   5. Carburetor
2. Exhaust manifold   4. Primary throttle   6. Preheating chamber

ber is, as the name implies, to warm and homogenize the air-fuel mixture before it is drawn into the intake ports, so that each cylinder receives an equally strong and thoroughly combustible mixture.

The throttle bypass or overrev valve serves to direct a regulated flow of fuel and air around the closed carburetor throttle, during engine deceleration (braking) from high speeds, and into the combustion chambers. This eliminates the over-rich surge condition that occurs when the throttle is finally opened after a period of engine braking.

The cold-start device on the rear carburetor is designed to improve the starting capabilities of a "lean" emissions engine during cold weather by providing extra fuel for starting and warm-up. Pulling out the choke lever turns a channelled disc, between the float chamber and the carburetor venturi, allowing additional fuel to enter the venturi. The choke restricts the intake air flow at the same time, further richening the mixture.

The constant intake air temperature device also aids in cold weather warm-up by providing exhaust manifold heat to the hose for the intake air. A thermostatically controlled flap regulates the mixture of intake air and exhaust heated air to an approximate temperature of 90° F.

In order to control emissions of NO_x, all 1973 140 series, 164 E and 1800 ES models with automatic transmission are equipped with an exhaust gas recirculation system. The system consists of a metering valve, a tubular pipe running from the exhaust manifold to the valve, another tubular pipe running from the valve to the inlet

EGR valve installed—B20F shown, B30F similar

duct, and a vacuum hose running from the valve's diaphragm to the inlet duct in front of the air regulator shutter. The valve permits a regulated amount of exhaust gases to enter the inlet duct and mix with the incoming intake air when the throttle is partly open. When the engine is idling, as well as under the full open throttle, the valve is closed, stopping the recirculation of the exhaust gases. Every 12 months or 12,000 miles, the system must be disassembled and cleaned. Every 24 months or 24,000 miles, the valve must be replaced with a new one.

Component Testing and Adjustment

TEMPERATURE COMPENSATOR

Zenith-Stromberg Carburetor

If the idle speed drops off sharply during extended periods of idling, especially

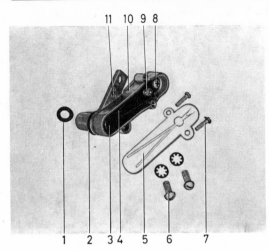

Temperature compensator

1. Rubber seal
2. Rubber seal
3. Valve
4. Bi-metal spring
5. Cover
6. Screws for temperature compensator

7. Screw for cover
8. Cross-slotted screw
9. Adjusting nut
10. Housing
11. Marking

BYPASS VALVE

Zenith-Stromberg Carburetor

If the engine does not return to idle speed soon after the throttle is released, and the throttle control linkage is properly adjusted, the bypass valve may be in need of adjustment or replacement.

1. If the engine still refuses to lower its rpm to idle speed when the throttle is released, turn the bypass adjusting screw on the front carburetor to the left, and manually lower the idle.

2. Run the engine briefly up to approximately 2000 rpm, then release the throttle. If the engine returns to idle speed, turn the screw ½ turn further to the left. If the engine does not return to idle, replace the bypass valve as a unit. See "Bypass Valve Replacement."

3. Remove the air cleaner. While peering into the carburetor bores, observe the air valves. Briefly race the engine and then release the throttle. The air valve of the front carburetor should normally go down to the bridge slower than the air valve of the rear carburetor. Turn the bypass ad-

during warm weather, the temperature compensator may be in need of adjustment or replacement.

1. Remove the one screw (7) retaining the plastic cover (5) to the compensator and remove the cover.

2. With the ambient temperature at or above 85° F, the valve (3) should be able to be pressed inward with light finger pressure and then return to its position without jamming. If the valve jams and is stiff in operation, the temperature compensator should be replaced as a unit. See "Temperature Compensator Replacement."

3. If properly adjusted, the valve will begin to open at 70–77° F, and be fully open at 85° F. If not properly adjusted, the valve may be adjusted while the temperature compensator is still on the carburetor by slackening one of the cross-slotted screws (8) for the bimetal spring (4), and centering the valve so that it opens and closes at the proper temperatures. If necessary, the temperature compensator may be removed and isolated at 70–77° F, then adjusted with the nut (9) for the bimetal spring so that the valve is loose in its seat at this temperature.

4. Replace the cover (5) and retaining screw on the compensator and check its operation during idling.

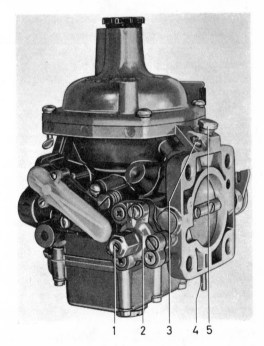

Stromberg carburetor—front, right side

1. Adjusting screw
2. By-pass valve
3. Plug for outlet for speed compensator (air conditioner)

4. Vacuum hose connection for distributor
5. Plug

justing screw to the right until the above-
mentioned normal function is obtained. If
the valve cannot be adjusted so that the
front air valve goes down to the bridge
slower than the rear air valve, the bypass
valve must be replaced as a unit. See "Bypass Valve Replacement."

HOT-START VALVE

Zenith-Stromberg Carburetor

When the throttle control is in the idling
position, adjust the valve control of the
hot-start valve so that the valve is against
the carburetor lever with the valve piston
in the upper position.

Coat the contact surfaces on the valve
and carburetor with high-temperature
white grease such a Molykote.

Test the operation of the hot-start valve
by determining that the engine returns to
idle speed after several brief periods of
racing the engine.

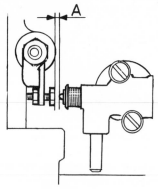

Hot start valve adjustment—SU carburetor

CONSTANT (INTAKE) AIR TEMPERATURE DEVICE

If the flap for the constant air temperature device sticks in one position, engine
operation will suffer. Normally, the flap is
closed to cold air (intake hose) at an ambient temperature of 70–77° F, and closed
to hot air (exhaust manifold heated) at
95–105° F.

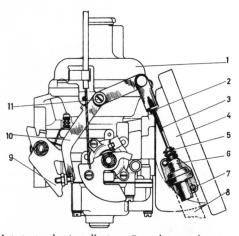

Hot start valve installation—Stromberg carburetor

1. Carburetor
2. Locknut
3. Control rod
4. Air cleaner, lower section
5. Rubber seal
6. Hot start valve
7. Attaching rivet
8. Venting filter hose.
   (Only on vehicle
   with gas evaporative
   unit)
9. Throttle lever
10. Valve control
11. Screw for valve control

SU Carburetor

To adjust the hot-start valve, press the
control rods down to the bottom position
and measure the distance (A) between the
rod and the adjusting screw. Adjust the
distance to a maximum of 0.04 in.

Test the operation of the control rods—
making sure that they do not jam.

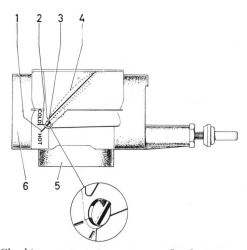

Checking constant air temperature flap function

1. HOT = open for warm
   air
2. COLD = open for cold
   air
3. Tab
4. Flap
5. Hot air intake
6. Cold air intake

1. The operation of the flap may be
checked with the flap housing installed in
position. When the small tab on the flap
housing points toward the mark closest the
exhaust heat hose, the flap is open for cold
(unheated) air. When the tab points to the
mark nearest the cold air intake, the flap is
open for warm (exhaust heated) air. If the
tab indicates that the flap is opening and

closing the air sources at the right temperatures, you may rest your soul. If not, check the operation of the flap control thermostat.

2. Disconnect the flap housing from the air intake hoses. Immerse the thermostat in lukewarm water. At a water temperature of 70–77° F, the thermostat should be in its upper (toward the flap housing) position. At 95–105° F, the thermostat should be in its lower position (away from the flap housing). If correct operation cannot be obtained, replace the thermostat and flap housing as a unit.

3. Replace the flap housing and thermostat assembly, making sure that the thermostat is centered in the middle of the air flow. Secure the hose clamp screw on top of the flap.

Component Replacement

TEMPERATURE COMPENSATOR

Zenith-Stromberg Carburetor

1. Remove the retaining screws (6) and lift off the compensator.

2. Discard the old rubber seals (1, 2) and replace them with new ones.

3. Position the compensator to the side of the carburetor and install the retaining screws.

4. Check the operation of the compensator during idle as outlined in "Temperature Compensator Testing and Adjustment."

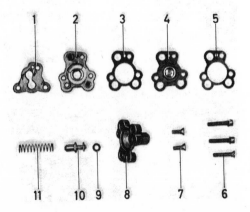

By-pass valve disassembled

1. Gasket	7. Screw for cover
2. Housing	8. Cover
3. Gasket	9. Rubber ring
4. Diaphragm	10. Adjusting screw
5. Gasket	11. Spring
6. Screw for by-pass valve	

BYPASS VALVE

Zenith-Stromberg Carburetor

1. Remove the three retaining screws (6) and lift off the bypass valve.

2. Discard the old bypass valve-to-carburetor housing gasket.

3. Position a new gasket and bypass valve to the carburetor, making sure that the orifices and mating surfaces of the valve and gasket align, then install the three retaining screws.

4. Check the operation of the bypass valve as outlined in "Bypass Valve Testing and Adjustment."

HOT-START VALVE

Zenith-Stromberg Carburetor

The hot-start valve on the Stromberg carburetor is riveted to the air cleaner. If cleaning is to be performed on the valve, it must be accomplished with the valve in place on the air cleaner.

Hot start valve removed—SU carburetor

1. Channel, connected to air cleaner
2. Channel, connected to floatchamber
3. Gasket (in assembly position)

SU Carburetor

1. Remove the two retaining screws and lift off the valve.

2. Discard the old gasket and clean the channels in the carburetor with a low-pressure air line.

3. Position the valve and new gasket to the carburetor, making sure that the gasket is aligned properly, then install the two retaining screws.

4. Adjust the position of the control rod and test the operation of the valve as outlined in "Hot-Start Valve Testing and Adjustment."

Constant Air Temperature Device Flap Housing

1. Loosen the hose clamps, and disconnect the flap housing and thermostat assembly from the hoses for the intake air, exhaust heated air, and intake manifold.

2. Install the new flap housing assembly in position and reconnect the three hoses. Make sure that the thermostat is centered in the middle of the intake air flow. Secure the hose clamp screw on top of the flap.

3. Check the operation of the new flap housing as outlined in "Constant Air Temperature Device Testing and Adjustment."

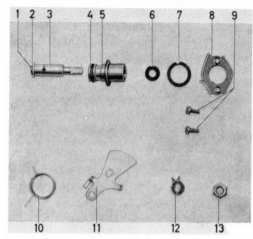

Cold start device disassembled—SU carburetor

1. Circlip
2. Washer
3. Spindle
4. Rubber ring
5. Housing
6. Rubber seal for spindle
7. Gasket
8. Spring retainer
9. Screws for cold start device
10. Return spring
11. Fast idle screw
12. Tab washer
13. Nut

Constant air temperature flap

1. Thermostat
2. Lock
3. Air cleaner connection
4. Flap control
5. Flap
6. Hot air intake
7. Cold air intake

Cold-Start Device Seals

SU Carburetor

1. Pry off the lockwasher (12) for the cold-start device and unscrew the channel disc nut (13).

2. Disconnect the return spring (10) and remove the channel disc and spring.

3. Remove the two retaining screws (9) and the spring retainer (8).

4. Lift the cold-start device away from the carburetor. Press the spindle (3) out of the cold-start device housing (5). Remove the gasket (7), the rubber ring (4), and rubber seal (6) from the spindle, and discard them. Clean all metal parts in kerosine, and clean the fuel channels with an air line.

5. Install a new rubber ring and seal on the housing and oil them with light (10W) engine oil. Install the spindle into the housing.

6. Position the housing assembly, with a new gasket, to the carburetor, fit the spring retainer, and install the retaining screws.

7. Position the return spring in its retainer so that the spring's short end fits into the retainer slot.

8. Hook the channel disc onto the spring's longer end and install the disc on the spindle. Install the channel disc retaining nut and snap on the lockwasher.

Component Service

Positive Crankcase Ventilation System

The only service required for the PCV system is the cleaning of the hoses, nipples, and metal filter every two years or 24,000 miles. Detailed maintenance of the system is outlined in the "Routine Maintenance" section of chapter 1.

Fuel Evaporative Control System

The only items requiring service in the evaporative control system are the foam plastic filter in the bottom of the charcoal canister and the hot-start valve. The canister filter is replaced every two years or 24,000 miles, as outlined in the "Routine Maintenance" section of chapter 1. The hot-start valve is serviced when hard starting in warm weather occurs. Adjust the control rods and lubricate the contact surfaces as outlined in "Hot-Start Valve Testing and Adjustment." On models equipped with SU carburetors, the valve may be removed and the passages cleaned of all impurities with compressed air.

Fuel System

FUEL PUMP

Volvo has used two different mechanical and two different electrical fuel pumps on its 1970–73 models. The mechanical units are used with carbureted engines, and the electrical units with fuel-injection. The procedure for replacing the two mechanical types is the same and the procedure for replacing the two electrical types is the same.

Mechanical Type

The Pierburg PV 3025 fuel pump used on the 164, and the Pierburg APG fuel pump used on the 140 series models are all camshaft-driven diaphragm types. When the fuel pump rocker arm is lifted by the camshaft, the diaphragm is pulled downward, drawing fuel from the tank into the pump. On the return action of the rocker arm, the diaphragm spring forces the diaphragm upward, feeding fuel to the carburetor float chamber. When the fuel level in the float chamber reaches its operating level, the float chamber valve closes, raising the pressure in the fuel feed line. When this pressure on the upper side of the diaphragm exceeds the spring pressure, the pumping action ceases, until more fuel is needed by the float chamber. The fuel pump is located on the left (driver's) side of the engine block.

TESTING AND ADJUSTMENT

No adjustments may be made to the fuel pump. Before removing and overhauling the old fuel pump, the following test may be made while the pump is still installed on the engine.

CAUTION: *To avoid accidental ignition of fuel during the test, first remove the coil high-tension wire from the distributor and the coil.*

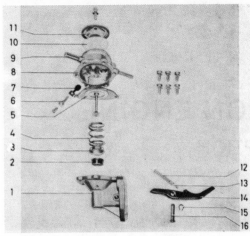

Pierburg APG fuel pump disassembled

1. Lower pump housing
2. Rubber seal
3. Guide
4. Diaphragm spring
5. Diaphragm
6. Stop arm
7. Spring
8. Upper pump housing
9. Inlet pipe
10. Strainer
11. Cover with gasket
12. Return spring
13. Spring holder
14. Lever
15. Circlip
16. Lever shaft

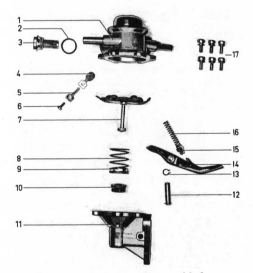

Pierburg PV 3025 fuel pump disassembled

1. Upper pump housing
2. Sealing washer
3. Plug with strainer
4. Inlet valve
5. Stop arm
6. Screw
7. Diaphragm
8. Spring
9. Spring guide
10. Rubber seal
11. Lower pump housing
12. Lever pin
13. Circlip
14. Lever
15. Spring retainer
16. Return spring
17. Screw

1. If a fuel pressure gauge is available, connect the gauge to the engine and operate the engine until the pressure stops ris-

ing. Stop the engine and take the reading. If the reading is within the specifications given in the "Tune-Up Specifications" chart in chapter 2, the malfunction is not in the fuel pump. Also check the pressure drop after the engine is stopped. A large pressure drop below the minimum specification indicates leaky valves. If the pump proves to be satisfactory, check the tank and inlet line.

2. If a fuel pressure gauge is not available, disconnect the fuel line at the pump outlet, place a vessel beneath the pump outlet, and crank the engine. A good pump will force the fuel out of the outlet in steady spurts. A worn diaphragm spring may not provide proper pumping action.

3. As a further test, disconnect and plug the fuel line from the tank at the pump, and hold your thumb over the pump inlet. If the pump is functioning properly, a suction should be felt on your thumb. No suction indicates that the pump diaphragm is leaking, or that the diaphragm linkage is worn.

4. Check the crankcase for gasoline. A ruptured diaphragm may leak fuel into the engine.

REPLACEMENT

1. Disconnect and plug the inlet and outlet lines to the fuel pump.

2. Remove the two fuel pump retaining bolts and carefully pull the pump and old gasket away from the block.

3. Discard the old gasket and position a new one on the pump.

4. Mount the fuel pump and gasket to the engine block, being careful to insert the pump lever (rocker arm) in the engine block, aligning it correctly above the camshaft.

5. While holding the pump securely against the block, install the two fuel pump retaining bolts, and tighten them securely.

6. Unplug and reconnect the fuel lines to the pump.

7. Start the engine and check for fuel leaks. Also check for oil leaks where the pump attaches to the block.

OVERHAUL

1. Remove the fuel pump from the engine, as described above, and scribe alignment marks on the upper and lower housing.

2. Remove the housing retaining screws and separate the parts.

3. Remove the rocker arm pin lockring and press out the pin. Pull out the rocker arm and the return spring.

4. Remove the diaphragm with its spring, guide, and rubber seal. The spring can be removed after the rubber seal has been pulled up over the nylon washer.

5. Remove the screw on the underside of the upper housing, and remove the stop arm and spring valve. The inlet valve cannot be removed.

6. Replace any worn or broken parts. Replace all gaskets and seals.

7. To reassemble, position the leaf spring and stop arm in the upper housing recess (A). Tighten the screw just enough for the leaf spring to contact the upper housing properly.

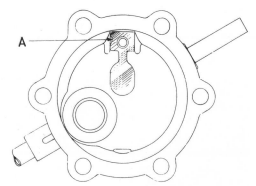

Correct location of leaf spring—Pierburg APG

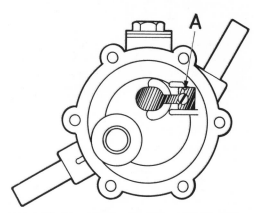

Correct location of leaf spring—Pierburg PV 3025

8. Install the diaphragm spring and guide, and then pull on the rubber seal with the flange inward, facing the guide.

9. Install the diaphragm unit in the lower housing. Press downward so that the

rubber seal seats properly. Press down the diaphragm and push in the rocker arm. Make sure that the rocker arm is installed in correct relation to the diaphragm rod.

10. Install the rocker arm pin, lockring, spring retainer, and return spring.

11. Assemble the upper and lower housing halves and install the retaining screws, taking note of the alignment marks.

12. Fit the fuel pump to the engine, making sure that the rocker arm is located in its correct position above the cam lobe.

Electric Type

Volvo has used electric fuel pumps on all of its fuel-injected models. On pre-1972 models, a Bosch unit with a 2.5 ampere current consumption and a 13 gallon per hour capacity is used. Post-1971 models use another Bosch unit with a 5 ampere current consumption and a 26 gallon per hour capacity. For purposes of description, testing, and replacement, the two units may be grouped together.

Electric fuel pump installed—1970–71 1800E shown

The electric pump and pumping motor are completely enclosed in the fuel pump housing. The electric rotor and brushes operate in fuel. The pump draws fuel from the tank and sends it under pressure to the pressure regulator, which limits the fuel pressure to 28 psi. If, for some reason such as the fuel line becoming blocked, or the pressure regulator malfunctioning, the pressure in the fuel pump builds up to 64 psi, a relief valve opens. On pre-1972 models, this relief valve conveys the excess fuel back to the tank. On post-1971 models, the relief valve shuts off the fuel supply and re-cycles the fuel inside the pump until the pressure is reduced. When the ignition switch is turned on, the pump operates briefly for about 1 or 2 seconds, and then shuts off. This will prevent the engine from being flooded by a leaking cold-start valve or injector. The pump then only works when the starter motor is engaged, or the engine is running. The fuel pump is located beneath the car, either in front of the fuel tank (1800), or on the right side of the fuel tank (140 series, 164).

NOTE: *Reports from the field indicate that a no-start condition may occasionally occur when the car has not been started for an extended period of time. This may be due to the fuel pump sticking in one position because of foreign matter entering the pump, or corrosion forming on the rotor shaft or commutator and brushes. It is, therefore, very important to replace the in-line fuel filter at its regular intervals on pre-1972 fuel-injected models, and clean the fuel tank pick-up screeen every 12 months or 12,000 miles on post-1971 fuel-injected models to prevent corrosion causing water condensation and foreign matter from entering the pump. As an additional corrosion prevention measure, add an alcohol solution or "dry gas" to the fuel, especially in winter months. If, however, the pump does become "stuck" in one position for any of the above reasons, it may be "unstuck" by lightly rapping on the pump casing with a length of hardwood such as a hammer handle, while the ignition is switched on.*

TESTING AND ADJUSTMENT

No adjustments may be made to the fuel pump. If the pump is not functioning properly, it must be discarded and replaced. To check the function of the fuel pump, the pump should be connected to a pressure gauge. Be careful not to switch the electrical leads. If the pump fails to pump its normal capacity, or if it cannot pump that capacity at its specified rate of current consumption, it must be replaced. Because of the highly technical nature of this operation, it is best to have this task delegated to your local Volvo or Bosch agency.

REPLACEMENT

1. Remove the electrical lead from the pump as well as the template to which the pump is mounted.

2. Clean around the hose connections. Pinch the fuel lines, loosen the hose clamps, and disconnect the lines.

3. Loosen the retaining nuts and remove the pump from its rubber mounts.

4. Install the new pump on its rubber mounts and tighten the retaining nuts.

5. Reconnect the fuel lines, tighten the hose clamps, and remove the pinchers.

6. Mount the template beneath the car and connect the electrical lead.

7. Start the engine and check for leaks.

CARBURETORS

Two different types of carburetors have been used on 1970–72 Volvos. A pair of sidedraft Zenith-Stromberg 175 CD2 SE units were used on 1970 140 series models, and on 1970–72 164 models. A pair of sidedraft SU HIF units were used on 1971–72 140 series models.

Principle of Operation

Both the Zenith-Stromberg and SU carburetors used on 1970–72 Volvos imported into this country are of the variable venturi, air valve type. The venturi area is determined by an air valve (suction piston) sliding up or down within a suction chamber which responds to changing engine vacuum and atmospheric pressure. The speed of the intake air remains relatively constant, assuring proper fuel atomization. The fuel delivery system is extremely simple with a single, tapered, metering needle regulating a single jet during idling, as well as acceleration, and full throttle conditions.

When the throttle plate is opened, the engine vacuum increases, permitting the

Stromberg carburetors installed—B30A shown

1. Cold air hose	13. Hose for fuel fumes to	23. Air hose for crankcase gases
2. Constant temperature device	carburetors	24. Hose for crankcase gases
flap	14. Venting filter	25. Idle trimming screw
3. Warm air hose	15. Air valve	26. Throttle control
4. Temperature compensator	16. Vacuum hose for vacuum for air	27. Bracket
5. Front carburetor	valve and distributor	28. Throttle stop screw
6. Clasp for air cleaner cover	17. Hose between fuel tank and	29. Manifold with preheating
7. Air cleaner	venting filter	chamber
8. Fuel hoses	18. Vacuum hose for distributor	30. Vacuum connection
9. Temperature compensator	(negative vacuum setting)	31. Idle trimming screw
10. Rear carburetor	19. Vacuum hose for brake booster	32. Throttle by-pass valve
11. Hot start valve	20. Choke wire	
12. Hose between hot start valve	21. Secondary throttle	
and venting filter	22. Throttle stop screw	

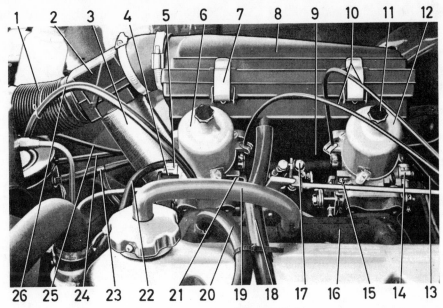

SU carburetors installed—B20B shown

1. Cold air hose
2. Constant temperature device flap
3. Warm air hose
4. Guard for throttle spindle
5. Hot start valve
6. Front carburetor
7. Clamp for air cleaner cover
8. Air cleaner
9. Fuel hose
10. Choke wires
11. Hydraulic damper
12. Rear carburetor
13. Vacuum hose for distributor (negative vacuum setting)
14. Hot start valve
15. Idle trimming screw
16. Manifold
17. Throttle control
18. Fresh-air intake for crankcase ventilation
19. Hose for crankcase gases
20. Hose for brake booster
21. Idle trimming screw
22. Fuel hose
23. Hoses connected to hot start valves
24. Hose to fuel tank
25. Vacuum hose (joined to "negative connection" on carburetor)
26. Hose for fuel fumes

air valve (suction piston) to overcome its calibrated return spring, raising the air valve and enlarging the venturi area. At the same time, the tapered metering needle, which is attached to the bottom of the air valve and is seated in the fuel jet, is raised, allowing more fuel to be sucked into the venturi. A damping piston enclosed in an oil-filled damping cylinder prevents the air valve from raising too suddenly, thus causing a temporarily richer mixture.

When the throttle plate is closed, the decreasing engine vacuum allows the return spring to overcome and lower the air valve, reducing the venturi area and restricting the air flow. At the same time, the tapered metering needle is further inserted into the fuel jet, reducing fuel flow.

Removal and Installation

1. On the Zenith-Stromberg carburetor, disconnect the hot-start valve control. Sep-

arate the air cleaner halves and remove the inner half from the carburetors.

2. Disconnect the throttle linkage by removing the link rod ball joints from the carburetors. Disconnect the choke cable, taking note of its proper location.

3. Disconnect and plug the fuel lines at the float chambers. Remove the vacuum hose for the distributor. On the SU carburetor, disconnect the hot-start valve hose.

4. Remove the four (each) nuts retaining the carburetors to the intake manifold. Remove the carburetors, gaskets, and protection plate.

5. Position the protection plate, new gaskets, and carburetors on the intake manifold studs. Install the carburetor retaining nuts and tighten them evenly until they are snug against the manifold.

6. Connect the vacuum hose, fuel hoses, choke, and throttle linkage. On the SU carburetor, connect the hot-start valve hose.

7. Install the inner half of the air cleaner to the carburetors. Adjust the idle speed and mixture of the carburetors as outlined in the "Tune-Up" section of chapter 2.

8. Fit the air cleaner halves together and, on the Stromberg carburetor, connect the hot-start valve control.

Carburetor Overhaul

Carburetors are relatively complex. Proper performance depends upon the cleanliness and proper adjustment of all internal and external components. In addition to the usual adjustments performed at the regular tune-up intervals, it eventually becomes necessary to remove, disassemble, clean, and overhaul the entire carburetor(s), in order to restore its original performance. To overhaul a carburetor, first purchase the proper rebuilding kit. Read the instructions and study the exploded view of the carburetor thoroughly prior to the actual removal and disassembly.

After reading the detailed carburetor rebuilding instructions, the following general procedure may be used. Remove the carburetor and place it on a clean work table. Disassemble the carburetor by removing the screws securing the upper and lower sections together. Remove the damping piston, air valve, spring, metering needle, fuel jet (SU only), and float assembly, and soak all metal parts in carburetor cleaning solvent. Scrape all old gasket material from the mating surfaces. After the metal parts have been soaked to remove all gum, varnish, and dirt, rinse them off with a clean, uncontaminated, solvent solution. Blow out all passages with compressed air and allow them to air dry. Do not use drills or wire to clean the passages. Check the throttle shaft and choke disc for excessive wear. Inspect the float hinge pins for distortion. All non-metal parts that are not being replaced should be wiped clean with a lint-free cloth. After all of the parts have been sufficiently cleaned or replaced, assemble the carburetor using new gaskets and seals, and, on Zenith-Stromberg carburetors, a new air valve diaphragm. If any of the replacement seals in the SU carburetor are cork, they must first be soaked in penetrating oil for a minimum of a half hour to avoid splitting during installation. Assemble the float chamber and adjust the float height. Assemble the air valve, spring, and metering needle into the upper housing. Join the upper and lower housing together, taking care to properly align the metering needle and fuel jet. When the jet and needle are installed correctly, the air valve should drop to the bridge with a distinctive click. Any binding of these two parts will result in poor carburetor performance. Install the damping piston. Install the carburetor on its manifold with a new gasket. Adjust the choke and throttle linkage, and the idle speed and mixture.

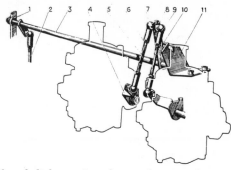

Throttle linkage—Stromberg carburetors shown

1. Bushing	7. Ball joint
2. Link rod for pedal	8. Lever
3. Control shaft	9. Lock wire
4. Lever	10. Stop for lever
5. Link rod	11. Bracket
6. Locknut	

Throttle Linkage Adjustment

On each carburetor, the link rods should maintain a 0.004 in. clearance "A" between the lever and the throttle spindle flange when the throttle control is against its stop

Throttle linkage adjustment—Stromberg carburetor

2. Body
3. Throttle plate spindle
4. Throttle plate
5. Throttle plate set screws
6. Seal
7. Return spring
8. Lever
9. Bushing
10. Lever
11. Spacing washer
12. Lockwasher
13. Nut
14. Lever
15. Lever
16. Adjuster screw
17. Spring
18. Cold start device assembly
19. Cold start device housing
20. Shaft
21. Circlip
22. Spring
23. Return spring
24. Fast idle choke lever
25. Choke cable attaching screw
26. Spacing washer
27. Lockwasher
28. Nut
29. Screw
30. Lockwasher
31. Choke cable support

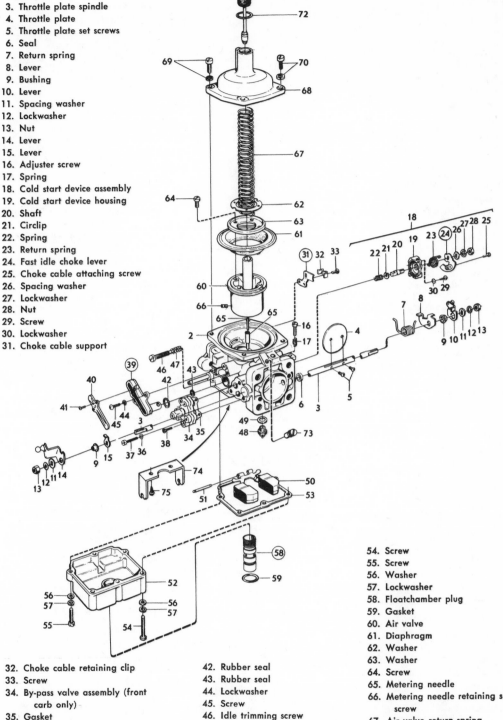

32. Choke cable retaining clip
33. Screw
34. By-pass valve assembly (front carb only)
35. Gasket
36. Lockwasher
37. Screw
38. Screw
39. Temperature compensator housing
40. Temperature compensator cover
41. Screw

42. Rubber seal
43. Rubber seal
44. Lockwasher
45. Screw
46. Idle trimming screw
47. Spring
48. Needle valve with seat
49. Gasket
50. Float
51. Float hinge pin
52. Floatchamber cover
53. Gasket

54. Screw
55. Screw
56. Washer
57. Lockwasher
58. Floatchamber plug
59. Gasket
60. Air valve
61. Diaphragm
62. Washer
63. Washer
64. Screw
65. Metering needle
66. Metering needle retaining set screw
67. Air valve return spring
68. Suction chamber cover
69. Screw and washer
70. Screw and washer
71. Damping piston assembly
72. Damping piston gasket
73. Plug for air conditioner speed compensator

Stromberg carburetor—disassembled

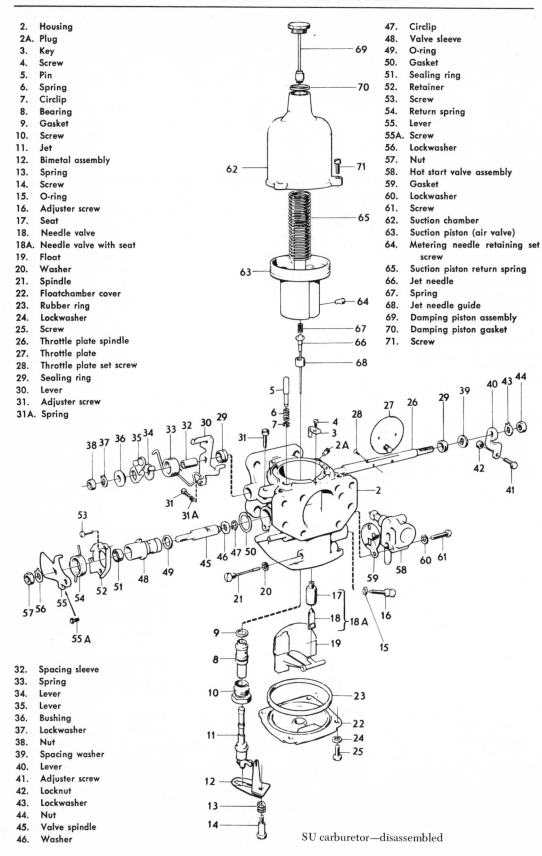

2. Housing
2A. Plug
3. Key
4. Screw
5. Pin
6. Spring
7. Circlip
8. Bearing
9. Gasket
10. Screw
11. Jet
12. Bimetal assembly
13. Spring
14. Screw
15. O-ring
16. Adjuster screw
17. Seat
18. Needle valve
18A. Needle valve with seat
19. Float
20. Washer
21. Spindle
22. Floatchamber cover
23. Rubber ring
24. Lockwasher
25. Screw
26. Throttle plate spindle
27. Throttle plate
28. Throttle plate set screw
29. Sealing ring
30. Lever
31. Adjuster screw
31A. Spring

47. Circlip
48. Valve sleeve
49. O-ring
50. Gasket
51. Sealing ring
52. Retainer
53. Screw
54. Return spring
55. Lever
55A. Screw
56. Lockwasher
57. Nut
58. Hot start valve assembly
59. Gasket
60. Lockwasher
61. Screw
62. Suction chamber
63. Suction piston (air valve)
64. Metering needle retaining set
    screw
65. Suction piston return spring
66. Jet needle
67. Spring
68. Jet needle guide
69. Damping piston assembly
70. Damping piston gasket
71. Screw

32. Spacing sleeve
33. Spring
34. Lever
35. Lever
36. Bushing
37. Lockwasher
38. Nut
39. Spacing washer
40. Lever
41. Adjuster screw
42. Locknut
43. Lockwasher
44. Nut
45. Valve spindle
46. Washer

SU carburetor—disassembled

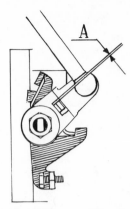

Throttle linkage adjustment—SU carburetor

on the intake manifold bracket. To adjust this clearance, remove the link rod ball socket from the carburetor lever ball stud, and turn the socket on the threaded link rod until the adjustment is correct.

Float Adjustment

ZENITH-STROMBERG CARBURETOR

1. Remove the carburetor as outlined in "Carburetor Removal and Installation."

Float level adjustment—Stromberg carburetor

2. Invert the carburetor and remove the float chamber.
3. The float is correctly adjusted when the high point of the float is ⅝ in. (distance B), and the low point of the float is ½ in. (distance A) from the sealing surface of the carburetor housing.
4. To adjust the float level, bend the tag at the float chamber inlet valve. Do not bend the arm between the float and the pin.
5. When the proper adjustment has been made, install the float chamber to the housing with a new gasket.
6. Install the carburetor on the intake manifold as outlined in "Carburetor Removal and Installation."

SU CARBURETOR

1. Remove the carburetor as outlined in "Carburetor Removal and Installation."

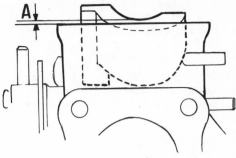

Float level adjustment—SU carburetor

2. Invert the carburetor and remove the float chamber.
3. The float is correctly adjusted when the distance "A" between the float "valley" and the housing flange is approximately 0.02–0.06 in.
4. The float is adjusted by bending the metal tab at the float chamber inlet valve.
5. When the correct adjustment has been made, install the float chamber to the housing with a new gasket.
6. Install the carburetor as outlined in "Carburetor Removal and Installation."

Fast Idle Adjustment

ZENITH-STROMBERG CARBURETOR

Pull out the choke control one inch from the dash. If the choke is adjusted correctly, the mark on the rapid idle cam (see illustration) should be opposite the centerline

Fast idle—Stromberg carburetor

of the fast idle screw. Adjust the fast idle with the fast idle screws to 1100–1300 rpm on both carburetors.

SU Carburetor

Pull out the choke control 0.8 in. from the dash. Adjust the fast idle with the fast idle screws to 1100–1600 rpm on both carburetors.

Damping Piston Replacement

If the engine stumbles upon acceleration, and the damping cylinders are filled to their proper level with oil, the problem may be with the damping pistons themselves. Unscrew the black knobs on top of the carburetors and remove the damping pistons. If the axial clearance "A" between the bottom of the piston and the retaining clip is not 0.04–0.07 in., the piston must be replaced as a unit.

FUEL INJECTION

Volvo has made Bosch electronic fuel injection available since 1970, when it was standard equipment on the 1800 series. The system was optional on the 140 series in 1971, and on the 164 in 1972. For 1973, all Volvos imported into the U.S. will be equipped with the system. The decision to utilize electronic fuel injection, despite the

Damping piston clearance

fact that it has increased the base price of the cars, has been made by many European manufacturers who desire to retain a modicum of performance while still conforming to stringent federal emission regulations. The electronic fuel injection system is inherently cleaner than carbureted systems because of its precise regulation of fuel under varying conditions of atmospheric temperature, and engine temperature, load, and rpm.

The complete system contains the following components: electronic control unit (brain), electric fuel pump, fuel filter, fuel pressure regulator, fuel injectors, cold-start

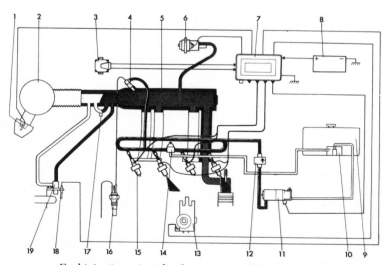

Fuel injection principle of operation—1972–73 B20F shown

1. Temperature sensor for induction air
2. Air cleaner
3. Throttle valve switch
4. Cold start valve
5. Inlet duct
6. Pressure sensor
7. Control unit (electronic)
8. Battery
9. Fuel tank
10. Fuel filter, suction side
11. Fuel pump
12. Fuel filter, discharge side
13. Triggering contacts in distributor
14. Pressure regulator
15. Injectors
16. Thermal timer contact
17. Idling adjusting screw
18. Temperature sensor for coolant
19. Auxiliary air regulator

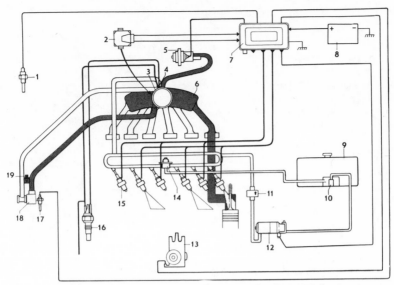

Fuel injection principle of operation—1972–73 B30F shown

1. Temperature sensor for induction air
2. Throttle valve switch
3. Throttle housing
4. Cold start valve
5. Pressure sensor
6. Inlet duct
7. Control unit (electronic)
8. Battery
9. Fuel tank
10. Fuel filter, suction side
11. Fuel filter, discharge side
12. Fuel pump
13. Triggering contacts in distributor
14. Pressure regulator
15. Injectors
16. Thermal timer contact
17. Temperature sensor for coolant
18. Auxiliary air regulator
19. Idling adjusting screw

valve, inlet duct (for intake air), throttle valve switch, auxiliary air regulator, intake air temperature sensor, coolant temperature sensor, intake air pressure sensor, and the triggering contacts in the ignition distributor.

Briefly, the system operates as follows:

Fuel is drawn from the fuel tank by the electric fuel pump and forced through the fuel lines and filter to the pressure regulator. The pressure regulator supplies fuel at a constant pressure of 28 psi to the injectors. If the fuel pressure for some reason exceeds 28 psi, a relief valve opens, allowing the excess fuel to return to the fuel tank. The electromagnetic fuel injectors are mounted in the intake ports of the cylinder head.

The duration of fuel injection, and, consequently, fuel quantity, is controlled by engine rpm and load. Engine rpm information is supplied to the electronic brain via the distributor triggering contacts. Engine load information is supplied by the intake air pressure sensor. The electronic brain uses this information to determine the length of time the injectors will remain open. During warm-up periods, the cold-start valve injects extra fuel into the intake air stream when the starter is operated. At the same time, the auxiliary air regulator supplies extra air until the engine reaches operating temperature.

When the engine is accelerated, the throttle valve switch sends electrical impulses to the brain to increase the time the injectors are open. When decelerating, the throttle valve switch sends another impulse to the brain, closing off the fuel flow. When engine speed drops to approximately 1,000 rpm, the fuel supply is turned on again, allowing a smooth transition to idle speed.

Component Description

The electronic control unit (brain) receives electrical impulses from the intake air pressure and temperature sensors, and determines the duration of the opening interval for the injectors. In addition, on 1970–71 models, the control unit determines if, and for how long, the cold-start valve should be open. Another function of the control unit is to determine when the fuel pump should be operated. The control unit is located beneath the passenger's front seat on 140 series and 164 models, and behind the instrument panel on 1800 series models. Repair of the control unit requires the use of special test equipment which is available on the dealer level only.

The fuel pump relay receives impulses from the control unit to operate the electrical fuel pump. The main relay feeds current from the charging system to the control unit, and also protects the injection system from damage should the battery leads be switched. On 1970–71 models, a cold-start valve relay receives impulses from the control unit to operate the cold-start valve. The relays are located on the right front wheel well in the engine compartment.

The pressure regulator is connected to the fuel distributing pipe, and is located at the firewall on 1970–71 models, and between the second and third injectors (four-cylinder) or the third and fourth injectors (six-cylinder) on 1972–73 models. It is a purely mechanical unit, pressurizing the fuel to 28 psi for purposes of injecting it into the cylinders. The regulator is adjustable.

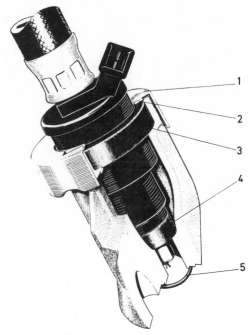

Injector with holder

1. Lock ring   4. Rubber seal
2. Steel washer   5. O-ring
3. Rubber seal

Pressure regulator installed—1972–73 shown

The fuel injectors pass fuel directly into the intake ports of the cylinder head (one for each intake port). Fuel is injected in two cycles. On four-cylinder engines, injectors one and three operate simultaneously, then injectors two and four operate. On six-cylinder engines, injectors one, three, and five operate together, then injectors two, four, and six operate. The injector operates when a pulse from the control unit energizes the magnetic winding of the injector, drawing the sealing needle up from the seat. When the pulse stops and

the magnetic winding de-energizes, the sealing needle is pushed against the seat by the return spring. A valve opening time interval of 0.002–0.010 second regulates the amount of fuel injected.

The cold-start valve is located in the inlet duct downstream from the air throttle. Its purpose is to provide extra fuel during cold starts. On 1970–71 models, the cold-start valve is operated by the cold-start valve relay which receives information from the temperature sensor via the control unit. On 1970–71 models, the valve

Cold start valve installed—B20E, B20F

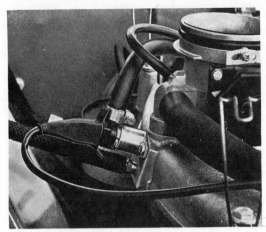

Cold start valve installed—B30F

Thermal timer installed—B30F

supplies additional fuel during starting for a period of 10 seconds when the coolant temperature is −4° F or colder, and stops providing the fuel during starting at a temperature of 132° F. On 1972–73 models, the cold-start valve is actuated by a temperature-sensitive thermal timer. On these models, extra fuel is provided during starting for a period of 12 seconds when the coolant temperature is −4° F or colder, and the additional fuel supply is cut off when the temperature reaches 95° F. On all models, the fuel is cut off when the starter stops running, regardless of the temperature.

The thermal timer is installed in 1972–73 models, on the right-hand side of the engine block. The timer, which is sensitive to engine temperature, supplies electrical current to the cold-start valve when the engine temperature is less than 95° F, and the starter is engaged. The duration of time that the timer feeds current to the cold-start valve varies from a fraction of a second at the higher temperatures to 12 seconds at −4° F and lower. Regardless of the temperature, the timer ceases operating the cold-start valve when the starter is disengaged.

The throttle valve switch is mounted at the mouth of the inlet duct and is connected to the throttle shaft. Its function is to increase the fuel supply during acceleration by sending additional and longer impulses to the electromagnetic fuel injectors, and to shut off the fuel supply during deceleration by withholding the impulses. At idle, the throttle valve switch regulates the carbon monoxide content of the exhaust gases.

The one-piece, cast aluminum inlet duct is bolted to the cylinder head. Its function is to supply intake air (and occasionally a few drops of fuel when the cold-start valve

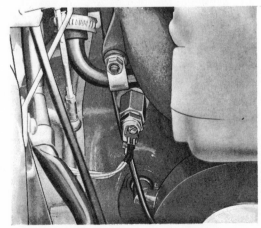

Thermal timer installed—B20F

Throttle valve switch installed—B20E, B20F

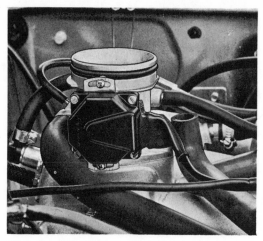

Throttle valve switch installed—B30F

Auxiliary air regulator installed—B30F

is activated) metered to the engine's needs by the throttle valve to each individual induction port in the cylinder head. The idle adjustment screw is located at the mouth of the inlet duct.

The auxiliary air regulator is located at the right front end of the cylinder head. It is a temperature-sensitive device with an expanding element projecting into the cooling system. The air regulator's operating range is from −13° F, fully open, to 140° F, fully closed. At the cold-start, the expanding element is temporarily contracted, allowing the auxiliary air hose to admit additional air into the inlet duct. Gradually, as the engine heats up, the element expands, closing off the auxiliary air hose.

The temperature sensor for the intake air provides the control unit with intake

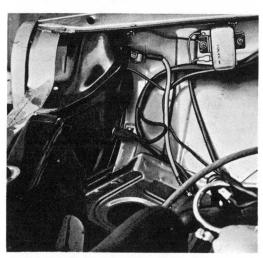

Temperature sensor for intake air installed

air temperature information so that the control unit can increase the injection frequency and duration somewhat at low intake air temperature. Compensation ceases when the temperature of the intake air becomes greater than 68° F (1970–71 models), or 86° F (1972–73 models). The sensor is located at the radiator crossbar, adjacent to the intake air hose on 140 and 1800 series Volvos, and at the radiator crossbar, near the right front headlight housing on the 164.

The coolant temperature sensor (not to be confused with the temperature gauge sensor) also provides the control unit with engine temperature information so that the control unit can regulate the injection in-

Auxiliary air regulator installed—B20E, B20F

Temperature sensor for coolant installed

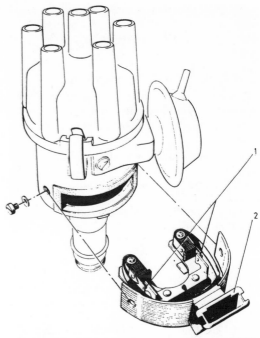

Distributor with control device—B30F shown, B20E and B20F similar

1. Triggering contacts   2. Electrical connection

terval and duration. On 1970–71 models, the sensor also provides the control unit with information determining if, and for how long, the cold-start valve will operate. This sensor is located in the cylinder head next to the auxiliary air regulator.

The pressure sensor monitors the atmospheric pressure present in the inlet duct, and supplies the control unit with information concerning engine load. The unit is located on the right front wheel housing and is connected to the inlet duct by means of a hose.

Pressure sensor installed

The triggering contacts supply the control unit information concerning engine speed (rpm). The control unit then determines when the injection shall begin, and what the duration will be, with the help of information received from the pressure sensor. The triggering contacts are located beneath the centrifugal governor in the distributor.

Fuel Injection System Precautions

Due to the highly sensitive nature of the Bosch electronic fuel injection system, the following special precautions must be strictly adhered to in order to avoid damage to the system.

1. Do not operate the engine with the battery disconnected.

2. Do not utilize a high-speed battery charger as a starting aid.

3. When using a high-speed battery charger to charge the battery while it is installed in the vehicle, at least one battery cable must be disconnected.

4. Do not allow the control unit to be subjected to temperatures exceeding 185° F, such as when the vehicle is being baked after painting. If there is a risk of the temperature exceeding 185° F, the control unit must be removed.

5. The engine must not be started when the ambient temperature exceeds 158° F, or damage to the control unit will result.

6. The ignition must be in the off position when disconnecting or connecting the control unit.

7. When working on the fuel system, take care not to allow dirt to enter the system. Small dust particles may jam fuel injectors.

Component Replacement

The fuel injection system is repaired simply by replacing the defective component. There are adjustments that can be made to the pressure regulator, throttle valve, throttle valve switch, throttle stopscrew, and the fuel mixture. To make resistance checks, use an ohmmeter, and for continuity checks, a 12 V test light. If the control unit is defective, return it to a qualified repair agency and install a new unit.

CONTROL UNIT

1. On 1800 series models, disconnect the defroster hose, remove the control unit bracket retaining screws, and lower the unit to the floor. On 140 series and 164 models, move the passenger's front seat all the way back, unscrew the bolt securing the seat's front, move the seat forward while folding the seat bottom to the rear, remove the control unit retaining screws, and draw out the unit.

2. Remove the screw for the cap holding the cable harness to the unit. Pull out the plastic cover strip.

3. Construct a puller out of $5/64$ in. welding wire (see illustration) to disconnect the main plug contact. Insert the puller in the rear of the control unit and pull out the plug carefully.

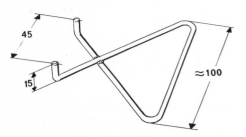

Puller for control unit plug contact

4. Press the plug contact firmly into the new or reconditioned control unit. Fit the plastic cover strip, retaining cap, and screw.

5. Fit the control unit into place and install its retaining screws. On 1800 series models, connect the defroster hose. On 140 series and 164 models, secure the seat front.

PRESSURE REGULATOR

If the pressure regulator cannot be adjusted to 28 psi with its adjusting nut, it must be replaced.

1. Place pinch clamps on the three fuel hoses connected to the regulator.

2. Loosen the hose clamps and remove the hoses.

3. On 1970–71 models, remove the regulator from its bracket and replace it with a new one.

4. Connect the fuel hoses to the new regulator, tighten the hose clamps, and remove the pinch clamps.

5. Start the engine and check for fuel leaks.

FUEL INJECTORS

1. On 164 models, remove the air cleaner.

2. Pinch shut the fuel hose to the header pipe.

3. Loosen the hose clamps for the injectors and lift up the header pipe.

4. Remove the plug contacts from the injectors. Disconnect the cable harness from the distributing pipe.

5. Turn the lockrings on the injectors counterclockwise so that they loosen from their bayonet fittings. Lift out the injectors.

Removing injector

6. Place the new injectors, with new washers and rubber sealing rings, in position and secure them by turning the lockrings clockwise.

7. Connect the cable harness at the distributing pipe. Connect the plug contacts to the injectors.

8. Place the header pipe in position, and tighten the hose clamps. Remove the pinch clamps.

9. On 164 models, install the air cleaner.

Cold-Start Valve

1. On 164 models, remove the air cleaner.
2. Pinch shut the fuel line to the valve.
3. Remove the plug contact and the fuel hose from the valve.
4. Remove the two retaining screws and the cold-start valve from the inlet duct.
5. Place the new cold-start valve in position with packing and install the retaining screws.
6. Connect the plug contact and fuel hose to the valve. Remove the pinch clamp.
7. On 164 models, install the air cleaner.

Thermal Timer

1. Drain the cooling system.
2. Disconnect the plug contacts and unscrew the thermal timer from the cylinder head.
3. Install a new timer and connect the plug contacts.
4. Refill the cooling system.

Throttle Valve Switch

1. Disconnect the plug contact from the switch. Remove the two retaining screws and pull the switch straight out of the inlet duct.
2. Fit the new switch to the inlet duct and install the retaining screws. Connect the plug contact.
3. Adjust the switch as outlined in "Throttle Valve Switch Adjustment."

Auxiliary Air Regulator

1. Drain the cooling system.
2. Remove the plug contact from the temperature sensor and disconnect the air hoses from the regulator.
3. Remove the two retaining bolts and draw out the regulator.
4. Using a new sealing ring, position the new regulator to the cylinder head and install the retaining bolts.
5. Connect the plug contact and the two air hoses.
6. Refill the cooling system.

Intake Air Temperature Sensor

1. On 164 models, remove the right drip protection, and the air hose from the right side.
2. Disconnect the four-way plug contact from the sensor.
3. Unscrew the old sensor and install a new one, taking care not to overtighten it.
4. Plug in the four-way contact for the sensor.
5. On 164 models, install the right air hose and drip protection.

Coolant Temperature Sensor

1. Drain a portion of the cooling system so that the coolant level in the radiator and engine is below the temperature sensor.
2. Disconnect the plug contact from the sensor.
3. Unscrew the old sensor and install a new one with a new sealing ring.
4. Connect the plug contact.
5. Top up the cooling system.

Pressure Sensor

1. Disconnect the four-way plug contact and the air hose from the sensor.
2. Remove the three screws retaining the sensor to the right wheel housing.
3. Transfer the attaching bracket to the new pressure sensor.
4. Position the new sensor to the wheel well and install the retaining screws.
5. Connect the plug contact and the air hose to the sensor.

Triggering Contacts

1. Remove the distributor as outlined under "Distributor Removal and Installation" in chapter 3.
2. Remove the two screws securing the triggering contacts holder to the distributor and then pull out the holder.
3. Lubricate the fiber pieces of the contact breaker lever on the new holder with Bosch Ft 1V4 or similar silicone cam lobe grease.
4. Check to see that the rubber ring is not damaged. Replace if necessary.
5. Install the new holder in the distributor and tighten the retaining screws.
6. Install the distributor as outlined in "Distributor Removal and Installation" in chapter 3.

Component Testing and Adjustment

Control Unit

The idle mixture may be adjusted with the slotted knob on the control unit. This operation is best performed with the use of a CO meter, which is available on the dealer level. Refer to the "Fuel Injection System Idle Mixture Adjustment" in chapter 2 for details.

The control unit may be tested only with the help of sophisticated test equipment available, again, only at the dealer level.

PRESSURE REGULATOR

The regulator may be adjusted with its adjusting nut. Pinch and disconnect the flexible fuel hose between the pressure regulator and the header pipe and insert a tee fitting and pressure gauge. Tighten the fuel connections and start the engine. Slacken the locknut and adjust the pressure to 28 psi. If the regulator cannot be adjusted properly, it must be replaced. Remove the tee fitting and gauge, and connect the fuel hoses.

THROTTLE VALVE

The throttle valve may be adjusted with its stopscrew near the mouth of the inlet duct. Release the stopscrew locknut for the throttle valve switch, and back off the screw several turns so that it does not lie against the throttle valve spindle stop. Make sure that the valve is completely closed. Screw in the stopscrew so that it contacts the spindle stop. At this point, turn the stopscrew 1/4–1/3 additional turn and tighten the locknut. Check to see that the switch does not jam in the closed position. Proceed to adjust the throttle valve switch as follows.

NOTE: *The stopscrew must not be used for idle adjustment.*

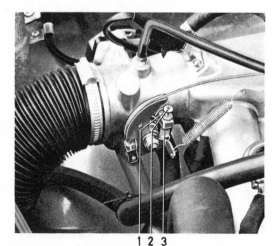

1 2 3
Throttle valve adjustment—B20E, B20F

1. Locknut   2. Stop screw
3. Stop on throttle valve spindle

1 2 3
Throttle valve adjustment—B30F

1. Stop screw   2. Locknut
3. Stop on valve spindle

THROTTLE VALVE SWITCH

The throttle valve switch may be adjusted with an ohmmeter. Connect the ohmmeter to the control unit (contacts 14 and 17 for four-cylinder, and contacts 9 and 14 for six-cylinder). Loosen the screws slightly so that the switch may be rotated. Scribe a mark at the upper switch screw on the inlet duct if one is not there already. Close the throttle valve by turning the switch clockwise as far as it will go. Then, observing the ohmmeter, carefully turn the switch counterclockwise until the ohmmeter registers 0 (zero). At this point, the switch is turned a further 1° counterclockwise (1/2 graduation mark at upper screw), and both switch screws are tightened. Check to make sure that the ohmmeter reading rises to infinity when the throttle valve opens approximately 1°.

AUXILIARY AIR REGULATOR

To check the operation of the auxiliary air regulator, start the engine and allow it to reach operating temperature (176° F). Make a note of the idle speed and then disconnect the hose between the inlet duct and the regulator. While covering the hose opening with your hand, check to see that the idle speed does not drop significantly over the first reading. A drop in idle speed indicates a leak in the regulator, requiring its replacement.

Chapter Five

Chassis Electrical

Heater

Heater Unit Removal and Installation
140 SERIES, 164

1970–72

1. Remove the lower radiator hose, open the engine drain plug, and drain the cooling system. Disconnect the negative battery cable.

2. Remove the control valve hoses.

3. Remove the heater control panel below the dashboard by removing the two retaining screws. Tilt the top of the panel back so that it loosens from the dashboard clips and clears the hood release.

4. Remove the transmission tunnel mat, defroster hoses, heater control cables, and fan switch wires.

5. Remove the two screws which retain the fuse box to the heater.

6. Remove the control valve, being careful not to damage the copper capillary tube. Loosen the upper hose to the heater.

7. Plug the heater outlets to avoid spilling coolant upon removal. Loosen the heater unit ground cables, remove the four retaining screws, loosen the drain hose, and lift out the heater unit and control valve from their brackets.

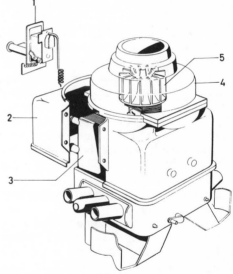

Heater unit disassembled—1970–72 140 series, 164

1. Heat control valve	4. Fan casing
2. Heater casing	5. Fan
3. Heater core	

8. Reverse the above procedure to install.

1973 Standard Heating System

1. Remove the lower radiator hose, open the engine drain plug, and drain the cooling system. Disconnect the negative battery cable.

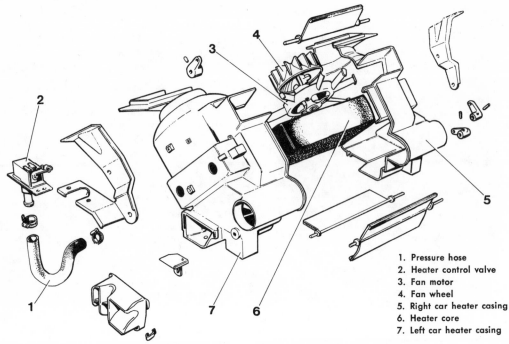

1. Pressure hose
2. Heater control valve
3. Fan motor
4. Fan wheel
5. Right car heater casing
6. Heater core
7. Left car heater casing

Standard heater unit disassembled—1973 140 series, 164

2. Remove the center panel and the left-hand defroster hose.

3. Lift up the driveshaft tunnel mat, disconnect the front and rear attaching screws of the rear seat heater ducts, and then remove the ducts from the heater.

4. Disconnect the heater control valve and air-mix cables from their shutters.

5. Disconnect and plug the pressure hose at the heater. Also plug the heater pipes to prevent residual coolant from spilling onto the carpet.

6. Remove the attaching screws which secure the left-hand upper bracket to the dashboard and the left-hand lower bracket to the transmission tunnel.

7. Remove the glovebox by unscrewing the four attaching screws, removing the glovebox door stop, and disconnecting the wires from the glovebox courtesy light.

8. Disconnect the defroster and floor heating cables from their levers.

9. Disconnect the fan motor wires at the switch contact plate.

10. Remove the attaching screws which secure the right-hand upper bracket to the dashboard and the right-hand lower bracket to the transmission tunnel.

11. Remove the right-hand defroster hose. Disconnect the hose between the heater and the dashboard circular vents.

Lift the heater unit to the right, and then out of the vehicle.

12. Reverse the above procedure to install, taking care to ensure that the air vent rubber seal is properly located, and that the fan motor ground cable is attached to the upper right-hand bracket attaching screw.

1973 Combination Heater-Air Conditioner System

1. Remove the lower radiator hose, open the engine drain plug, and drain the cooling system. Disconnect the negative battery cable.

2. Remove the heater hoses from the heater pipes at the engine side of the firewall. Plug the heater pipes.

3. Remove the evaporator hose brackets from their body mounts and disconnect the dryer from its bracket. Position the dryer as close to the firewall as the evaporator hose permits.

4. Remove the instrument cluster by removing the steering column molded casings, removing the bracket retaining screw and lowering it toward the steering column, removing the four instrument cluster retaining screws, disconnecting the speedometer cable, tilting the speedometer out of its snap fitting, moving the cluster for-

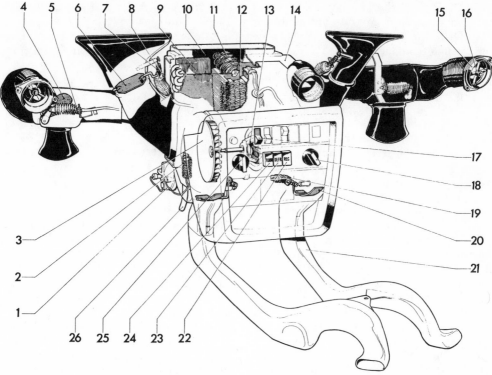

Combination heater-air conditioner system—1973 140 series, 164

1. Heater control valve
2. Capillary tube for heater control valve
3. Turbine
4. Shutter, air vent left floor
5. Vacuum motor
6. Shutter, left defroster nozzle
7. Return spring for vacuum motor
8. Vacuum motor
9. Evaporator (only on vehicles with air conditioning)
10. Air intake cover
11. Vacuum motor for air intake cover
12. Heater core
13. Fan motor
14. Central unit
15. Blow-in valve
16. Shutter knob
17. Air conditioning switch
18. Fan motor switch
19. Vacuum motor
20. Shutter, right air duct, rear floor
21. Air duct to rear floor
22. Knob, air intake cover
23. Knob, defroster shutter
24. Knob, floor shutter
25. Temperature controls
26. Drain hose

ward and disconnecting the electrical plug contacts, then lifting the cluster out of the vehicle.

5. Remove the air hose between the central unit and the left inner air vent. Remove the hose from the vacuum motor for the left defroster nozzle.

6. Remove the left-side panel from the central unit.

7. Lift up the driveshaft tunnel mat and disconnect the rear seat heater duct from the central unit.

8. Remove the heater pipes from the passenger side of the firewall.

9. Remove the upper and lower attaching screws for the left support leg. Remove the attaching screws which secure the upper bracket to the dashboard and the lower bracket to the transmission tunnel.

NOTE: *If the upper bracket screw holes are slotted, the screws need only be slackened a few turns.*

10. Remove the right-side panel from the central unit.

11. Remove the glovebox by unscrewing the four attaching screws, removing the glovebox door stop, and disconnecting the glovebox courtesy light wires.

12. Remove the right defroster nozzle, and also the air hose between the central unit and the right inner air vent.

13. Lift up the driveshaft tunnel mat and disconnect the rear seat heater duct from the central unit.

14. Remove the upper and lower attaching screws for the right support leg. Remove the lower attaching screws for the control panel.

15. Disconnect the fan motor wires and the ground wires from the control panel.

16. Disconnect the yellow lead cable from its plug contact.

17. Separate the halves of the vacuum hose connector and disconnect the vacuum tank hose at the connector.

18. Position the control panel as far back on the transmission tunnel as the cables permit.

19. Remove the screws which attach the upper brackets to the firewall and the lower brackets to the transmission tunnel.

20. Remove the thermostat clamp from the central unit, and the two evaporator cover retaining clamps.

21. Without disconnecting any of the refrigerant lines, remove the evaporator from the central unit, placing it on the right-hand side of the firewall.

22. Remove the molded dashboard padding from beneath the glovebox.

23. Remove the retaining clamps for the right outer vent duct, and remove the duct. Pry off the locking retainer for the turbine (blower), and remove the turbine. Remove the clamps which retain the blower housing (inner end) to the central unit and remove the housing.

24. Remove the passenger's front seat cushion and lift the central unit forward and onto the floor of the vehicle. Be careful not to place undue stress on the connected refrigerant lines.

25. Reverse the above procedure to install, taking care to ensure that the evaporator pipes and thermostat capillary are enclosed in sealing compound, that the drainage tubes are inserted in their respective transmission tunnel holes, and that the ground cables are connected.

1800 SERIES

1970–73

1. Disconnect the lower radiator hose, open the engine drain plug, and drain the cooling system. Disconnect the negative battery cable.

2. Disconnect the heater hoses from the heater core pipe and the control valve pipe. Disconnect the fan motor wires.

3. Disconnect the fresh air intake from the heater.

4. On 1970–71 models, remove the pressure regulator bracket retaining screws and allow the pressure regulator to hang free while still connected to the hoses.

5. Remove the four heater-to-firewall attaching nuts.

6. Remove the defroster hoses. Disconnect the heater control valve and the control cables.

7. Lift out the heater and control valve as a unit.

8. Reverse the above procedure to install.

Blower Motor Removal and Installation

140 SERIES, 164

1970–72

1. Remove the heater unit as outlined in "Heater Unit Removal and Installation."

2. Remove the four rubber bushings on the sides of the heater unit.

3. Scribe marks on both sides of the fan housing to facilitate assembly. Remove the spring clips and separate the housing halves.

4. Mark the mounting plate's relative position to the fan housing. Straighten the tabs and separate the mounting plate from the housing.

5. Remove the retaining screws and separate the fan motor from the mounting plate.

6. Reverse the above procedure to install, being careful to apply soft sealer to the housing halves.

1973 Standard Heating System

1. Remove the heater unit as outlined in "Heater Unit Removal and Installation."

2. Place the unit on its side with the control valve facing upward. Remove the spring clips and separate the housing halves.

3. Lift out the old fan motor and replace

Standard system blower motor location in housing —1973 140 series, 164

it with a new unit, making sure that the support leg without the "foot" points to the output for the defroster channel. (See illustration.)

4. Assemble the heater housing halves with new spring clips, and seal the joint without clips with soft sealing compound.

5. Install the heater unit as outlined in "Heater Unit Removal and Installation."

1973 Combination Heater-Air Conditioner System

In order to remove the blower motor, both the right and left turbines (blower wheels) must first be removed. The heater unit does not have to be removed.

1. Disconnect the negative battery cable.

2. Lift the carpet and remove the central unit side panels.

3. Remove the retaining screws for the control panel and move the panel as far back on the transmission tunnel as the electrical cables will permit.

4. Remove the attaching screws for the rear seat heater ducts and disconnect the ducts from the central unit.

5. Remove the instrument cluster as outlined in "Instrument Cluster Removal and Installation."

6. Remove the glovebox by unscrewing the four attaching screws, removing the glovebox door stop, and disconnecting the wires from the glovebox courtesy light. Remove the molded dashboard padding from beneath the glovebox.

7. Disconnect the vacuum hoses to the left and right defroster nozzle vacuum motors, then remove the nozzles and the left and right air ducts.

8. Remove the air hoses between the left and right inside air vents.

9. Remove the clamps on the central unit outer ends, and remove the ends.

10. Pry off the locking retainer for the turbines (blower wheels), and remove both left and right turbines.

11. Position the heater control valve capillary tube to one side.

12. Remove the left inner end (blower housing) from the central unit.

13. Unscrew the three retaining screws and remove the fan motor retainer.

14. Disconnect the plug contact from the fan motor control panel. Release the tabs of the electric cables from the plug contact, and, removing the rubber grommet, pull the electrical cables down through the central unit right opening.

15. Remove the fan motor from the left opening.

16. Reverse the above procedure to install.

1800 SERIES

1970–73

NOTE: *The fan motor and fan are replaced as a unit.*

1. Remove the valve cover and place a rag over the rocker arm assembly.

2. On 1970–71 models, remove the pressure regulator bracket from the heater and allow it to hang freely.

3. Disconnect the fan motor wires at the fan terminals.

4. Remove the six retaining screws and remove the fan motor from the heater assembly.

5. Reverse the above procedure to install.

Removing blower motor—1800 series

Heater Core Removal and Installation

140 SERIES, 164

1970–72

1. Remove the heater unit as outlined in "Heater Unit Removal and Installation."

2. Remove the four rubber bushings on the sides of the heater unit.

3. Scribe marks on both sides of the fan housing to facilitate assembly. Remove the spring clips and separate the housing halves.

4. Separate the heater core from the housing half, taking care not to damage the sensitive body of the control valve.

5. Reverse the above procedure to install, being careful to apply soft sealer to the housing halves.

1973 Standard Heating System

1. Remove the heater unit as outlined in "Heater Unit Removal and Installation."

2. Place the unit on its side with the control valve facing upward. Remove the spring clips and separate the housing halves.

3. Disconnect the capillary tube from the heater core and then lift out the core.

4. Reverse the above procedure to install, being careful to transfer the foam plastic packing to the new heater core, and to install the fragile capillary tube carefully on the core.

1973 Combination Heater-Air Conditioner System

1. Remove the combination heater-air conditioner unit as outlined under "Heater Unit Removal and Installation."

2. Remove the left outer end of the central unit. Remove the locking retainer and the turbine (blower wheel).

3. Remove the two retaining screws for the left transmission tunnel bracket.

4. Remove the lockring for the left intake shutter shaft.

5. Remove the three retaining screws and lift off the inner end.

6. Remove the three retaining screws for the fan motor retainer.

7. Disconnect the heater hoses at the heater core.

8. Remove the clamps which retain the central unit halves together, lift off the left half, and remove the heater core.

9. Reverse the above procedure to install, taking care to transfer the foam plastic packing to the new heater core.

1800 SERIES

1970–73

1. Remove the heater unit as outlined in "Heater Unit Removal and Installation."

2. Remove the fan motor as outlined in "Blower Motor Removal and Installation."

3. Remove the screws securing the heater housing halves together and then separate the halves.

4. Remove the heater core from the housing.

5. Install the new or reconditioned core

in the housing. Check the operation of the shutters for binding or looseness.

6. Install the thermostat capillary tube on the core. (See illustration.)

7. Apply new soft sealing compound to the housing halves prior to assembly.

8. Reverse the above procedure to install.

Radio

Radio Removal and Installation

1. Disconnect the negative battery cable.

2. Remove the radio control knobs by pulling them straight out. Remove the control shaft retaining nuts.

3. Disconnect the speaker wires, the power lead (either at the fuse box or the in-line fuse connection), and the antenna cable from its jack on the radio.

4. Remove the hardware which attaches the radio to its mounting (support) bracket(s), and slide it back and down from the dash.

5. Reverse the above procedure to install.

Windshield Wipers

Motor Removal and Installation

140 SERIES, 164

1970–72

1. Disconnect the negative battery cable.

2. Remove the wiper arm and blade assemblies.

3. Remove the molded panel from under the dash.

4. Remove the heater switch.

5. Remove the instrument cluster as outlined in "Instrument Cluster Removal and Installation."

6. Remove the intermediate defroster nozzle and disconnect the hoses.

7. Remove the retaining bolts and lower the wiper motor.

8. Reverse the above procedure to install.

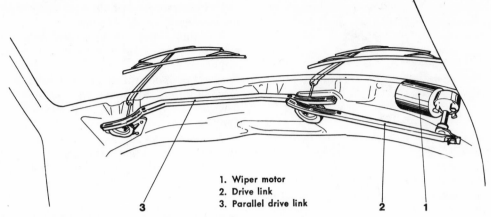

1. Wiper motor
2. Drive link
3. Parallel drive link

Windshield wiper unit—1973 140 series, 164

1973

1. Disconnect the negative battery cable.

2. Disconnect the drive link from the wiper motor lever by unsnapping the locking tab underneath the dashboard.

3. Open the hood and disconnect the plug contact from the motor, located on the firewall.

4. Remove the three attaching screws and lift out the motor.

5. Reverse the above procedure to install, taking care to transfer the rubber seal, rubber damper, and spacer sleeves to the new motor.

Linkage Removal and Installation

140 SERIES, 164

1970–72

1. Remove the wiper motor as outlined in "Wiper Motor Removal and Installation."

2. Disconnect the heater control cable.

3. Remove the fuse box from its bracket and allow it to hang free.

4. Disconnect the ground cables.

5. On carburetted versions, remove the choke control.

6. Release the attaching screws for the wiper frame and lower the frame.

7. Reverse the above procedure to install.

DRIVE LINK

1973

1. On vehicles equipped with a combination heater-air conditioner unit, remove the glovebox and the right defroster nozzle.

2. Remove the right-hand side panel and the defroster hoses.

3. Remove the locking tab for the wiper motor lever connection, loosen the nut for the cable stretcher, and remove the drive link.

4. Reverse the above procedure to install, carefully placing the cable around the wiper arm drive segment with the cable nipple inserted in the segment recess.

PARALLEL DRIVE LINK

1. On vehicles equipped with a combination heater-air conditioner unit, remove the glovebox and the right defroster nozzle.

2. Remove the right-hand side panel and the defroster hoses.

3. Remove the drink link by releasing the locking tab for the wiper motor lever connection and loosening the cable stretcher.

4. Remove each cable stretcher nut and disconnect both ends of the cable from their wiper arm drive segments.

5. Lift forward and remove the parallel drive link.

6. Reverse the above procedure to install, taking care to place each cable end around its respective wiper drive arm segments with the cable nipple inserted in the segment recess.

CABLE

1. Remove the drive link and parallel drive link as outlined in "Drive Link Re-

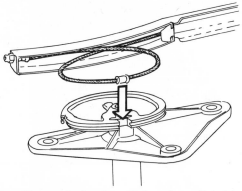

Installing cable for drive link and parallel drive link—left-hand side, 1973, 140 series, 164

moval and Installation" and "Parallel Drive Link Removal and Installation."

2. Pry up and remove the cable retaining lockwasher. Remove the old cable.

3. Position the new cable on its wiper arm drive segments and secure it with a new retaining lockwasher.

4. Install the cable stretcher in the drive link. The tensioning nut should not be tightened until the drive link and parallel drive link are installed.

5. Install the drive link and parallel drive link.

Windshield Wiper Unit (complete) Removal and Installation
1800 SERIES
1970–73

1. Disconnect the negative battery cable.

2. Remove the wiper arm and blade assemblies. Unscrew the wiper arm shaft retaining nuts, and then lift off the washers and rubber seals.

3. Disconnect the electrical wires at the wiper motor.

4. Remove the two wiper motor retaining bolts and lower the motor and linkage assembly out from under the dash.

5. Reverse the above procedure to install.

Tailgate Window Wiper

Motor Removal and Installation
145
1970–73

1. Disconnect the negative battery cable.

2. Remove the upholstered finish panel on the inside of the tailgate.

3. Remove the screws which retain the reinforcing bracket beneath the wiper motor.

4. Disconnect the wiper link arm. Bend the reinforcing bracket to one side and lower the wiper motor until it is clear of the bracket.

5. Disconnect the electrical wires from the motor and remove the motor.

6. Reverse the above procedure to install.

Instruments

Instrument Cluster Removal and Installation

A voltage stabilizer feeds a 10 V current to both the temperature gauges and the fuel gauge. Electrical malfunctions in these gauges must be checked with an ohmmeter, not a 12 V test light. If malfunctions occur simultaneously in all three of the gauges that are fed by the stabilizer, the stabilizer itself is probably malfunctioning. When replacing the voltage stabilizer, the new unit must fit in the same position as the old one. If the stabilizer is not located correctly in the dash, the voltage output may be altered.

140 SERIES, 164
1970–72

1. Disconnect the negative battery cable.

2. Remove the two screws which retain the control panel.

3. Remove the two retaining screws and lower the molded panel beneath the dashboard.

4. Pull the upper section of the cluster outward so it loosens from its retaining clips. Loosen the panel from the hood release mechanism.

5. Move the control panel—with the short side first—through the dashboard opening.

6. Disconnect the heater controls and the speedometer cable. Remove the flange nuts for the instrumentation.

7. Rotate the instrument cluster slightly, so that the electrical connections may be removed from the reverse side.

8. Lift out the cluster from the dashboard.

9. Reverse the above procedure to install.

1973

1. Disconnect the negative battery cable.

2. Remove the molded plastic casings from the steering column.

3. Remove the bracket retaining screw and lower the bracket toward the steering column.

4. Remove the cluster attaching screws.

5. Disconnect the speedometer cable.

6. Tilt the cluster out of its snap fitting and disconnect the plug contact. On vehicles equipped with a tachometer, disconnect the tachometer sending wire.

7. Lift the cluster out of the dashboard.

8. Reverse the above procedure to install.

1800 SERIES

1970–73

The 1800 series Volvos are equipped with a tachometer, coolant temperature gauge, oil temperature gauge, speedometer (with odometer, tripmeter, and warning lamps), fuel gauge, oil pressure gauge, and clock. Each of these instruments must be removed separately. When replacing an instrument, first disconnect the negative battery cable, then disconnect the electrical connections on the instrument's reverse side, remove the retaining nuts and attaching bracket, and pull the instrument straight out.

Headlights

All Volvos manufactured for sale in the U.S. are equipped with sealed beam headlights.

Removal and Installation

140 SERIES

1. Open the hood and remove the headlight contact by pulling it straight out.

2. Slacken the three phillips screws so that the plastic headlight retainers can be removed.

3. Remove the sealed beam from the engine compartment.

4. Reverse the above procedure to install, and recheck headlight alignment.

Removing headlight retaining screws—140 series

164

1. Remove the headlight outer trim rim by pulling it upward and away from the car.

2. Slacken the three phillips screws a few turns so that the inner trim ring may be rotated and removed.

3. Pull out the sealed beam slightly and remove the headlight contact.

4. Reverse the above procedure to install, and recheck headlight alignment.

1800 SERIES

1. Remove the headlight outer chrome rim by removing the retaining screw at the lower part of the rim.

2. Remove the three phillips screws retaining the inner rim.

3. Pull out the sealed beam slightly and remove the headlight contact.

4. Reverse the above procedure to install, and recheck the headlight alignment.

Removing headlight retaining screws—1800 series, 164 similar

Light Bulb Chart

140 series, 164	Wattage (candlepower)	Type
Headlights	40/50 W	Sealed Beam
Parking lights, front (140 series)	5 W	S 8.5
Parking lights, front (164)	5 W (4 cp)	Ba 15 s
Parking lights, rear (taillights)	5 W (4 cp)	Ba 15 s
Turn signal flashers, front & rear	32 cp	Ba 15 s
Stop lights	25 W (32 cp)	Ba 15 s
Back-up lights	15 W (32 cp)	Ba 15 s
License plate light	5 W	S 8.5
Side marker lights	5 W	Ba 15 s
Interior lighting	10 W	S 8.5
Glovebox light	2 W	Ba 9 s
Instrument cluster lighting	3 W	W 2.2 d
Heater control lighting	1.2 W	W 1.8 d
Gear selector lighting (automatic)	1.2 W	W 1.8 d
Clock light	2 W	Ba 7 s
Rear window defroster warning light		
142, 144, 164	1.2 W	W 1.8 d
145	2 W	Ba 7 s
Warning lights for: charging, turn signals, parking brake, high beams, oil pressure, overdrive, choke, brake system failure, emergency flashers, tailgate wiper/washer, and seat belts.	1.2 W	W 1.8 d

1800 series	Wattage (candlepower)	Type
Headlights	45/50 W	Sealed Beam
Parking lights and turn signals, front	32/4 cp	BAY 15 d
Stop and taillights (1800 E)	32/4 cp	BAY 15 d
Stop lights (1800 ES)	20 W (32/4 cp)	Ba 15 s
Taillights (1800 ES)	4 cp	Ba 9 s
Turn signals, rear	32 cp	Ba 15 s
Back-up lights	32 cp	Ba 15 s
License plate lighting	4 cp	Ba 9 s
Side marker lights (1970–72)	32/4 cp	BAY 15 d
(1973)	5 W	Ba 15 s
Interior lighting	10 W	SW 8.5
Map reading lamp	2 W	Ba 9 s
Instrument lights, heater control light	3 W	W 2.1 d
Clock light	2 W	Ba 7 s
Control switch illumination (1800 ES)	1.2 W	W 1.8 d
Gear selector lighting (automatic)	1.2 W	W 1.8 d
Warning lights for: charging, turn signals, and high beams.	3 W	W 2.1 d
Warning lights for: overdrive, brakes, and seat belts.	1.2 W	Ba 9 s
Warning lights for: rear window defroster and emergency flashers.	1.2 W	W 1.8 d
Oil pressure warning light	2 W	Ba 7 s

Fuses

All electrical equipment is protected from overloading, by fuses. Each fuse has a rating that will allow it to transmit a predetermined amount of resistance before its filament melts, thereby stopping the excessive current flow. If a fuse blows repeatedly, the trouble is probably in the electrical component that the fuse protects. Never replace a fuse with another of a higher ampere rating. Sometimes, a fuse will blow when all of the electrical equipment protected by the fuse is operating, especially under severe weather conditions. For this reason, it is wise to carry a few spare fuses of each type in the car. Consult the fuse chart for ampere ratings.

On 1970–71 140 series and 164 models, the fuse box is located behind a snap-out panel in the dashboard above the transmission tunnel, and on 1972 140 series and 164 models, the fuse box is located behind the control panel for the clock, rear defroster, and emergency flashers, over the transmission tunnel. To tilt-down the control

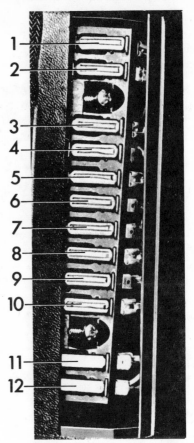

Fusebox—1973 140 series, 164

1. Windshield wipers/washer Horn	8 A
2. Heater fan Cigarette lighter	16 A
3. Rear defroster Overdrive	16 A
4. Back-up lamps Buzzer seat belts	8 A
5. Turn signals Instrument	5 A
6. Reminder light seat belts Buzzer ignition switch	8 A
7. Clock Glove box lighting Extra interior lighting	5 A
8. Brake lights Interior lighting	5 A
9. High beam headlights	5 A
10. Instrument panel lighting	5 A
11. Left parking light License plate lighting	5 A
12. Right parking light	5 A

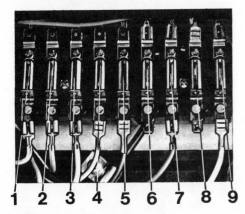

Fusebox—1970–72 140 series, 164

1. Windshield wipers, washer	8 A
2. Warning lamp, high beam headlights	5 A
3. Heater fan, temperature and fuel gauges Warning lamps for brakes, oil pressure, battery charging, choke. Shift positions lighting, automatic transmission	8 A
4. Turn indicators, back-up lights, overdrive	8 A
5. Horn, electrically heated rear window, cigarette lighter	16 A
6. Interior lighting, glove box lighting, warning buzzer for ignition key	5 A
7. Stop lights, clock, warning light	8 A
8. Parking light left, rear light left, license plate lighting, clock lighting	5 A
9. Instrument panel lighting Parking light, right Rear light, right	5 A

panel and gain access to the fuse box, remove the two retaining screws at the upper corners of the panel.

On 1973 140 series and 164 models, the fuse box is located beneath a protective cover, below the dashboard, in front of the driver's door.

On all 1800 series models, the fuse box is located under the dashboard, to the left of the driver.

On fuel-injected models, an additional fuse box is located in the engine compartment on the left wheel wall. It houses a single fuse protecting the electrical fuel pump.

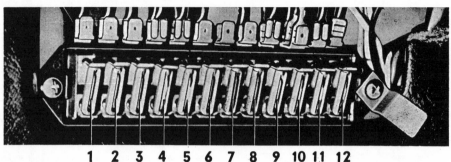

Fusebox—1800 series

1. Heater fan — 8 A	6. Horn relay — 8 A	11. Instrument panel light — 5 A
2. Windshield wipers—washers — 8 A	Reminder light and buzzer, seat belt	Rear light, left, and side marking light
3. Cigarette lighter — 8 A	Back-up light	License plate light
Overdrive (M41)	7. Spare — 16 A	Parking light, left, and side marking light
4. Flashers — 5 A	8. Electrically heated tailgate window — 16 A	Light, heater controls
Warning lamps, brakes, charging oil pressure	9. Brake lights — 8 A	Light, switches
Instruments	Electric clock	12. Rear light, right, side marking light — 5 A
Light, seat belts	10. Map reading lamp — 5 A	Parking light, right, side marking light
5. Relay for electrically heated tailgate window	Warning buzzer, ignition key	Shift positions light (BW 35 automatic transmission)
Relay for fuel pump	Interior lighting	
	Dimmer relay	

Pos.	Title	Data	Pos.	Title	Data
1.	Dir. ind. flashers	32 CP	22.	Charging warning lamp	1.2 W
2.	Parking lights	5 W	23.	Connector	
3.	Headlight low beam	40 W	24.	Glove compartment lighting	2 W
4.	Headlight high beam	45 W	25.	Overdrive warning lamp	1.2 W
5.	Horn		26.	Switch for headlights signalling and emergency flashers	
6.	Distributor firing order	1-3-4-2	27.	Fuel gauge	
7.	Ignition coil		28.	Voltage stabilizer	
8.	Battery	12 V 60 Ah	29.	Temperature gauge	
9.	Starter motor	1.0 hp	30.	Oil pressure lamp	
10.	Switch for reversing lights only for M 40 and M 41		31.	Switch for overdrive on transmission	
11.	High beam warning lamp	1.2 W	32.	Flashers warning lamp	1.2 W
12.	Dipper relay for high and low beams and headlight flasher		33.	Instrument lighting	2 x 1.2 W
13.	Horn ring		34.	Temperature gauge, sensitive head	
14.	Alternator		35.	Heater control lighting	3 x 1.2 W
15.	Relay for back-up light on M 40, M 41 and starter relay on BW 35		36.	Heater	
16.	Fuse box		37.	Windshield wipers	
17.	Voltage regulator		38.	Windshield washer	
18.	Brake contact		39.	Solenoid for overdrive	
19.	Warning flashers		40.	Interior lamp	10 W
20.	Brake warning lamp	1.2 W	41.	Switch for heater	
21.	Oil pressure warning lamp	1.2 W	42.	Switch for windshield wipers and washer	
			43.	Instrument lighting rheostat	
			44.	Light switch	

Wiring Diagrams

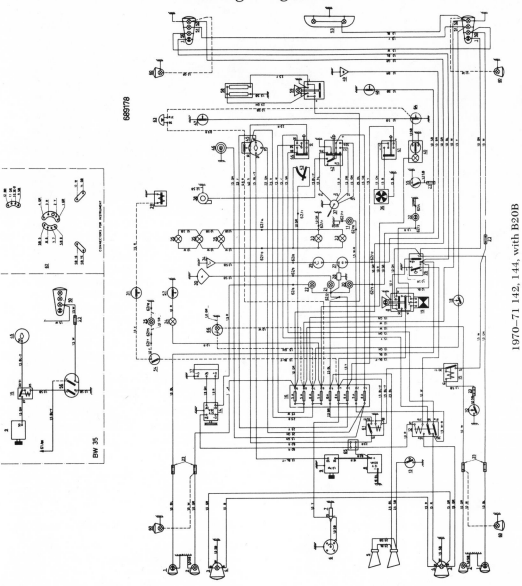

689178

1970-71 142, 144, with B20B

BW 35

Pos.	Title	Data
45.	Ignition switch	
46.	Cigarette lighter	
47.	Door contact	
48.	Switch for parking brake control	
49.	Fuel gauge tank unit	
50.	Back-up lights	15 W
51.	Brake stoplights	25 W
52.	Tail lights	5 W
53.	Number plate lighting	2 x 5 W
54.	Switch for overdrive	
55.	Brake warning contact	

Pos.	Title	Data
56.	Switch on transmission BW 35	
57.	Switch glove compartment lighting	
58.	Electrically heated rear window	
59.	Switch for electrically heated rear window	
60.	Side marker lamps, only for USA	5 W
61.	Relay for electrically heated rear window	
62.	Connection at instrument	
63.	Buzzer	
64.	Door switch on driving seat side	
65.	Connection plate	
66.	Clock	

Color code:

SB	Black	BL	Blue
W	White	R	Red
Y	Yellow	BR	Brown
GN	Green	W-R	White-Red
GR	Grey	BL-Y	Blue Yellow

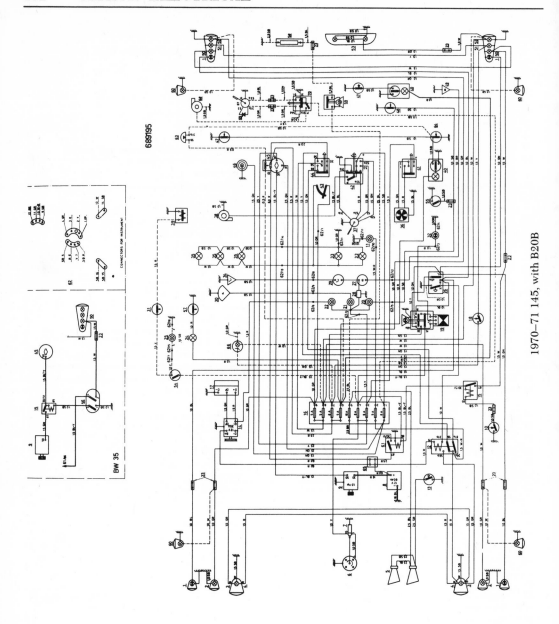

1970–71 145, with B20B

68195

BW 35

Pos.	Title	Data	Pos.	Title	Data
1.	Dir. ind. flashers	32 CP	34.	Temperature gauge, sensitive head	
2.	Parking lights	5 W	35.	Heater control lighting	3 x 1.2 W
3.	Headlight low beam	40 W	36.	Heater	
4.	Headlight high beam	45 W	37.	Windshield wipers	
5.	Horn		38.	Windshield washer	
6.	Distributor firing order	1-3-4-2	39.	Solenoid for overdrive	
7.	Ignition coil		40.	Interior lamp	10 W
8.	Battery	12 V 60 Ah	41.	Switch for heater	
9.	Starter motor	1.0 hp	42.	Switch for windshield wipers and washer	
10.	Switch for back-up lights only for M 40 and M 41		43.	Instrument lighting rheostat	
11.	High beam control lamp	1.2 W	44.	Light switch	
12.	Dipper relay for high and low beams and headlight flasher		45.	Ignition switch	
			46.	Cigarette lighter	
13.	Horn ring		47.	Door switch	
14.	Alternator		48.	Switch for parking brake control	
15.	Relay for back-up lights on M 40, M 41 and starter relay on BW 35		49.	Fuel gauge tank unit	
			50.	Back-up lights	15 W
16.	Fuse box		51.	Brake stoplights	25 W
17.	Voltage regulator		52.	Tail lights	5 W
18.	Brake contact		53.	Number plate lighting	2 x 5 W
19.	Warning flashers		54.	Switch for overdrive	
20.	Brake warning lamp	1.2 W	55.	Brake warning contact	
21.	Oil pressure warning lamp	1.2 W	56.	Switch on transmission BW 35	
22.	Charging warning lamp	1.2 W	57.	Switch glove compartment lighting	
23.	Connector		58.	Electrically heated rear window	
24.	Glove compartment lighting	2 W	59.	Switch for electrically heated rear window	
25.	Overdrive warning lamp	1.2 W	60.	Side marker lamps, only for USA	5 W
26.	Switch for headlights signalling and emergency flashers		61.	Relay for electrically heated rear window	
			62.	Connection at instrument	
27.	Fuel gauge		63.	Buzzer	
28.	Voltage stabilizer		64.	Door switch on driving seat side	
29.	Temperature gauge		65.	Connection plate	
30.	Oil pressure warning light		66.	Clock	
31.	Switch for overdrive on transmission		67.	Rear window wiper	
32.	Flashers warning lamp	1.2 W	68.	Rear window washer	
33.	Instrument lighting	2 x 1.2 W	69.	Diode	
			70.	Switch for rear window wiper	

Color code:

SB	Black
W	White
Y	Yellow
GN	Green
GR	Grey
BL	Blue
R	Red
BR	Brown
W-R	White-Red
BL-Y	Blue Yellow

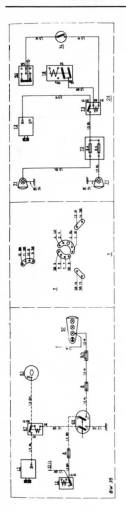

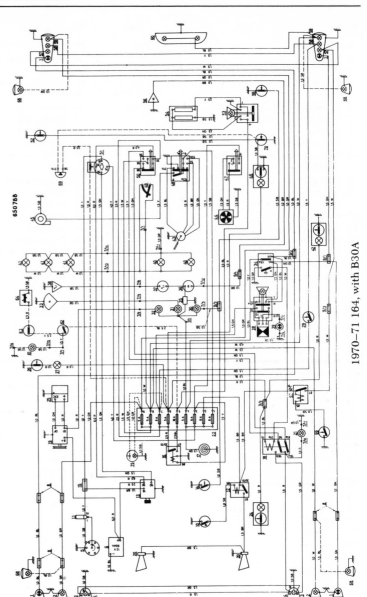

650788

1970–71 164, with B30A

Pos.	Title	Data	Pos.	Title	Data
1.	Dir. ind. flashers	32 CP	39.	Emergency flashers warning lamp	1.2 W
2.	Parking lights	5 W	40.	Instrument lighting	2 x 3 W
3.	Headlight low beam	40 W	41.	Heater control lighting	3 x 1.2 W
4.	Headlight high beam	45 W	42.	Luggage compartment light	18 W
5.	Distributor firing order	1-5-3-6-2-4	43.	Windshield wipers	
6.	Battery	12 V 60 Ah	44.	Heater	
7.	Conn. at instrument		45.	Windshield washer	
8.	Junction		46.	Interior light	10 W
9.	Part of 6-pole connector		47.	Switch for heater	
10.	Horn ring		48.	Switch for windshield wipers and washer	
11.	Ignition coil		49.	Instrument lighting rheostat	
12.	Relay for horn		50.	Light switch	
13.	Starter motor	1.0 hp	51.	Ignition switch	
14.	Brake warning valve contact		52.	Door contact	
15.	Resistor		53.	Switch for electrically heated rear window	
16.	Relay for heated rear window		54.	Electrically heated rear window	
17.	Cigarette lighter		55.	Switch for parking brake control	
18.	Dipped relay for high and low beams and headlight flasher		56.	Fuel gauge tank unit	
19.	Alternator	12 V 55 A	57.	Back-up lights	15 W
20.	Horn		58.	Brake stoplights	25 W
21.	High beam control lamp	1.2 W	59.	Rear lights	5 W
22.	Fusebox		60.	Number plate lighting	2 x 5 W
23.	Wiring of foglights		61.	Overdrive warning lamp	1.2 W
24.	Engine compartment lighting	18 W	62.	Switch for overdrive	
25.	Voltage regulator		63.	Switch for overdrive on transmission	
26.	Switch, glove compartment lighting		64.	Solenoid for overdrive	
27.	Glove compartment lighting	2 W	65.	Switch on transmission BW 35	
28.	Emergency warning flashers		66.	Switch for back-up lights only for M 400 and M 410	
29.	Brake contact		67.	Relay for back-up on M 400, M 410 and starter relay on BW 35	
30.	Brake warning lamp	1.2 W	68.	Side marker lamps	5 W
31.	Oil pressure warning lamp	1.2 W	69.	Buzzer, ignition key	
32.	Charging warning lamp	1.2 W	70.	Door contact on driving seat side	
33.	Oil pressure warning lamp		71.	Foglights	
34.	Switch for headlight signalling and turn indicators		72.	Fusebox for foglights	
35.	Voltage stabilizer		73.	Relay for foglights	
36.	Fuel gauge		74.	Switch for foglights	
37.	Temperature gauge		75.	Clock	
38.	Temperature gauge sensitive head				

Color code:

SB	Black
W	White
Y	Yellow
GN	Green
GR	Grey
BL	Blue
R	Red
BR	Brown

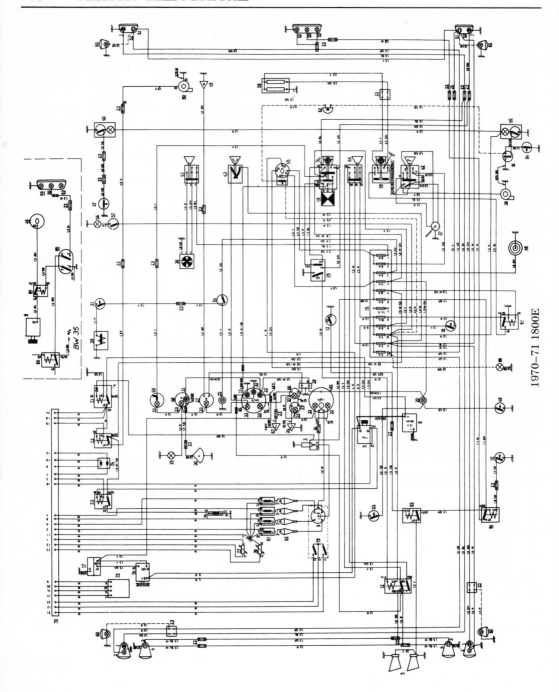

1970-71 1800E

Pos.	Title	Data	Pos.	Title	Data
1.	Directional indicators	23 CP	43.	Rheostat for instrument lighting	
2.	Parking lights	4 CP	44.	Lighting switch	
3.	Low beam headlights	40 W	45.	Ignition	
4.	High beam headlights	45 W	46.	Cigarette lighter	
5.	Horn		47.	Door switch	
6.	Distributor (firing order 1-3-4-2)		48.	Switch for parking brake control	
7.	Ignition coil		49.	Fuel level pickup	
8.	Battery	12 V 60 Ah	50.	Rear lights	
9.	Starter motor	1.0 hp	51.	Stop lights	32 CP
10.	Switch for back-up light		52.	Back-up lights	4 CP
11.	Warning lamp for high beam	3 W	53.	License plate lighting	2 x 4 CP
12.	Step relay for high beam and low beam headlights		54.	Switch for overdrive	
13.	Horn control		55.	Brake warning switch	
14.	Alternator 35 A		56.	Map-reading lamp	
15.	Switch, courtesy lighting		57.	Switch for map-reading lamp	
16.	Fusebox		58.	Electrically heated read window	150/40 W
17.	Voltage regulator		59.	Switch for electrically heated rear window	
18.	Brake switch		60.	Side marker lights (only USA)	5 W
19.	Emergency warning flashers		61.	Relay for electrically heated rear window	
20.	Warning lamp for brakes	2 W	62.	Spark plugs	
21.	Warning lamp for oil pressure	2 W	63.	Warning buzzer (only USA)	
22.	Warning lamp for battery charging	3 W	64.	Door switch on driver's side	
23.	Connector		65.	Horn relay	
24.	Connector (only right-hand drive)		66.	Oil temperature gauge	
25.	Warning lamp for overdrive	2 W	67.	Oil temperature sender	
26.	Switch for directional indicators and flashers		68.	Oil pressure gauge	
27.	Fuel gauge		69.	Lock	
28.	Voltage stabilizer		70.	Control unit for fuel injection	
29.	Temperature gauge		71.	Main relay for fuel injection	
30.	Oil pressure pickup		72.	Relay for fuel pump	
31.	Overdrive switch on transmission		73.	Relay for cold start valve	
32.	Warning lamp for directional indicators		74.	Pressure sensor	
33.	Instrument lighting		75.	Throttle switch	
34.	Temperature pickup		76.	Cold start valve	
35.	Lighting for heating controls		77.	Temperature sensor I (induction air)	
36.	Heater		78.	Temperature sensor II (coolant)	
37.	Windshield wipers		79.	Triggering contacts	
38.	Windshield washer		80.	Fuel pump	
39.	Control solenoid for overdrive, on transmission		81.	Injectors	
40.	Courtesy lighting	2 x 5 W	82.	Tachometer	
41.	Switch for heater		83.	Speedometer	
42.	Switch for windshield wipers and washer		84.	Relay for rear lights	
			85.	Switch for automatic transmission BW 35	
			86.	Quadrant lighting (only BW 35)	

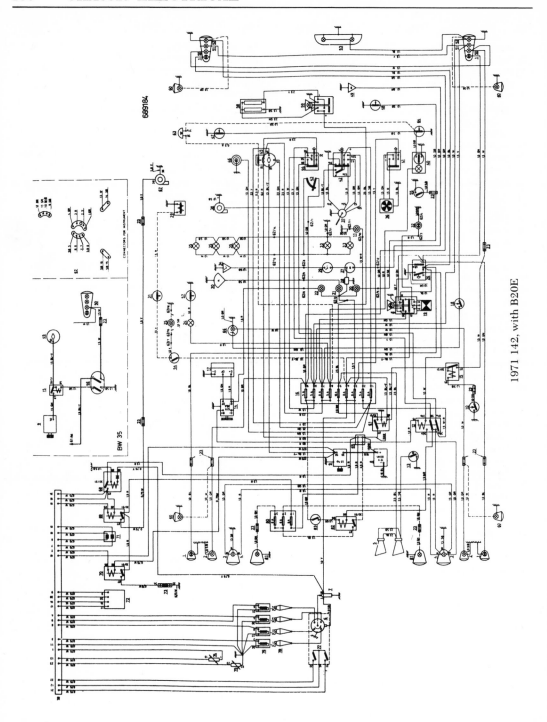

1971 142, with B20E

Pos.	Title	Data	Pos.	Title	Data
1.	Dir. ind. flashers	32 CP	41.	Switch for heater	
2.	Parking lights	5 W	42.	Switch for windshield wipers and washer	
3.	Headlight low beam	40 W	43.	Instrument lighting rheostat	
4.	Headlight high beam	45 W	44.	Light switch	
5.	Horn		45.	Ignition switch	
6.	Distributor firing order	1-3-4-2	46.	Cigarette lighter	
7.	Ignition coil		47.	Door switch	
8.	Battery	12 V 60 Ah	48.	Switch for parking brake control	
9.	Starter motor	1.0 hp	49.	Fuel gauge tank unit	
10.	Switch for back-up lights only for M 40 and M 41		50.	Back-up lights	15 W
11.	High beam warning lamp	1.2 W	51.	Brake stoplights	25 W
12.	Dipper relay for high and low beams and headlight flasher		52.	Taillights	5 W
13.	Horn ring		53.	Number plate lighting	2 x 5 W
14.	Alternator		54.	Switch for overdrive	
15.	Relay for back-up lights on M 40, M 41 and starter relay on BW 35		55.	Brake warning contact	
16.	Fuse box		56.	Switch on transmission BW 35	
17.	Voltage regulator		57.	Switch glove compartment lighting	
18.	Brake contact		58.	Electrically heated rear window	
19.	Warning flashers		59.	Switch, electrically heated rear window	
20.	Brake warning lamp	1.2 W	60.	Side marker lamps, only for USA	5 W
21.	Oil pressure warning lamp	1.2 W	61.	Relay for electrically heated rear window	
22.	Charging warning lamp	1.2 W	62.	Connection at instrument	
23.	Connector		63.	Buzzer	
24.	Glove compartment lighting	2 W	64.	Door switch on driving seat side	
25.	Overdrive warning lamp	1.2 W	65.	Connection plate	
26.	Switch for headlights signalling and emergency flashers		66.	Clock	
27.	Fuel gauge		67.	Fuel pump	
28.	Voltage regulator		68.	Main relay for fuel injection	
29.	Temperature gauge		69.	Relay for fuel pump	
30.	Oil pressure tell-tale		70.	Relay for starting valve	
31.	Switch for overdrive on transmission		71.	Pressure sensor	
32.	Flashers warning lamp	1.2 W	72.	Flap valve contact	
33.	Instrument lighting	2 x 1.2 W	73.	Start valve	
34.	Temperature gauge, sensitive head		74.	Temperature sensor, intake air	
35.	Heater control lighting	3 x 1.2 W	75.	Temperature sensor, coolant	
36.	Heater		76.	Injection valves	
37.	Windshield wipers		77.	Release contact	
38.	Windshield washer		78.	Electronic unit	
39.	Solenoid for overdrive		79.	Spark plugs	
40.	Interior lamp	10 W	80.	Fuse box	
			81.	Foglights	2 x 55 W
			82.	Relay for foglights	
			83.	Switch for foglights	

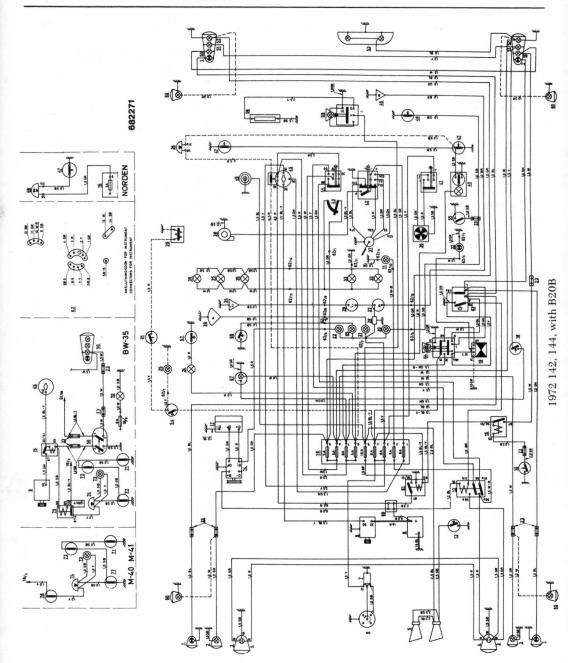

682271

NORDEN

ANSLUTNINGSDON FÖR INSTRUMENT
CONNECTORS FOR INSTRUMENT

BW-35

M-40 M-41

1972 142, 144, with B20B

Pos.	Title	Data	Pos.	Title	Data
1.	Dir. ind. flashers	32 CP	38.	Windshield washers	
2.	Parking lights	5 W	39.	Solenoid for overdrive on M 41 transmission	
3.	Headlight low beams	40 W	40.	Interior light	10 W
4.	Headlight high beams	45 W	41.	Switch for heater	
5.	Horn		42.	Switch for windshield wipers and washers	
6.	Distributor firing order	1-3-4-2	43.	Panel light rheostat	
7.	Ignition coil		44.	Light switch	
8.	Battery	12 V 60 Ah	45.	Ignition switch	
9.	Starter motor	1.0 hp	46.	Cigarette lighter	
10.	Contact for back-up light (M 40 and M 41 only)		47.	Door switch	
11.	High beam warning lamp	1.2 W	48.	Switch for parking brake control	
12.	Step relay for high and low beams and headlight flashers		49.	Fuel gauge tank unit	
13.	Horn ring		50.	Back-up lights	15 W
14.	Alternator	12 V 35 A	51.	Brake stoplights	25 W
15.	Relay for back-up light on M 40, M 41 and starter relay on BW 35		52.	Taillights	5 W
16.	Fusebox		53.	License plate light	2 x 5 W
17.	Voltage regulator		54.	Switch for overdrive M 41	
18.	Brake contact		55.	Brake warning switch	
19.	Flasher unit		56.	Contact on transmission BW 35	
20.	Brake warning lamp	1.2 W	57.	Switch glove box light	
21.	Oil pressure warning lamp	1.2 W	58.	Electrically heated rear window	
22.	Battery charging warning lamp	1.2 W	59.	Switch, electrically heated rear window	
23.	Connector		60.	Side marker lights (USA only)	5 W
24.	Glove box light	2 W	61.	Main relay, starter switch	
25.	Overdrive warning lamp M 41	1.2 W	62.	Terminal at instrument	
26.	Warning buzzer, ignition key		63.	Switch for dir. ind. and headlight flashers	
27.	Fuel gauge		64.	Switch for hazard warning flasher	
28.	Voltage stabilizer		65.	Choke warning lamp	
29.	Temperature gauge		66.	Choke control contact	
30.	Oil pressure sender		67.	Clock	
31.	Contact for overdrive on M 41 transmission		68.	Warning buzzer, headlights	
32.	Flashers warning lamp	1.2 W	69.	Connector	
33.	Instrument lighting	2 x 3 W	70.	Shift positions light	
34.	Temperature gauge sensor		71.	Switch, seat buckle, passenger	
35.	Heater control light	3 x 1.2 W	72.	Switch, passenger seat	
36.	Heater		73.	Warning lamp, seat belts	
37.	Windshield wipers		74.	Buzzer, seat belts	
			75.	Relay, seat belts	
			76.	Contact, M 40, M 41 transmission	
			77.	Switch, seat buckle, driver	

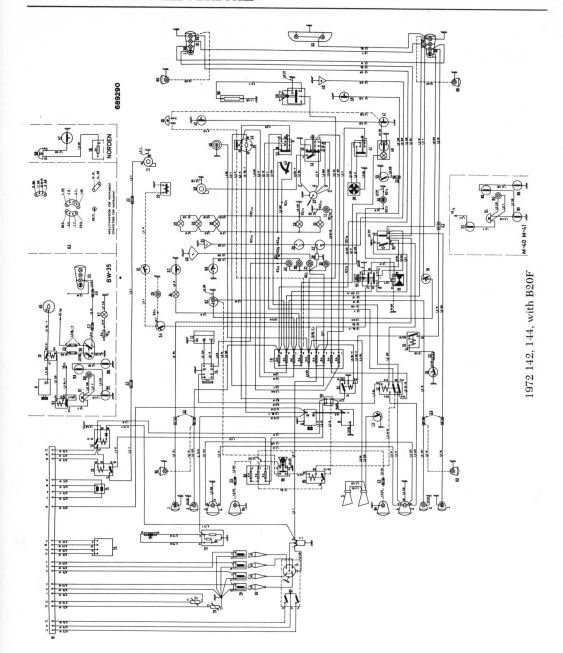

689290

NORDEN

BW-35

M-40 M-41

1972 142, 144, with B20F

Pos.	Title	Data	Pos.	Title	Data
1.	Dir. ind. flashers	32 CP	46.	Cigarette lighter	
2.	Parking lights	5 W	47.	Door switch	
3.	Headlight low beams	40 W	48.	Switch for parking brake control	
4.	Headlight high beams	45 W	49.	Fuel gauge tank unit	
5.	Horn		50.	Back-up light	15 W
6.	Distributer firing order	1-3-4-2	51.	Brake stoplights	25 W
7.	Ignition coil		52.	Taillights	5 W
8.	Battery	12 V 60 Ah	53.	License plate light	2 x 5 W
9.	Starter motor	1.0 hp	54.	Switch for overdrive M 41	
10.	Contact for back-up light (M 40 and M 41 only)		55.	Brake warning switch	
			56.	Contact on transmission BW 35	
11.	High beam warning lamp	1.2 W	57.	Switch glove box light	
12.	Step relay for high and low beams and headlight flashers		58.	Electrically heated rear window	
			59.	Switch, electrically heated rear window	
13.	Horn ring		60.	Side marker lights (USA only)	5 W
14.	Alternator	12 V 55 A	61.	Main relay, starter switch, rear window	
15.	Relay for back-up light on M 40, M 41 and starter relay on BW 35		62.	Terminal at instrument panel	
			63.	Switch for dir. ind. and headlight flashers	
16.	Fusebox		64.	Switch for hazard warning flashers	
17.	Voltage regulator		65.	Choke warning lamp	
18.	Brake switch		66.	Choke control contact	
19.	Flasher unit		67.	Clock	
20.	Brake warning lamp	1.2 W	68.	Warning buzzer, headlights	
21.	Oil pressure warning lamp	1.2 W	69.	Connector	
22.	Battery charging warning lamp	1.2 W	70.	Thermal timer contact	
23.	Connector		71.	Fuel pump	
24.	Glove box light	2 W	72.	Main relay for fuel injection	
25.	Overdrive warning lamp M41	1.2 W	73.	Relay for fuel pump	
26.	Warning buzzer, ignition key		74.	Pressure sensor	
27.	Fuel gauge		75.	Throttle valve switch	
28.	Voltage stabilizer		76.	Start valve	
29.	Temperature gauge		77.	Temperature sensor, intake air	
30.	Oil pressure switch		78.	Temperature sensor, coolant	
31.	Switch for overdrive on M 41 transmission		79.	Injection valves	
32.	Headlight flashers warning lamp	1.2 W	80.	Triggering contacts	
33.	Instrument lighting	2 x 3 W	81.	Electronic control unit	
34.	Temperature gauge sensor		82.	Spark plugs	
35.	Heater controls light	3 x 1.2 W	83.	Fusebox	
36.	Heater		84.	Foglights	2 x 55 W
37.	Windshield wipers		85.	Relay for foglights	
38.	Windshield washers		86.	Switch for foglights	
39.	Solenoid for overdrive on M 41 transmission		87.	Shift positions light, aut. trans.	
			88.	Switch, seat buckle, passenger	
40.	Interior light	10 W	89.	Switch, passenger seat	
41.	Switch for heater		90.	Seat belts warning lamp	
42.	Switch for windshield wipers and washers		91.	Warning buzzer, seat belts	
43.	Instrument panel light rheostat		92.	Relay, seat belts	
44.	Light switch		93.	Switch, M 40, 41 transmission	
45.	Ignition switch		94.	Switch, seat buckle, driver	

Color code:

SB	Black
W	White
Y	Yellow
GN	Green
GR	Grey
BL	Blue
R	Red
BR	Brown
BL-Y	Blue-yellow
W-R	White-red
GN-R	Green-red

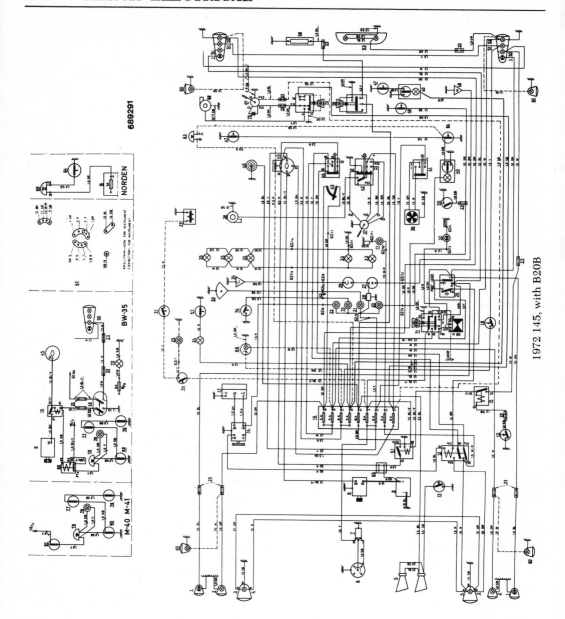

689291

NORDEN

BW-35

M-40 M-41

1972 145, with B20B

Pos.	Title	Data	Pos.	Title	Data
1.	Dir. ind. flashers	32 CP	40.	Interior light	10 W
2.	Parking lights	5 W	41.	Switch for heater	
3.	Headlight low beams	40 W	42.	Switch for windshield wipers and washers	
4.	Headlight high beams	45 W	43.	Panel light rheostat	
5.	Horn		44.	Light switch	
6.	Distributor firing order	1-3-4-2	45.	Ignition switch	
7.	Ignition coil		46.	Cigarette lighter	
8.	Battery	12 V 60 Ah	47.	Door switch	
9.	Starter motor	1.0 hp	48.	Switch for parking brake control	
10.	Contact for back-up light (M 40 and M 41 only)		49.	Fuel gauge tank unit	
11.	High beam warning lamp	1.2 W	50.	Back-up lights	32 CP
12.	Step relay for high and low beams and headlight flashers		51.	Brake stoplights	32 CP
13.	Horn ring		52.	Taillights	5 W
14.	Alternator	12 V 55 A	53.	License plate light	2 x 5 W
15.	Relay for back-up light on M 40, M 41 and starter relay on BW 35		54.	Switch for overdrive M 41	
16.	Fusebox		55.	Brake warning switch	
17.	Voltage regulator		56.	Contact on transmission BW 35	
18.	Brake contact		57.	Switch, glove box light	
19.	Flasher unit		58.	Electrically heated rear window	
20.	Brake warning lamp	1.2 W	59.	Switch, electrically heated rear window	
21.	Oil pressure warning lamp	1.2 W	60.	Side marker lights (USA only)	5 W
22.	Battery charging warning lamp	1.2 W	61.	Main relay, starter switch rear window	
23.	Connector		62.	Terminal at instrument	
24.	Glove box light	2 W	63.	Warning buzzer, ignition key	
25.	Overdrive warning lamp M 41	1.2 W	64.	Door switch on driver's side	
26.	Switch for dir. ind. and headlight flashers		65.	Connector	
27.	Fuel gauge		66.	Clock	
28.	Voltage stabilizer		67.	Tailgate window wiper	
29.	Temperature gauge		68.	Tailgate window washer	
30.	Oil pressure sender		69.	Warning buzzer, headlights	
31.	Contact for overdrive on M 41 transmission		70.	Switch for tailgate window wiper	
32.	Flashers warning lamp	1.2 W	71.	Switch for hazard warning flasher	
33.	Instrument lighting	2 x 3 W	72.	Shift positions light	
34.	Temperature gauge sensor		73.	Choke warning lamp	
35.	Heater control light	3 x 1.2 W	74.	Choke control contact	
36.	Heater		75.	Diode	
37.	Windshield wipers		76.	Switch, seat buckle, passenger	
38.	Windshield washers		77.	Switch, passenger seat	
39.	Solenoid for overdrive on M 41 transmission		78.	Warning lamp, seat belts	
			79.	Buzzer, seat belts	
			80.	Relay, seat belts	
			81.	Contact, M 40, M 41 transmission	
			82.	Switch, seat buckle, driver	

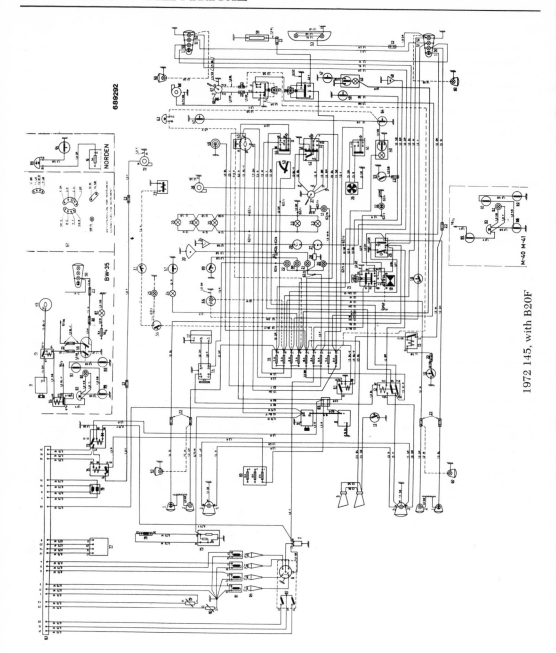

689292

NORDEN

BW-35

M-40 M-41

1972 145, with B20F

Pos.	Title	Data
1.	Dir. ind. flashers	32 CP
2.	Parking lights	5 W
3.	Headlight low beams	40 W
4.	Headlight high beams	45 W
5.	Horn	
6.	Distributor firing order	1-3-4-2
7.	Ignition coil	
8.	Battery	12 V 60 Ah
9.	Starter motor	1.0 hp
10.	Contact for back-up light (M 40 and M 41 only)	
11.	High beam warning lamp	1.2 W
12.	Step relay for high and low beams and headlight flashers	
13.	Horn ring	
14.	Alternator	12 V 55 A
15.	Relay for back-up light on M 40, M 41 and starter relay on BW 35	
16.	Fusebox	
17.	Voltage regulator	
18.	Brake contact	
19.	Flasher unit	
20.	Brake warning lamp	1.2 W
21.	Oil pressure warning lamp	1.2 W
22.	Battery charging warning lamp	1.2 W
23.	Connector	
24.	Glove box light	2 W
25.	Overdrive warning lamp M 41	1.2 W
26.	Switch for dir. ind. and headlight flashers	
27.	Fuel gauge	
28.	Voltage stabilizer	
29.	Temperature gauge	
30.	Oil pressure sender	
31.	Contact for overdrive on M 41 transmission	
32.	Flashers warning lamp	1.2 W
33.	Instrument lighting	2 x 3 W
34.	Temperature gauge sensor	
35.	Heater control light	3 x 1.2 W
36.	Heater	
37.	Windshield wipers	
38.	Windshield washers	
39.	Solenoid for overdrive on M 41 transmission	
40.	Interior light	10 W
41.	Switch for heater	
42.	Switch for windshield wipers and washers	
43.	Panel light rheostat	
44.	Light switch	
45.	Ignition switch	
46.	Cigarette lighter	

Color code:

SB	Black
W	White
Y	Yellow
GN	Green
GR	Grey
BL	Blue
R	Red
BR	Brown
W-R	White-red
BL-Y	Blue-yellow
GN-R	Green-red

Pos.	Title	Data
47.	Door switch	
48.	Switch for parking brake control	
49.	Fuel gauge tank unit	
50.	Back-up lights	32 CP
51.	Brake stoplights	32 CP
52.	Taillights	5 W
53.	License plate light	2 x 5 W
54.	Switch for overdrive M 41	
55.	Brake warning switch	
56.	Contact on transmission BW 35	
57.	Switch, glove box light	
58.	Electrically heated tailgate window	
59.	Switch, electrically heated tailgate window	
60.	Side marker lights (USA only)	5 W
61.	Main relay, starter switch tailgate window	
62.	Terminal at instrument	
63.	Warning buzzer, ignition key	
64.	Door switch on driver's side	
65.	Connector	
66.	Clock	
67.	Tailgate window wiper	
68.	Tailgate window washer	
69.	Diode	
70.	Switch for tailgate window wiper	
71.	Switch for hazard warning flasher	
72.	Fuel pump	
73.	Main relay for fuel injection	
74.	Relay for fuel pump	
75.	Thermal timer contact	
76.	Pressure sensor	
77.	Throttle valve switch	
78.	Start valve	
79.	Temperature sensor, intake air	
80.	Temperature sensor, coolant	
81.	Injection valve	
82.	Triggering contacts	
83.	Electronic control unit	
84.	Spark plugs	
85.	Fusebox	
86.	Warning buzzer, headlights	
87.	Shift positions light	
88.	Choke warning lamp	
89.	Choke control contact	
90.	Switch, seat buckle, passenger	
91.	Switch, passenger seat	
92.	Warning lamp, seat belts	
93.	Buzzer, seat belts	
94.	Relay, seat belts	
95.	Contact transmission M 40, M 41	
96.	Switch, seat buckle, driver	

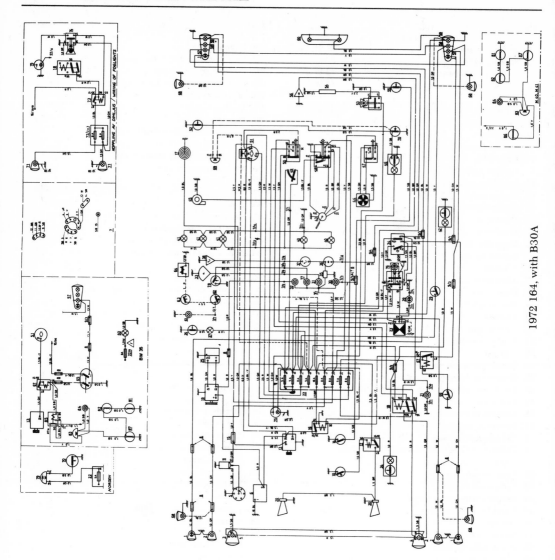

1972 164, with B30A

Pos.	Title	Data	Pos.	Title	Data
1.	Dir. ind. flashers	32 CP	46.	Interior lamp	
2.	Parking lights	5 W	47.	Switch for heater	10 W
3.	Headlight low beams	40 W	48.	Switch for windshield wipers and washer	
4.	Headlight high beams	45 W	49.	Rheostat, instrument panel light	
5.	Distributor firing order	1-5-3-6-2-4	50.	Light switch	
6.	Battery	12 V 60 Ah	51.	Ignition switch	
7.	Conn. at instrument		52.	Door switch	
8.	Connector		53.	Switch, electrically heated rear window	
9.	Part of 6-pole conn. unit		54.	Electrically heated rear window	
10.	Horn ring		55.	Switch for parking brake control	
11.	Ignition coil		56.	Fuel gauge tank unit	
12.	Relay for horn		57.	Back-up lights	
13.	Starter motor	1.0 hp	58.	Brake stoplights	32 CP
14.	Brake warning switch		59.	Taillights	32 CP
15.	Resistor		60.	License plate light	5 W
16.	Main relay, ignition switch		61.	Overdrive warning lamp	2 x 5 W
17.	Cigarette lighter		62.	Switch for overdrive	1.2 W
18.	Dip relay for high and low beams and headlight flasher		63.	Switch, overdrive on transmission	
19.	Alternator	12 V 55 A	64.	Solenoid for overdrive	
20.	Horn		65.	Contact on transmission BW 35	
21.	Warning lamp for high beams	1.2 W	66.	Contact for back-up lights (M 400 and M 410 only)	I
22.	Fusebox		67.	Relay for back-up lights on M 400, M 410 and starter relay on BW 35	
23.	Flasher unit		68.	Side marker lights	
24.	Engine comp. light	18 W	69.	Warning buzzer, ignition key	5 W
25.	Voltage regulator		70.	Door switch on driving side	
26.	Contact, glove compartment light		71.	Foglights	
27.	Glove compartment light	2 W	72.	Fusebox for foglights	
29.	Brake contact		73.	Relay for foglights	
30.	Brake warning lamp		74.	Switch for foglights	
31.	Oil pressure warning lamp	1.2 W	75.	Clock	
32.	Battery charging warning lamp	1.2 W	76.	Switch for emergency warning flashers	
33.	Oil pressure switch	1.2 W	77.	Choke warning lamp	
34.	Switch for dir. ind. and headlight flashers		78.	Choke contact	
35.	Voltage stabilizer		79.	Warning buzzer, lights	
36.	Fuel gauge		80.	Shift positions light, aut. trans.	
37.	Temperature gauge		81.	Contact, seat buckle, passenger	
38.	Temperature gauge sensor		82.	Contact, passenger seat	
39.	Flashers, warning lamp		83.	Warning buzzer, safety belts	
40.	Instrument panel light	1.2 W	84.	Warning lamp, safety belts	
41.	Heater control light	2 x 3 W	85.	Relay, safety belts	
42.	Luggage comp. light	3 x 1.2 W	86.	Contact, transmission M 41	
43.	Windshield wipers	18 W	87.	Contact, seat buckle, driver	
44.	Heater				
45.	Windshield washer				

Color code:

GN-R	Green-red
SB	Black
W	White
Y	Yellow
GN	Green
GR	Grey
BL	Blue
R	Red
BR	Brown
BL-Y	Blue-yellow
W-R	White-red

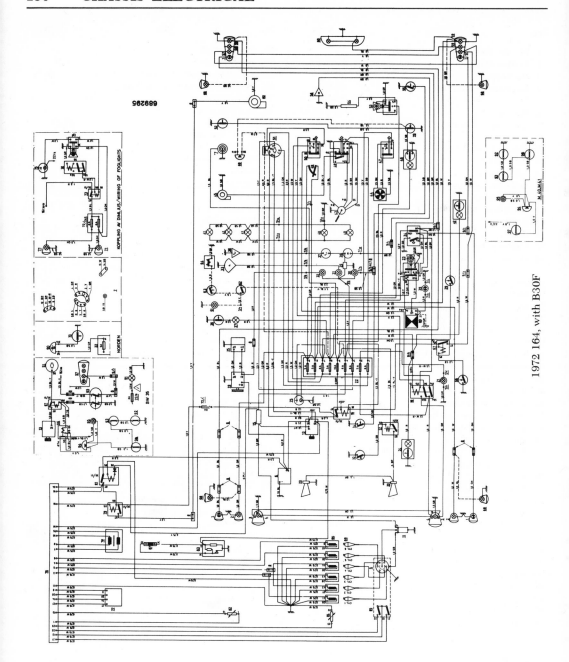

KOPPLING AV DIMLJUS/WIRING OF FOGLIGHTS

NORDEN

BW 35

689295

1972 164, with B30F

Pos.	Title	Data	Pos.	Title	Data
1.	Dir. ind. flashers	32 CP	51.	Ignition switch	
2.	Parking lights	5 W	52.	Door contact	
3.	Headlight low beams	40 W	53.	Switch, electrically heated rear window	
4.	Headlight high beams	45 W	54.	Electrically heated rear window	
5.	Distributor firing order	1-5-3-6-2-4	55.	Contact for parking brake warning lamp	
6.	Battery	12 V 60 Ah	56.	Fuel gauge tank unit	
7.	Conn. at instrument		57.	Back-up lights	32 CP
8.	Connector		58.	Brake stoplights	32 CP
9.	Part of 6-pole conn. unit		59.	Taillights	5 W
10.	Horn ring		60.	License plate light	2 x 5 W
11.	Ignition coil		61.	Overdrive warning lamp	1.2 W
12.	Relay for horn		62.	Switch for overdrive	
13.	Starter motor	1.0 hp	63.	Switch for overdrive on transmission	
14.	Brake warning contact		64.	Solenoid for overdrive	
15.	Resistor		65.	Contact on aut. trans. BW 35	
16.	Main relay, ignition switch		66.	Contact for reversing lights (M 400 and M 410 only)	
17.	Cigarette lighter		67.	Relay for reversing lights on M 400, M 410 and starter relay on BW 35	
18.	Dipped relay for high and low beams and headlight flashers		68.	Side marker lights	5 W
19.	Alternator	12 V 55 A	69.	Warning buzzer, ignition key	
20.	Horn		70.	Door contact on driving seat side	
21.	High beams warning lamp	1.2 W	71.	Foglights	
22.	Fusebox		72.	Fusebox	
23.	Switch, emergency warning flashers		73.	Relay for foglights	
24.	Engine comp. light	18 W	74.	Switch for foglights	
25.	Voltage regulator		75.	Clock	
26.	Switch, glove box light		76.	Electronic control unit	
27.	Glove light	2 W	77.	Throttle valve switch	
29.	Brake contact		78.	Pressure sensor	
30.	Brake warning lamp	1.2 W	79.	Relay for fuel pump	
31.	Oil pressure warning lamp	1.2 W	80.	Fuel pump	
32.	Battery charging warning lamp	1.2 W	81.	Main relay for fuel injection	
33.	Oil pressure sensor		82.	Temperature sensor, intake air	
34.	Switch for dir. ind. and headlight flashers		83.	Thermal timer contact	
35.	Voltage stabilizer		84.	Temperature sensor, coolant	
36.	Fuel gauge		85.	Triggering contacts	
37.	Temperature gauge		86.	Injection valves	
38.	Temperature gauge sensor		87.	Cold start valve	
39.	Flashers warning lamp	1.2 W	88.	Spark plugs	
40.	Instrument panel light	2 x 3 W	89.	Flasher unit	
41.	Heater control light	3 x 1.2 W	90.	Warning buzzer, lights	
42.	Luggage comp. light	18 W	91.	Shift positions light	
43.	Windshield wipers		92.	Contact, seat buckle, passenger	
44.	Heater		93.	Contact, passenger seat	
45.	Windshield washer		94.	Warning buzzer, safety belts	
46.	Interior light	10 W	95.	Warning lamp, safety belts	
47.	Switch for heater		96.	Relay, safety belts	
48.	Switch for windshield wipers and washer		97.	Contact, transmission M 41	
49.	Instrument panel light rheostat		98.	Contact, seat buckle, driver	
50.	Light switch				

Color code:

SB	Black
W	White
Y	Yellow
GN	Green
GR	Grey
BL	Blue
R	Red
BR	Brown
BL-Y	Blue-yellow
R-W	Red-white

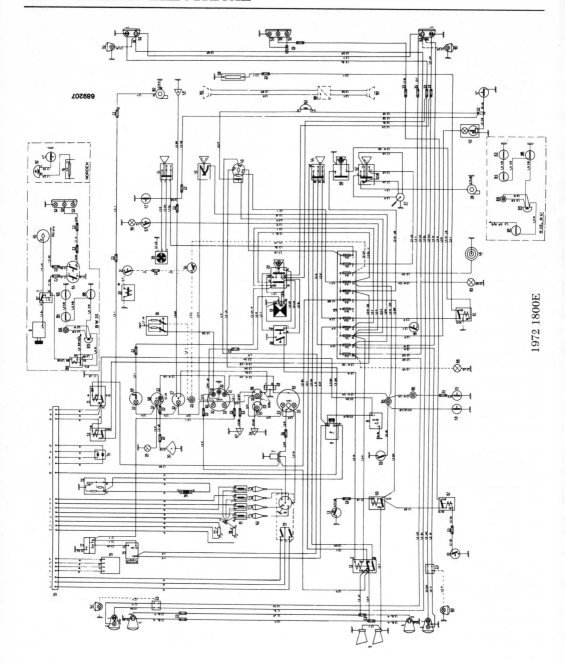

689207

NORDEN

BW 35

1972 1800E

Pos.	Title	Data	Pos.	Title	Data
1.	Dir. ind. flashers	32 CP	50.	Back-up lights	32 CP
2.	Parking lights	5 W	51.	Rear lights	4 CP
3.	Headlight low beams	40 W	52.	Brake stoplights	32 CP
4.	Headlight high beams	45 W	53.	License plate light	2 x 4 CP
5.	Horn		54.	Switch for overdrive M 41	
6.	Distributor firing order	1-3-4-2	55.	Brake warning contact	
7.	Ignition coil		56.	Map light	
8.	Battery	12 V 60 Ah	57.	Switch for map light	
9.	Starter motor	1.0 hp	58.	Electrically heated rear window	
10.	Contact for back-up light M 41		59.	Switch, electrically heated rear window	
11.	High beams warning lamp		60.	Side marker lights (USA only)	5 W
12.	Dipper relay for high and low beams and headlight flashers		61.	Relay for electrically heated rear window	
13.	Horn ring		62.	Spark plugs	
14.	Alternator	35 A	63.	Warning buzzer	
15.	Contact seat belt		64.	Contact on transmission BW 35	
16.	Fusebox		65.	Horn relay	
17.	Voltage regulator		66.	Oil temperature gauge	
18.	Brake contact		67.	Oil temperature sensor	
19.	Flasher unit		68.	Oil pressure gauge	
20.	Switch for emergency warning flashers		69.	Clock	
21.	Battery charging warning lamp	3 W	70.	Electronic unit	
22.	Oil pressure warning lamp	2 W	71.	Main relay for fuel injection	
23.	Connector		72.	Relay for fuel pump	
24.	Connector (R-H drive only)		73.	Thermal timer contact	
25.	Overdrive warning lamp M 41	1.2 W	74.	Pressure sensor	
26.	Switch for dir. ind. and headlight flashers		75.	Throttle valve switch	
27.	Fuel gauge		76.	Start valve	
28.	Voltage stabilizer		77.	Temperature sensor, intake air	
29.	Temperature gauge		78.	Temperature sensor, coolant	
30.	Oil pressure sender		79.	Triggering contacts	
31.	Contact for overdrive on transmission M 41		80.	Fuel pump	
32.	Flashers warning lamp	3 W	81.	Injection valves	
33.	Instrument panel light		82.	Tachometer	
34.	Coolant temperature sensor		83.	Speedometer	
35.	Heater control light	3 W	84.	Brake warning lamp	2 W
36.	Heater		85.	Seat belts light	1.2 W
37.	Windshield wipers		86.	Seat belt warning lamp	1.2 W
38.	Windshield washer		87.	Relay for back-up lights starter relay on BW 35	
39.	Solenoid for overdrive on transmission M 41		88.	Shift positions light (BW 35 only)	1.2 W
40.	Interior lamp	10 W	89.	Radio	
41.	Switch for heater		90.	Speaker	
42.	Switch for windshield wipers and washer		91.	Dimmer switch for overdrive warning lamp M 41	
43.	Instrument panel light rheostat		92.	Warning buzzer light	
44.	Light switch		93.	Contact, seat buckle, passenger	
45.	Starter switch		94.	Contact, passenger seat	
46.	Cigarette lighter		95.	Warning buzzer, safety belts	
47.	Door switch		96.	Relay, safety belts	
48.	Switch for parking brake control		97.	Contact, transmission M 41	
49.	Fuel gauge tank unit		98.	Contact, seat buckle, driver	

Color code:

SB	Black
W	White
Y	Yellow
GN	Green
GR	Grey
BL	Blue
R	Red
BR	Brown
W-SB	White-black
W-GN	White-green
BL-R	Blue-red
BL-W	Blue-white
BL-Y	Blue-yellow
GN-R	Green-red

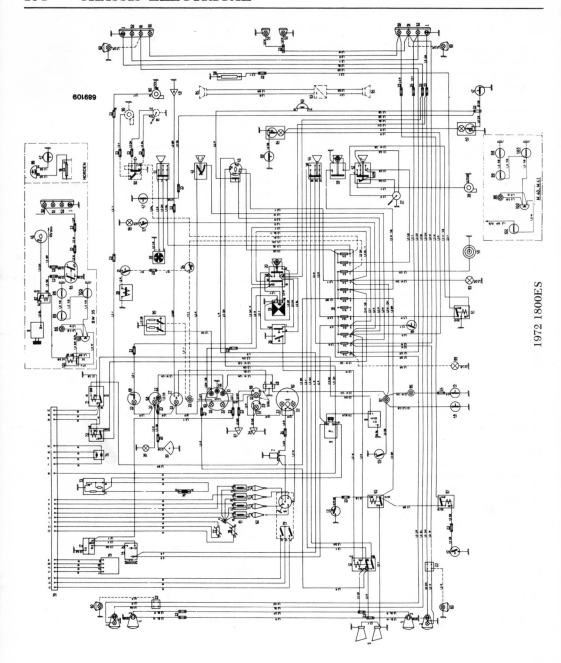

689109

1972 1800ES

Pos.	Title	Data	Pos.	Title	Data
1.	Dir. ind. flashers	32 CP	52.	Brake stoplights	32 CP
2.	Parking lights	4 CP	53.	License plate light	2 x 4 CP
3.	Headlight low beams	40 W	54.	Switch for overdrive M 41	
4.	Headlight high beams	45 W	55.	Brake warning contact	
5.	Horn		56.	Map light	
6.	Distributor firing order	1-3-4-2	57.	Switch for map light	
7.	Ignition coil		58.	Electrically heated rear window	
8.	Battery	12 V 60 Ah	59.	Switch, electrically heated rear window	
9.	Starter motor	1.0 hp	60.	Side marker lights (USA only)	5 W
10.	Contact for back-up light M 41		61.	Relay for electrically heated rear window	
11.	High beams warning lamp		62.	Spark plugs	
12.	Dipper relay for high and low beams and headlight flashers		63.	Warning buzzer	
13.	Horn ring		64.	Contact on transmission BW 35	
14.	Alternator	35 A	65.	Horn relay	
15.	Contact seat belt		66.	Oil temperature gauge	
16.	Fusebox		67.	Oil temperature sensor	
17.	Voltage regulator		68.	Oil pressure gauge	
18.	Brake contact		69.	Clock	
19.	Flasher unit		70.	Electronic unit	
20.	Switch for emergency warning flashers		71.	Main relay for fuel injection	
21.	Battery charging warning lamp	3 W	72.	Relay for fuel pump	
22.	Oil pressure warning lamp	2 W	73.	Thermal timer contact	
23.	Connector		74.	Pressure sensor	
24.	Connector (R-H drive only)		75.	Throttle valve switch	
25.	Overdrive warning lamp M 41	1.2 W	76.	Start valve	
26.	Switch for dir. ind. and headlight flashers		77.	Temperature sensor, intake air	
27.	Fuel gauge		78.	Temperature sensor, coolant	
28.	Voltage stabilizer		79.	Triggering contacts	
29.	Temperature gauge		80.	Fuel pump	
30.	Oil pressure sender		81.	Injection valves	
31.	Contact for overdrive on transmission M 41		82.	Tachometer	
32.	Flashers warning lamp	3 W	83.	Speedometer	
33.	Instrument panel light		84.	Interior light, rear	10 W
34.	Coolant temperature sensor		85.	Seat belts light	2 W
35.	Heater control light	3 W	86.	Seat belt warning lamp	1.2 W
36.	Heater		87.	Relay for back-up lights starter relay on BW 35	
37.	Windshield wipers		88.	Shift positions light (BW 35 only)	1.2 W
38.	Windshield washer		89.	Door switch, rear	
39.	Solenoid for overdrive on transmission M 41		90.	Tailgate washer	
40.	Interior lamp	10 W	91.	Tailgate wiper	
41.	Switch for heater		92.	Switch for tailgate wiper and washer	
42.	Switch for windshield wipers and washer		93.	Radio	
43.	Instrument panel light rheostat		94.	Speaker	
44.	Light switch		95.	Dimmer switch for overdrive warning lamp M 41	
45.	Starter switch		96.	Warning buzzer light	
46.	Cigarette lighter		97.	Brake warning lamp	1.2 W
47.	Door switch		98.	Contact, seat buckle, passenger	
48.	Switch for parking brake control		99.	Contact, passenger seat	
49.	Fuel gauge tank unit		100.	Warning buzzer, safety belts	
50.	Back-up lights	32 CP	101.	Relay, safety belts	
51.	Rear lights	4 CP	102.	Contact, transmission M 41	
			103.	Contact, seat buckle, driver	

Color code:

SB	Black	BR	Brown
W	White	W-SB	White-black
Y	Yellow	W-GN	White-green
GN	Green	BL-R	Blue-red
GR	Grey	BL-W	Blue-white
BL	Blue	BL-Y	Blue-yellow
R	Red	GN-R	Green-red

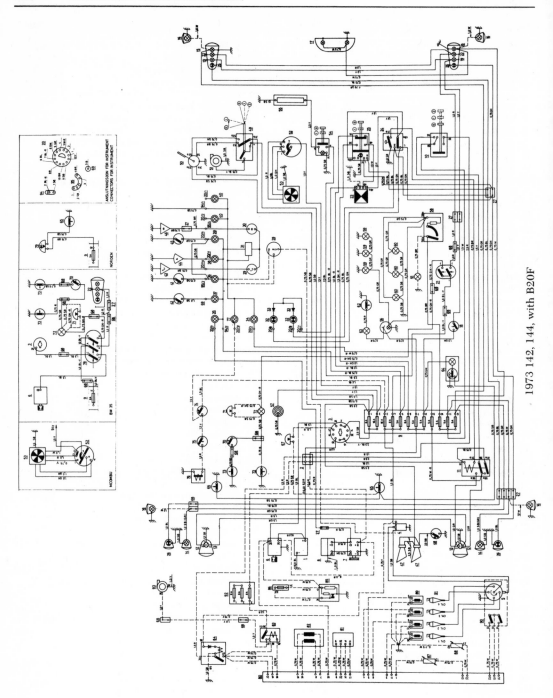

1973 142, 144, with B20F

Pos.	Title	Data
1.	Battery	12 V 60 Ah
2.	Connection box	
3.	Ignition switch	
4.	Ignition coil	
5.	Distributor, firing sequence	1-3-4-2
6.	Starter motor	
7.	Alternator	
8.	Voltage regulator	
9.	Fusebox	
10.	Light switch	
11.	Dip relay for high and low beams	
12.	Headlights	45 W
13.	Low beams	40 W
14.	Position light	5 W
15.	Rear light	5 W
16.	Side marking lights	5 W
17.	Plate light	2 x 5 W
18.	Brake stop light contact	
19.	Brake stop lights	32 CP
20.	Connection at instrument	
21.	Contact on transmission M 40, M 41	
22.	Back-up lights	32 CP
23.	Flasher unit	
24.	Dir. ind. switch	
25.	Switch, emergency warning flashers	
26.	Flasher lights	32 CP
27.	Part of 6-pole connection block	
28.	Tachometer	
29.	Temperature gauge	
30.	Fuel gauge	
31.	Voltage stabilizer	
32.	Flasher light warning lamp	1.2 W
33.	Diode	
34.	Warning lamp for high beams	1.2 W
35.	Warning lamp for battery charging	1.2 W
36.	Parking brake warning lamp	1.2 W
37.	Choke warning lamp	1.2 W
38.	Oil pressure warning lamp	1.2 W
39.	Brake warning lamp	1.2 W
40.	Vacant warning lamp	
41.	Parking brake contact	
42.	Choke control contact	
43.	Temperature sensor	
44.	Oil pressure sensor	
45.	Brake warning contact	
46.	Brake level sender	
47.	Horn	
48.	Horn ring	
49.	Switch, windshield wipers/washer	

Pos.	Title	Data
50.	Windshield wipers	
51.	Windshield washer	
52.	Switch, fan	
53.	Fan	
54.	Switch, electrically heated rear window	
55.	Electrically heated rear window	
56.	Clock	
57.	Cigarette lighter	
58.	Rheostat for instrument panel lighting	
59.	Instrument panel lighting	3 x 2 W
60.	Lighting for controls	3 x 1.2 W
61.	Shift positions light, aut. trans.	1.2 W
62.	Glove box contact	
63.	Glove box lamp	
64.	Interior lamp	
65.	Door switch on left side	
66.	Door switch on right side	
67.	Reminder buzzer for ignition key	
68.	Joint	
69.	Connection at instrument	
70.	Passenger seat contact	
71.	Reminder buzzer for seat belt	
72.	Seat belt warning lamp	1.2 W
73.	Contact for seat belt	
74.	Switch for overdrive M 41	
75.	Contact for overdrive on transmission M 41	
76.	Solenoid for overdrive on transmission M 41	
77.	Overdrive warning lamp	1.2 W
78.	Contact on automatic transmission BW 35	
79.	Reminder buzzer for lights	
80.	Control unit	
81.	Throttle valve switch	
82.	Pressure sensor	
83.	Relay for fuel pump	
84.	Main relay for fuel injection	
85.	Thermal timer contact	
86.	Start valve	
87.	Temperature sensor, intake air	
88.	Temperature sensor, coolant	
89.	Injection valves	
90.	Cut-in contact	
91.	Spark plug	
92.	Fusebox	
93.	Fuel pump	
94.	Connection at instrument	
95.	Connection at instrument	

Color code:
SB	Black
Y	Yellow
BL	Blue
BL-Y	Blue-yellow
BL-R	Blue-red
GN-R	Green-red
R	Red
GN	Green
W-R	White-red
W	White
BR	Brown
GR	Grey

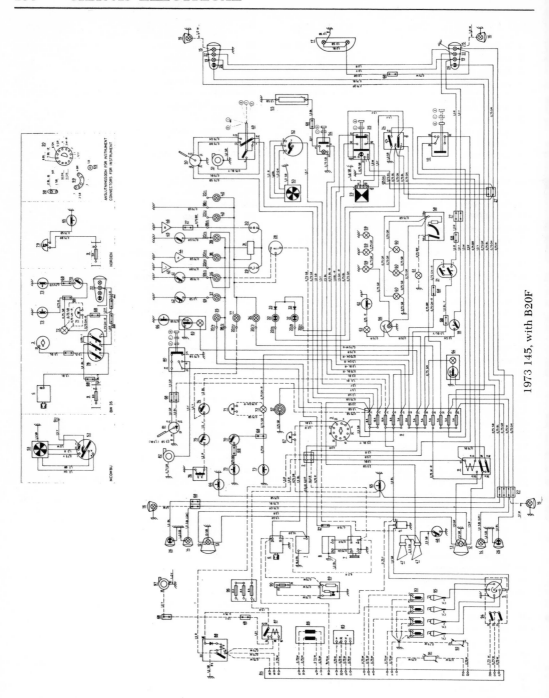

1973 145, with B20F

Pos.	Title	Data	Pos.	Title	Data
1.	Battery	12 V 60 Ah	52.	Switch, fan	
2.	Connection box		53.	Fan	
3.	Ignition switch		54.	Switch, electrically heated rear window	
4.	Ignition coil		55.	Electrically heated rear window	
5.	Distributor, firing sequence	1-3-4-2	56.	Clock	
6.	Starter motor		57.	Cigarette lighter	
7.	Alternator		58.	Rheostat for instrument panel lighting	
8.	Voltage regulator		59.	Instrument panel lighting	3 x 2 W
9.	Fusebox		60.	Lighting for control panel	3 x 1.2 W
10.	Light switch		61.	Shift positions light, aut. trans.	1.2 W
11.	Dip relay for high and low beams		62.	Glove box contact	
12.	Headlights	45 W	63.	Glove box lamp	
13.	Low beams	40 W	64.	Interior lamp	
14.	Position light	5 W	65.	Door switch on left side	
15.	Rear lights	5 W	66.	Door switch on right side	
16.	Side marking lights	5 W	67.	Reminder buzzer for ignition key	
17.	Plate light	2 x 5 W	68.	Joint	
18.	Brake stop light contact		69.	Connection at instrument	
19.	Brake stop lights	32 CP	70.	Passenger seat contact	
20.	Connection at instrument		71.	Reminder buzzer for seat belt	
21.	Contact on transmission M 40, M 41		72.	Seat belt warning lamp	1.2 W
22.	Back-up lights	32 CP	73.	Contact for seat belt	
23.	Flasher unit		74.	Switch for overdrive M 41	
24.	Dir. ind. switch		75.	Contact for overdrive on transmission M 41	
25.	Switch, emergency warning flashers		76.	Solenoid for overdrive on transmission M 41	
26.	Flasher lights	32 CP	77.	Overdrive warning lamp	1.2 W
27.	Part of 6-pole connection block		78.	Contact on automatic transmission BW 35	
28.	Tachometer		79.	Reminder buzzer for lights	
29.	Temperature gauge		80.	Switch for electrically heated tailgate window	
30.	Fuel gauge		81.	Tailgate window wiper	
31.	Voltage stabilizer		82.	Tailgate window washer	
32.	Flasher light warning lamp	1.2 W	83.	Rear roof light	10 W
33.	Diode		84.	Control unit	
34.	Warning lamp for high beams	1.2 W	85.	Throttle valve switch	
35.	Warning lamp for battery charging	1.2 W	86.	Pressure sensor	
36.	Parking brake warning lamp	1.2 W	87.	Relay for fuel pump	
37.	Choke warning lamp	1.2 W	88.	Main relay for fuel injection	
38.	Oil pressure warning lamp	1.2 W	89.	Thermal timer contact	
39.	Brake warning lamp	1.2 W	90.	Start valve	
40.	Vacant warning lamp		91.	Temperature sensor, intake air	
41.	Parking brake contact		92.	Temperature sensor, coolant	
42.	Choke control contact		93.	Injection valves	
43.	Temperature sensor		94.	Trip contact	
44.	Oil pressure sensor		95.	Spark plug	
45.	Brake warning contact		96.	Fusebox	
46.	Brake level sender		97.	Fuel pump	
47.	Horn		98.	Connection at instrument	
48.	Horn ring		99.	Connection at instrument	
49.	Switch, windshield wipers/washer				
50.	Windshield wipers				
51.	Windshield washer				

Color code:

SB	Black
Y	Yellow
BL	Blue
BL-Y	Blue-yellow
BL-R	Blue-red
GN-R	Green-red
R	Red
GN	Green
W-R	White-red
W	White
BR	Brown
GR	Grey

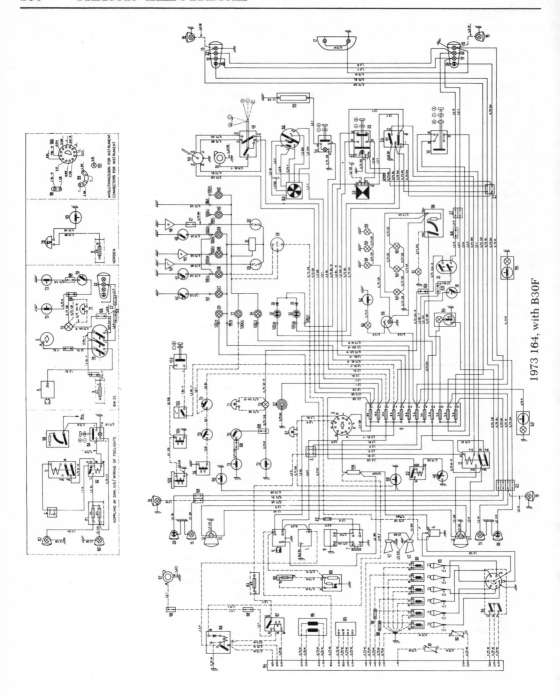

1973 164, with B30F

Pos.	Title	Pos.	Title

1. Battery
2. Connection box
3. Ignition switch
4. Ignition coil
5. Distributor, firing sequence
6. Starter motor
7. Alternator
8. Voltage regulator
9. Fusebox
10. Light switch
11. Dip relay for high and low beams
12. Headlights
13. Low beams
14. Position light
15. Rear lights
16. Side marking lights
17. Plate light
18. Brake stop light contact
19. Brake stop lights
20. Relay for horn
21. Contact on transmission M 40, M 41
22. Back-up lights
23. Flasher unit
24. Dir. ind. switch
25. Switch, emergency warning flashers
26. Flasher lights
27. Part of 6-pole connection block
28. Tachometer
29. Temperature gauge
30. Fuel gauge
31. Voltage stabilizer
32. Flasher light warning lamp
33. Diode
34. Warning lamp for high beams
35. Warning lamp for battery charging
36. Parking brake warning lamp
37. Choke warning lamp
38. Oil pressure warning lamp
39. Brake warning lamp
40. Vacant warning lamp
41. Parking brake contact
42. Choke control contact
43. Temperature sensor
44. Oil pressure sensor
45. Brake warning contact
46. Fuel level sender
47. Horn
48. Horn ring
49. Switch, windshield wipers/washer
50. Windshield wipers
51. Windshield washer
52. Switch, fan
53. Fan

Color code:

SB	Black
Y	Yellow
BL	Blue
BL-Y	Blue-yellow
BL-R	Blue-red
GN-R	Green-red
R	Red
GN	Green
W-R	White-red
W	White
BR	Brown
GR	Grey

54. Switch, electrically heated rear window
55. Electrically heated rear window
56. Clock
57. Cigarette lighter
58. Rheostat for instrument panel lighting
59. Instrument panel lighting
60. Lighting for controls
61. Shift positions light, aut. trans.
62. Glove box contact
63. Glove box lamp
64. Interior lamp
65. Door switch on left side
66. Door switch on right side
67. Warning buzzer for ignition key
68. Joint
69. Engine comp. lighting
70. Passenger seat contact
71. Warning reminder for seat belt
72. Seat belt warning lamp
73. Contact for seat belt
74. Switch for overdrive M 41
75. Contact for overdrive on transmission M 41
76. Solenoid for overdrive on transmission M 41
77. Overdrive warning lamp
78. Contact on automatic transmission BW 35
79. Warning buzzer for light
80. Fog light
81. Fusebox
82. Fog light relay
83. Fog light switch
84. Injection control unit
85. Throttle valve switch
86. Pressure sensor
87. Relay for fuel pump
88. Main relay for fuel injection
89. Thermal timer contact
90. Cold start valve
91. Temperature sensor, intake air
92. Temperaure sensor, coolant
93. Injectors
94. Triggering contacts
95. Spark plug
96. Luggage comp. light
97. Fuel pump
98. Connection at instrument
99. Connection at instrument
100. Connection at instrument
101. Connection at instrument
102. Switch for compressor
103. Thermostat
104. Solenoid on compressor
105. Solenoid valve
106. Resistor

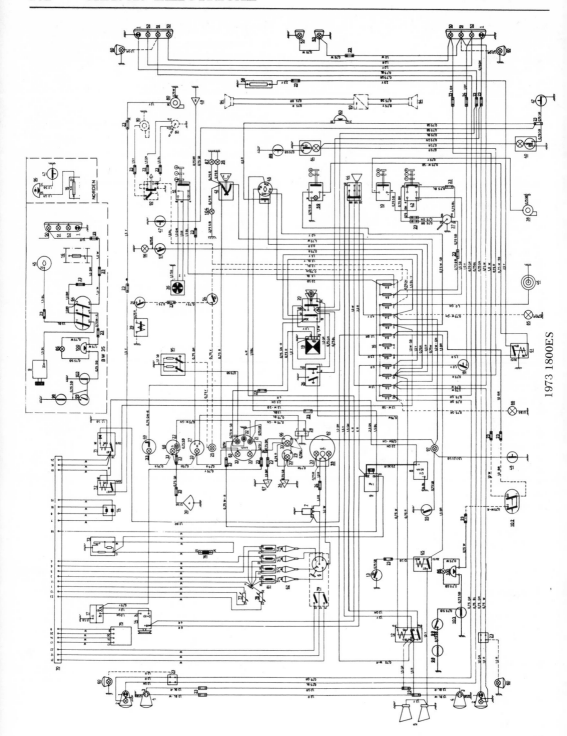

1973 1800ES

Pos.	Title	Data
1.	Dir. ind. flashers	32 CP
2.	Parking lights	4 CP
3.	Headlight low beams	40 W
4.	Headlight high beams	45 W
5.	Horn	
6.	Distributor firing order	1-3-4-2
7.	Ignition coil	
8.	Battery	12 V 60 Ah
9.	Starter motor	1.0 hp
10.	Switch for windshield washer	
11.	High beams warning lamp	
12.	Dipper relay for high and low beams and headlight flashers	
13.	Horn ring	
14.	Alternator	35 A
16.	Fusebox	
17.	Voltage regulator	
18.	Brake contact	
19.	Flasher unit	
20.	Switch for emergency warning flashers	
21.	Battery charging warning lamp	3 W
22.	Oil pressure warning lamp	2 W
23.	Connector	
24.	Connector (R-H drive only)	
25.	Overdrive warning lamp M 41	1.2 W
26.	Switch for dir. ind. and headlight flashers	
27.	Fuel gauge	
28.	Voltage stabilizer	
29.	Temperature gauge	
30.	Oil pressure sender	
31.	Contact for overdrive on transmission M 41	
32.	Flashers warning lamp	3 W
33.	Instrument panel light	
34.	Coolant temperature sensor	
35.	Heater control light	3 W
36.	Heater	
37.	Windshield wipers	
38.	Windshield washer	
39.	Solenoid for overdrive on transmission M 41	
40.	Interior lamp	10 W
41.	Switch for heater	
42.	Switch for windshield wipers and washer	
43.	Instrument panel light rheostat	
44.	Light switch	
45.	Starter switch	
46.	Cigarette lighter	
47.	Door switch	
48.	Switch for parking brake control	
49.	Fuel gauge tank unit	
50.	Back-up light	32 CP
51.	Rear lights	4 CP

Pos.	Title	Data
52.	Brake stoplights	32 CP
53.	License plate light	2 x 4 CP
54.	Switch for overdrive M 41	
55.	Brake warning contact	
56.	Map light	
57.	Switch for map light	
58.	Electrically heated rear window	
59.	Switch, electrically heated rear window	
60.	Side marker lights (USA only)	5 W
61.	Relay for electrically heated rear window	
62.	Spark plugs	
63.	Warning buzzer	
64.	Contact on transmission BW 35	
65.	Horn relay	
66.	Oil temperature gauge	
67.	Oil temperature sensor	
68.	Oil pressure gauge	
69.	Clock	
70.	Electronic unit	
71.	Main relay for fuel injection	
72.	Relay for fuel pump	
73.	Thermal timer contact	
74.	Pressure sensor	
75.	Throttle valve switch	
76.	Start valve	
77.	Temperature sensor I	
78.	Temperature sensor II	
79.	Triggering contact	
80.	Fuel pump	
81.	Injection valves	
82.	Tachometer	
83.	Speedometer	
84.	Interior light, rear	10 W
85.	Seat belts light	2 W
86.	Seat belt warning lamp	1.2 W
87.	Lighting for switch	
88.	Shift positions light (BW 35 only)	1.2 W
89.	Door switch, rear	
90.	Tailgate washer	
91.	Tailgate wiper	
92.	Switch for tailgate wiper and washer	
93.	Radio	
94.	Speaker	
95.	Dimmer switch for overdrive warning lamp M 41	
96.	Warning buzzer light	
97.	Brake warning lamp	1.2 W
98.	Contact, seat buckle, passenger	
99.	Contact, passenger seat	
100.	Warning buzzer, safety belts	
102.	Contact, transmission M 41	
103.	Contact, seat buckle, driver	
104.	Decal lighting (only USA)	

Color code:

SB	Black	BR	Brown
W	White	W-SB	White-black
Y	Yellow	W-GN	White-green
GN	Green	BL-R	Blue-red
GR	Grey	BL-W	Blue-white
BL	Blue	BL-Y	Blue-yellow
R	Red	GN-R	Green-red

Clutch and Transmission

Manual Transmission

Manual transmissions installed in 1970–73 Volvos are the M40, M41, M400, and the M410. All are fully synchronized four speed transmissions, with all forward gears in constant mesh. The M41 and M410 units are equipped with Laycock-de-Normanville overdrive units, and except for the overdrive engaging switch and push plate, are identical to their M40 and M400 counterparts. The heavy-duty, top cover, Volvo manufactured M40 is installed as standard equipment on 140 series models. The similar M41 overdrive transmission is optional on 140 series models, and standard equipment on most 1800E, and all 1800ES models. The extra heavy-duty, top cover, ZF manufactured M400 is standard equipment on 164 models. The similar M410 overdrive transmission is optional on the 164, and was installed on some early 1970 1800E models.

Removal and Installation

The transmission or the transmission-overdrive assembly may be removed with the engine installed in the vehicle.

140 SERIES

1. If an engine lifting (support) apparatus, such as SVO 2727, is available, install

Suspending engine

it in the engine compartment. If using an SVO 2727, secure the lifting hook around the exhaust pipe. The purpose of supporting the rear of the engine here is to prevent damage to the viscous fan, radiator, or front engine mounts by limiting the downward travel of the rear of the engine when the transmission support crossmember is removed. If no lifting apparatus is available, place a jack with a protective wooden block beneath the engine oil pan. Do not place the jack under the flywheel (clutch) housing.

2. Lift up the rubber boot, unscrew the protective cover, and remove the gearshift lever from the transmission.

3. Jack up the vehicle sufficiently to allow removal of the transmission. Maintain the car at a level attitude and place jackstands beneath the jack points for support. Remove the lower drain plug from the transmission and drain the oil.

4. Slowly loosen the nuts for the transmission support crossmember. Make sure that the supporting apparatus or the jack prevent the rear of the engine from lowering. Remove the crossmember. Disconnect the front universal joint from the transmission (or overdrive) output shaft flange. Disconnect the speedometer cable. Disconnect the rear engine mount and the exhaust pipe bracket.

5. Allow the rear of the engine to drop 0.8 in. Disconnect the back-up light wires, and the wires for the overdrive, if so equipped.

6. Remove the four bolts which retain the transmission to the flywheel (clutch) housing. It may be necessary to use a universal joint on the wrench to gain access to the two upper bolts. Before removing the transmission, keep in mind that it is quite heavy, and a hydraulic floor jack may offer some support and maneuverability as the box is being removed. To remove the transmission, pull it straight out to the rear.

7. While the transmission is removed, it is a good time to inspect the condition of the clutch and the throw-out bearing. Replace the throw-out bearing if it is scored or if it has been emitting metal–to–metal noises.

8. Reverse steps 1–6 to install, being careful to install two guide pins in the flywheel (clutch) housing. This will aid in

Transmission guide pins installed

aligning the transmission input shaft with the clutch spline when the transmission is being fitted to the flywheel housing. After two transmission–to–flywheel housing bolts are installed, the guide pins may be removed and the remaining two bolts installed. Torque the transmission–to–flywheel housing bolts to 45 ft lbs, and the universal joint–to–output shaft flange bolts to 25–30 ft lbs. Fill the transmission to the proper level with oil.

164

1. Follow steps 1–3 under "Transmission Removal and Installation" for the 140 series.

2. Remove the upper radiator bolts and the exhaust manifold flange nuts. Disconnect the negative battery cable, the throttle shaft and clutch cable from the flywheel (clutch) housing.

3. Slowly loosen the nuts for the transmission support crossmember. Making sure that the rear of the engine remains supported, remove the crossmember. Disconnect the exhaust pipe bracket and the speedometer cable. Disconnect the front universal joint from the transmission (or overdrive) output shaft flange.

4. Lower the rear of the engine approximately 1.8 in. Disconnect the back-up light wires and the wires for the overdrive, if so equipped.

5. Place a hydraulic floor jack beneath the transmission. Remove the bolts which retain the transmission and flywheel (clutch) housing assembly to the engine. Leave the starter connected but position it to one side. Remove the transmission by pulling it straight to the rear.

6. Prior to assembly, inspect the condition of the clutch and throw-out bearing. Replace the bearing if it is scored or noisy in operation.

7. Reverse steps 1–5 to install. Torque the flywheel (clutch) housing–to–engine bolts to 45 ft lbs, and the universal joint–to–output shaft flange bolts to 25–30 ft lbs. Fill the transmission to the proper level with oil.

1800 Series (M41)

1. Remove the storage console from the transmission tunnel. Lift up the boot, unscrew the protective cover and remove the gearshift lever.

2. Disconnect the negative battery

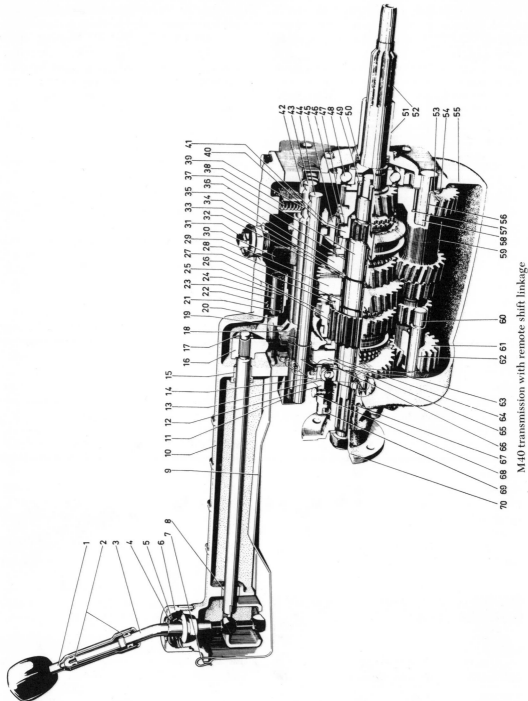

M40 transmission with remote shift linkage

1. Gear lever, upper section with knob	25. Insert	47. Synchronizing cone
2. Rubber bushings	26. Engaging sleeve and gear wheel for reverse	48. Ball bearing
3. Gear lever, lower section	27. Synchronizing cone	49. Roller bearing
4. Washer	28. Needle bearings	50. Sealing ring
5. Spring	29. Gear wheel for 2nd speed	51. Cover
6. Cover	30. Push plate for overdrive switch (only M 41)	52. Input shaft
7. Lock spring	31. Overdrive switch (only M 41)	53. Spacer washer
8. Bushing	32. Thrust washer	54. Thrust washer
9. Protective cover	33. Circlip	55. Housing
10. Gearbox cover	34. Thrust washer	56. Needle bearing
11. End casing	35. Gear wheel for 3rd speed	57. Spacer washer
12. Rear cover	36. Needle bearings	58. Countershaft
13. Ball bearing	37. Mainshaft	59. Idler gear
14. Striker (x-ray)	38. Spring	60. Reverse shaft
15. Bushing	39. Interlock ball	61. Reverse gear
16. Gear shifter rod	40. Synchronizing hub	62. Bushing
17. Circlip	41. Insert	63. Striker lever (x-ray)
18. Selector fork, 1st and 2nd speeds	42. Selector rail for 3rd and 4th speeds	64. Needle bearings
19. Gate	43. Selector rail for 1st and 2nd speeds	65. Gear wheel for 1st speed
20. Sliding plate	44. Selector rail for reverse	66. Thrust washer
21. Sleeve (reverse catch)	45. Engaging sleeve	67. Speedometer worm gear
22. Spring	46. Spring	68. Bleeder nipple
23. Sleeve		69. Oil seal
24. Spring		70. Flange

cable. Remove the radiator attaching bolts.

3. Jack up the vehicle sufficiently to allow removal of the transmission. Install jackstands. Remove the lower drain plug and drain the transmission oil.

4. Remove the bolts which retain the driveshaft to the flanges, and remove the attaching bolts for the support bearings. Pull the driveshaft approximately 0.4 in. to the rear.

5. Place a jack, with a protective wooden block, beneath the oil pan of the engine.

6. Disconnect the exhaust pipe bracket and the speedometer. Remove the rear engine mount. Slowly loosen the nuts for the transmission support crossmember, making sure that the jack supports the rear of the engine.

7. Lower the engine approximately 0.8 in. Disconnect the electric cables from the transmission.

8. Remove the four bolts which secure the transmission to the flywheel (clutch) housing. It may be necessary to use a universal joint to gain access to the two upper bolts. Support the weight of the transmission with another jack and pull the unit straight out to the rear.

9. Inspect the condition of the clutch and throwout bearing. Replace the bearing if it is scored or has been noisy in operation.

10. Reverse steps 1–8 to install, making sure to install two guide pins in the flywheel (clutch) housing to aid in aligning the transmission input shaft with the clutch spline when the transmission is being fitted to the flywheel housing. After two transmission–to–flywheel housing bolts are installed, the guide pins may be removed and the remaining two bolts installed. Torque the bolts to 45 ft lbs. Fill the transmission to the proper level with oil.

1800 SERIES (M410)

1. Disconnect the upper and lower radiator hoses and drain the cooling system. Disconnect the heater hoses and the air intake hose. Pull up the rubber boot, unscrew the protective cover and remove the gearshift lever.

2. Raise the vehicle sufficiently to remove the transmission, and install jackstands. Disconnect the driveshaft, exhaust pipe bracket, clutch cable, the electrical wires for the back-up lights and the overdrive.

3. Place a hydraulic floor jack beneath the transmission, and remove the transmission support crossmember.

4. Place a protective wooden block be-

tween the rear of the engine and the fire-wall. Lower the jack and the rear of the engine until the engine contacts the wooden block.

5. Remove the bolts which secure the flywheel (clutch) housing to the engine. Leave the starter connected but position it to one side. Remove the transmission by pulling it straight to the rear.

6. Prior to installation, inspect the condition of the clutch and throwout bearing. Replace the bearing if it is scored or has been noisy in operation.

7. Reverse steps 1–5 to install. Torque the flywheel (clutch) housing–to–engine bolts to 45 ft lbs. Fill the tranmission to the proper level with oil.

Linkage Adjustment

Shift linkage adjustments are neither necessary nor possible on Volvo transmissions. The linkage is mounted inboard and is permanently bathed in oil and insulated from the elements. On 1970–71 140 series, the shift lever mounts directly in the top of the transmission. This configuration, although providing for more direct shifting action by elimination of the levers and rods of conventional transmissions, required the use of a long wand-like shift lever with long throws required to change gears. This situation is remedied on 1972 and later 140 series cars, as well as all 164 and 1800 series, with the implementation of an inboard mounted, intermediate shifter rod. This rod allows the use of a much shorter, sportier shift lever and shorter throws between gears.

Overdrive

The overdrive unit for the M41 and M410 transmissions is a planetary gear type and is mounted on the rear of the transmission. When the overdrive is in the direct drive position (overdrive switched off) and the car is driven forward, power from the transmission mainshaft is transmitted through the freewheel rollers and uni-directional clutch to the overdrive output shaft. When the car is backing up or during periods of engine braking, torque is

transmitted through the clutch sliding member which is held by spring pressure against the tapered portion of the output shaft. When the overdrive is actuated, the clutch sliding member is pressed by hydraulic pressure against the brake disc (ring), which locks the sun wheel. As a result, the output shaft of the overdrive rotates at a higher speed than the mainshaft thereby accomplishing a 20% reduction in engine speed in relation to vehicle speed.

The overdrive is actuated by a switch located beneath the steering wheel. This switch energizes a solenoid on the overdrive unit, via a switch on the transmission, which is cut in only when 4th gear is engaged. The solenoid has two windings: a heavy control winding and a lower current, hold winding. When actuated, the control winding opens the overdrive control valve, whereupon the control winding is cut off and the valve is held in the open position by the hold winding. The control valve regulates the pressurized oil flow from the cam-operated pump to the hydraulic pistons which operate the overdrive clutch sliding member.

Removal and Installation

To facilitate removal, the vehicle should first be driven in 4th gear with the overdrive engaged, and then coasted for a few seconds with the overdrive disengaged and the clutch pedal depressed.

1. Remove the transmission from the vehicle as outlined in the applicable "Transmission Removal and Installation" section.

2. Disconnect the solenoid cables.

3. If the overdrive unit has not already been drained, remove the six bolts and the overdrive oil pan.
CAUTION: *Be careful to avoid spilling hot transmission fluid on the skin.*

4. Remove the bolts which retain the overdrive unit to the transmission intermediate flange. Pull the unit straight to the rear until it clears the transmission mainshaft.

5. Reverse the above procedure to install. Install the overdrive oil pan with a new gasket. After installation of the transmission and overdrive assembly, fill the transmission (which automatically fills the overdrive) to the proper level with the correct lubricant. Check the lubricant level in the transmission after driving 6–9 miles.

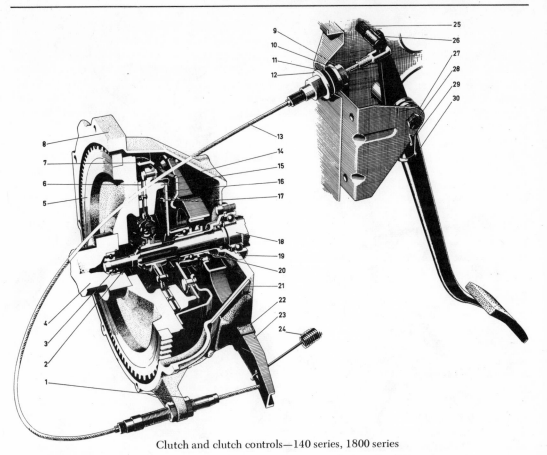

Clutch and clutch controls—140 series, 1800 series

1. Adjusting nuts	12. Washer	22. Dust cover
2. Circlip	13. Clutch wire	23. Release fork
3. Support bearing in crankshaft	14. Retainer	24. Return spring
4. Crankshaft	15. Pressure plate	25. Pedal stop
5. Flywheel	16. Thrust spring	26. Rubber sleeve
6. Clutch plate	17. Support rings	27. Bracket
7. Clutch cover	18. Clutch plate shaft (input shaft	28. Screw for pedal shaft
8. Flywheel housing	transmission)	29. Return spring
9. Nut	19. Cover, transmission	30. Clutch pedal
10. Washer	20. Release bearing	
11. Rubber bushing	21. Holding plate	

Clutch

All 1970 and later model Volvos are equipped with diaphragm spring clutches. The 140 and 1800 series use an 8½ in. disc, while the carbureted 164 uses a 9 in. disc, and the fuel-injected 164E uses a 9½ in. disc. The diaphragm spring serves a dual purpose: when engaging the clutch, it serves as a pressure spring, and when disengaging, it serves as a clutch lever. Clutch control, actuated by the foot pedal, is mechanical on all models imported into

this country. A flexible thrust cable is utilized to operate the release lever and throwout bearing.

Removal and Installation

M40, M41

1. Remove the transmission as outlined in the applicable "Transmission Removal and Installation" procedure.

2. Remove the upper bolt for the starter motor.

3. Remove the throwout bearing. Disconnect the clutch cable at the release

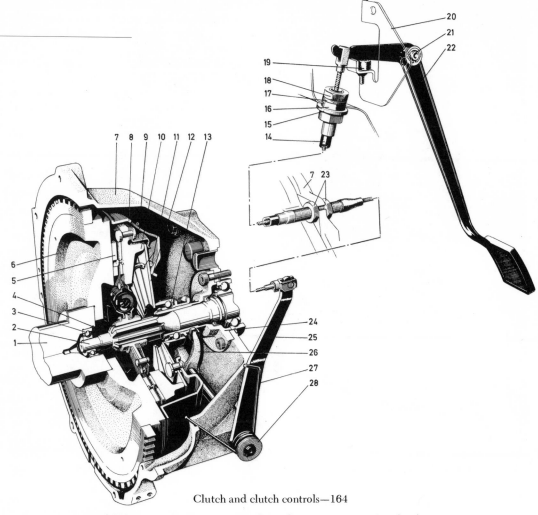

Clutch and clutch controls—164

1. Crankshaft	10. Thrust plate	20. Stop bracket
2. Clutch plate shaft	11. Support rings	21. Pedal shaft
(input shaft, transmission)	12. Pressure spring	22. Clutch pedal
3. Support bearing in crankshaft	13. Throw-out bearing	23. Adjusting nuts
4. Circlip	14. Clutch wire	24. Cover, transmission
5. Clutch plate	15. Washer	25. Lever and release shaft
6. Flywheel	16. Rubber bushing	26. Release fork
7. Flywheel housing	17. Washer	27. Return spring
8. Clutch cover	18. Nut	28. Washer
9. Retainer	19. Rubber stop	

lever (fork), and slacken the cable sleeve at its bracket.

4. Remove the bolts which retain the flywheel (clutch) housing to the engine, and lift off the housing.

5. Remove the bolt for the release fork ball joint, and remove the ball and release fork.

6. In order to prevent warpage, slowly loosen the bolts which retain the clutch to the flywheel diagonally in rotation. Re-

move the bolts and lift off the clutch and pressure plate.

7. Inspect the clutch assembly as outlined under "Clutch Inspection."

8. When ready to install, wash the clutch facings, pressure plate and flywheel with solvent to remove any traces of oil, and wipe them clean with a cloth.

9. Position the clutch assembly (the longest side of the hub facing backward) to the flywheel and align the bolt holes.

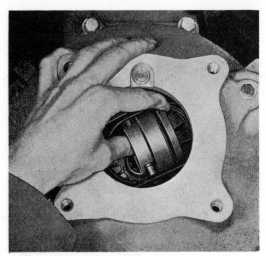

Removing throwout bearing

SVO 2824

Installing clutch

Insert a pilot shaft (centering mandrel), or an input shaft from an old transmission of the same type, through the clutch assembly and flywheel so that the flywheel pilot bearing is centered.

10. Install the six bolts which retain the clutch assembly to the flywheel and tighten them diagonally in rotation, a few turns at a time. After all of the bolts are tightened, remove the pilot shaft (centering mandrel).

11. Install the ball and release fork in the flywheel housing.

12. Place the upper starter bolt in the housing. Position the housing to the engine and first install the four upper bolts ($7/16$ in.), then the lower starter bolt, and finally the two lower bolts ($3/8$ in.).

13. Insert the cable sleeve in its bracket and install the rear nut. Connect the cable at the release lever (fork), and install the throwout bearing.

14. Install the nut for the upper starter motor bolt.

15. Install the transmission as outlined in the applicable "Transmission Removal and Installation" section.

16. Adjust the clutch pedal free travel.

M400, M410

1. Remove the transmission as outlined in the applicable "Transmission Removal and Installation" section.

2. In order to prevent warpage, slowly loosen the bolts which retain the clutch assembly to the flywheel diagonally in rotation. Remove the bolts and lift off the clutch and pressure plate.

3. Inspect the clutch assembly as outlined under "Clutch Inspection."

4. When ready to install, wash the clutch facings, pressure plate and flywheel with solvent to remove any traces of oil, and wipe them clean with a cloth.

5. Position the clutch assembly (the longest side of the hub facing backward) to the flywheel and align the bolt holes. Insert a pilot shaft (centering mandrel), or an input shaft from an old transmission of the same type, through the clutch assembly and flywheel so that the flywheel pilot bearing is centered.

6. Install the six bolts which retain the clutch assembly to the flywheel, and tighten them diagonally in rotation, a few turns at a time. After all of the bolts are tightened, remove the pilot shaft (centering mandrel).

7. Install the transmission as outlined in the applicable "Transmission Removal and Installation" section.

Clutch Inspection

Check the pressure plate for heat damage, cracks, scoring, or other damage to the friction surface. Check the curvature of the pressure plate with a $9\frac{1}{2}$ in. steel ruler. Place the ruler diagonally over the pressure plate friction surface and measure the distance between the straight edge of the ruler and the inner diameter of the pressure plate. This measurement must not be greater than 0.0012 in. In addition, there must be no clearance between the straight edge of the ruler and the outer diameter of the pressure plate. This check should be made at several points. Replace the clutch as a unit if it proves faulty.

Check the throwout bearing by rotating it several times while applying finger pressure, so that the ball bearing rolls against the inside of the races. If the bearing does not turn easily or if it binds at any point, replace it as a unit. Also make sure that the bearing slides easily on the guide sleeve from the transmission.

Clutch Pedal Play Adjustment

1. Loosen the locknut (2) for the fork (3) on the clutch cable.

2. Make the necessary adjustment and tighten the locknut. The free play (A) should be 0.12 in. for 140 series models, 0.12–0.16 for 1800 series, and 0.16–0.20 for the 164.

3. If this adjustment is insufficient, or if a new cable is installed, the sleeve attachment to the flywheel housing should be adjusted with the adjusting nuts (1).

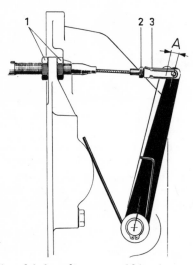

Clutch pedal play adjustment—164 series

Automatic Transmission

Automatic transmissions have been available on all 1970–73 140 series and 164 models, as well as 1971–73 1800 series Volvos. The transmission is a three-speed, dual-range, Borg-Warner model 35. The BW 35 consists of a three element torque converter coupling, planetary gear set, and

a valve control system. Until 1971, the BW 35 was equipped with a rear oil pump. In 1972 it was discontinued. Elimination of the rear pump reduced the hydraulic load on the gears, thereby improving response and fuel economy. However, the absence of the rear pump means that these Volvos cannot be push or tow started.

Oil Pan Removal and Installation

1. Place the transmission selector in Park.

2. Raise the vehicle and place jackstands underneath.

3. The drain plug is located on the oil pan. Place a container underneath to catch the fluid. If the vehicle has been driven for any length of time, be careful as the transmission fluid will be scalding hot. On 1970 models, use a 1/4 in. allen wrench to remove the plug. On 1971 and later models, the drain plug, with gasket, is removed with a screwdriver.

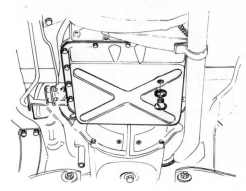

Oil pan drain plug—1971–73 shown

4. After the fluid has stopped draining, remove the 15 oil pan retaining bolts, and lower the pan and gasket.

5. Inspect the magnetic element in the pan for metal shavings or chips. A preponderance of these particles foreshadows a future trip to your dealer. Also remove any sludge or gum from the bottom of the pan. Clean the mating surfaces of the transmission case and oil pan.

6. Position the pan (with a new gasket) to the case and install the 15 retaining bolts. Step torque the bolts diagonally in rotation to 8–13 ft lbs. Coat the threads of the drain plug with Loctite. Install the plug (1971 and later models use a new plug gasket) and torque to 8–10 ft lbs.

7. Remove the jackstands and lower the

vehicle. Refer to the capacities chart in chapter 1 and fill the transmission to the proper level (between the MAX and MIN marks for a cold transmission) with type "F" automatic transmission fluid.

Oil Pump Strainer Service

1. Remove the oil pan as outlined in the "Oil Pan Removal and Installation" section.
2. Remove the four screws which retain the front oil pump wire-mesh strainer to the valve body, and lower the strainer. On 1970–71 models, remove the two screws and two bolts which retain the rear pump strainer to the valve body, and lower the strainer.

Location of oil pump strainer(s)—1970–71 shown

3. Clean the strainers in an alcohol based solvent solution.
4. Position the strainers to the valve body and install the retaining screws and bolts. Torque the screws to 1.7–2.5 ft lbs.
5. Install the oil pan with a new gasket as outlined in the "Oil Pan Removal and Installation" section.

Front Band Adjustment

1. Remove the oil pan as outlined in the "Oil Pan Removal and Installation" section.
2. Insert a 0.25 in. gauge block between the adjusting bolt and the servo cylinder. Tighten the bolt with an inch pound torque wrench to a torque of 10 in. lbs.
3. Adjust the position of the adjusting bolt spring. It should be 1–2 threads from the lever.
4. Remove the gauge block and torque wrench. Make sure that the long end of

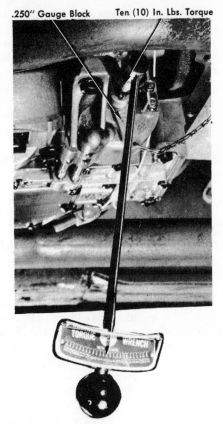

.250" Gauge Block   Ten (10) In. Lbs. Torque

Front band adjustment

the adjusting bolt spring is inserted in the cam for the front brake band.
5. Install the oil pan as outlined in the "Oil Pan Removal and Installation" section.

Rear Band Adjustment

1. An access hole is provided in the right side of the transmission tunnel. On some 140 series and 164 models, it is necessary to disconnect the right heater duct. Lift up the carpet and position it to one

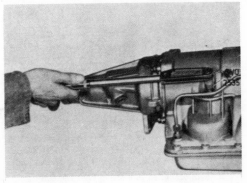

Rear band adjustment

side. Remove the rubber plug from the access hole.

2. Loosen the locknut for the adjusting screw located on the right side of the transmission case.

3. Using a 5/16 in. square socket and a foot pound torque wrench, tighten the adjusting screw to a torque of 10 ft lbs; then back off the adjusting screw one complete turn.

4. Without disturbing the adjustment, tighten the locknut.

5. Install the rubber plug, fit the carpet, and install the heater duct, if removed.

Neutral Start Switch Adjustment

The neutral start switches on 1970–72 Volvos are adjustable. If a switch on a 1973 or later model Volvo is not operating correctly it must be replaced complete with a new spacing washer, as it is not adjustable. The switch serves a dual function: first, it prevents the engine from being started while the gear selector is in any position other than Neutral or Park, and second, it closes the circuit that actuates the back-up lights when the selector is placed in Reverse. The following procedure is used to adjust the switch.

1. Check the adjustment of the gear selector as outlined under "Selector Linkage Adjustment." Place the gear selector in Drive. Firmly apply the parking brake.

2. On 1972 140 series and 164 models, remove the control lever from the transmission.

3. Loosen the locknut for the switch. Taking note of their positions, disconnect the electrical leads. Unscrew the switch until it is held on by just a few threads.

4. On 1970–71 models, first connect a 12 volt test light to the back-up light terminals (2 and 4), and screw in the switch until the test light goes out. Disconnect the light and mark this position on the switch and transmission with a pencil. Then connect the test light to the start inhibitor terminals (1 and 3), and screw out the switch until the light goes on. Disconnect the light and also mark this position. The proper adjustment is midway between these two marks.

5. On 1972 models, first connect a 12 volt test light to start inhibitor terminals (1 and 3), and screw in the switch until the test light goes out. Disconnect the light and mark this position on the switch and transmission with a pencil. Then connect the test light to the back-up light terminals (2 and 4), and screw out the switch until the light goes on. Disconnect the light and also mark this position. The proper adjustment is midway between these two marks.

6. When the proper adjustment is achieved, tighten the locknut, taking care

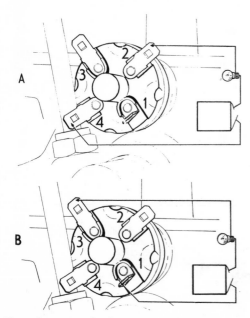

Neutral start switch adjustment—1970–71

A. Bulb connected to back-up light contacts
B. Bulb connected to starter inhibitor contacts

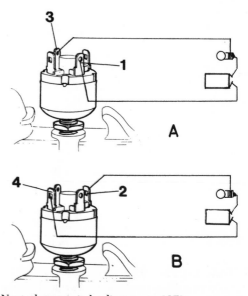

Neutral start switch adjustment—1972

A. Bulb connected to starter inhibitor contacts
B. Bulb connected to back-up light contacts

not to disturb the adjustment. Connect the four electrical leads.

7. On 1972 140 series and 164 models, install the control lever on the transmission.

8. Block the wheels so that the car cannot move either forward or backward. Make sure that the engine can only be started with the gear selector in Neutral or Park. Make sure that the back-up lights operate when the selector is placed in Reverse.

Gear Selector Linkage Adjustment
140 SERIES, 164

1970–71

1. Disconnect the pull rod from the selector shaft lever. Place the selector lever in Neutral.

2. Place the lever on the transmission in the central position. Adjust the length of the pull rod so that, on 140 series models, the ball socket can easily be snapped onto the lever ball, and so that, on 164 models, the pin can easily be pushed through the yoke and lever. When the pull rod is adjusted correctly, the distance to the link in

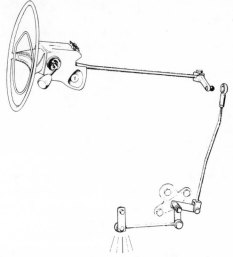

Gear selector linkage adjustment—1970 140 series, 164

the Neutral position should be equal to the distance to the link in the Drive position.

3. Make sure that the gear indicator points correctly on the scale (quadrant). Adjustments are made to the cable sleeve at the indicator.

4. Make sure that the output shaft is

1. Selector lever knob, upper section
2. Selector lever knob, lower section
3. Washer
4. Spring
5. Push rod
6. Selector lever
7. Shift positions cover
8. Shift positions lamp
9. Inhibitor plate
10. Housing
11. Shaft
12. Lever
13. Control rod
14. Lever
15. Bracket
16. Cable, shift positions lamp
17. Inhibitor
18. Button

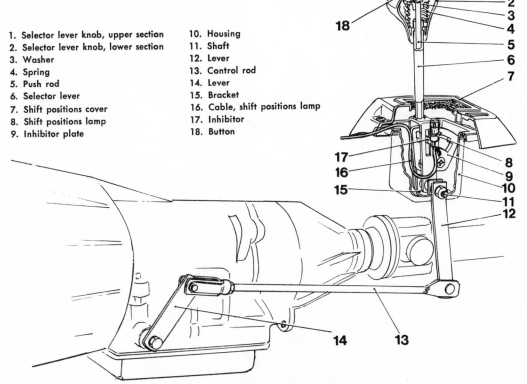

Gear selector linkage assembly—1972–73 140 series, 164

locked with the control lever in the Park position.

5. Connect the pull rod to the selector shaft lever.

1972–73

1. Disconnect the shift rod from the transmission lever. Place both the transmission lever and the gear selector lever in the "2" position.

2. Adjust the length of the shift control rod so that a small clearance (distance B) of 0.04 in. is obtained between the gear selector lever inhibitor and the inhibitor plate, when the shift control rod is connected to the transmission lever.

3. Position the gear selector lever in Drive and make sure that a similar small clearance (distance A) of 0.04 in. exists between the lever inhibitor and the inhibitor plate. Disconnect the shift control rod from the transmission lever and adjust, if necessary.

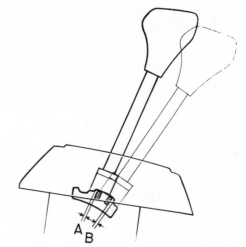

Gear selector linkage adjustment—1972–73 140 series, 164

1. Selector lever
2. Quadrant lighting
3. Lever
4. Control rod, upper
5. Lever arm with shaft
6. Bracket
7. Lever
8. Control rod, lower
9. Lever
10. Shaft
11. Lock pin
12. Bearing housing
13. Spring
14. Rubber bellows
15. Gating
16. Casing

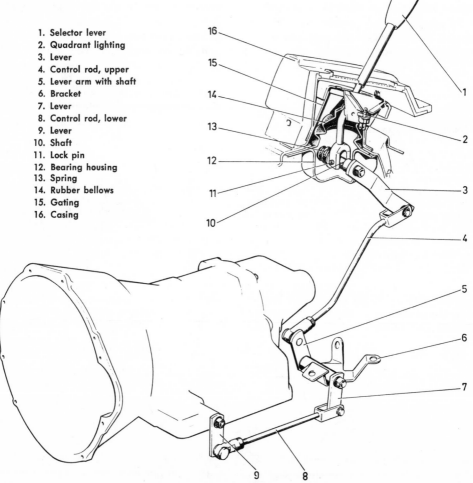

Gear selector linkage assembly—1800 series

Gear selector linkage adjustment—1800 series

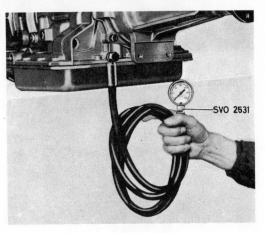

Connecting oil pressure gauge

4. Lock the control rod bolt with its safety clasp and tighten the locknut. Make sure that the control rod lug follows with the transmission lever.

5. After moving the transmission lever to the Park and "1" positions, make sure that the clearances A and B remain the same. In addition, make sure that the output shaft is locked with the selector lever in the Park position.

1800 SERIES

1971–73

1. Check to make sure that the transmission lever and the lever at the linkage bracket are parallel. If necessary, adjust the length of the lower control rod.

2. Disconnect the upper control rod from the intermediate lever (5). Place the gear selector in Neutral. Also set the transmission lever to its third (Neutral) position. Adjust the length of the upper control rod so that the ball socket aligns with the ball stud. Connect the control rod to the lever.

3. If the upper control rod adjustment is correct, the distances to the inhibitor plate in Neutral and Drive (A and B) should be equal.

4. Make sure that the output shaft is locked with the selector lever in the Park position.

Throttle Cable Adjustment

A correct adjustment of the throttle cable is imperative for the proper shifting operation of the transmission. Connect a tachometer to the engine and an oil pressure gauge (manometer) to the rear of the transmission (as shown) for this adjustment.

PROCEDURE A

1. Warm up the engine and check the idle speed against specifications in the "Tune-Up Chart." Make sure that the throttle cable and cable housing (outer cable) are attached correctly.

2. On dual-carbureted engines, the threaded sleeve is then screwed to within $1/32$ in. of the crimped stop on the cable.

3. Check the adjustment by making sure (with the accelerator pedal fully depressed), first, that the carburetor lever is at the full open stop position, and second, that the line pressure reading at converter stall speed (consult the converter stall speed chart) is a minimum of 160 psi.

PROCEDURE B

If the cable stop has been damaged, the adjustment disturbed, or if the transmission is not functioning properly, the throttle cable must be adjusted as follows.

1. Firmly apply the parking brake and place blocks in front and in back of the wheels.

2. Place the gear selector in Drive. Note the line pressure readings at 700 rpm and 1200 rpm. The line pressure increase between the two readings should be a minimum of 15 psi and a maximum of 20 psi for B20 engines, and 25–30 psi for B30 engines. The effective length of the outer cable (cable housing) must be increased if the pressure increase is lower than 15 psi (or 25 psi) and decreased if the pressure rise is greater than 20 psi (or 30 psi). The length of the outer cable is determined by the adjuster.

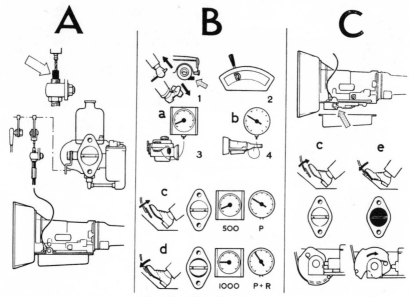

Throttle cable adjustment

A. Adjusting cable stop
B. Adjusting with tachometer and manometer
  1. Chock the wheels and apply the brakes
  2. Select position "D"
  3. Connect a tachometer (a)
  4. Connect a pressure gauge (b)

  c. Measure pressure (P) at 500 rpm
  d. Measure pressure (P + R) at 1000 rpm
  R. Should be (15–20 lb/sq in.)
C. Adjust the cam in transmission
  c. Accelerator pedal in idling position
  e. Accelerator pedal fully depressed

Procedure C

If the cable itself has been damaged and is in need of replacement, the transmission oil pan must be removed first. Refer to "Oil Pan Removal and Installation." Adjust the new cable as follows.

NOTE: *Do not lubricate the new cable as it is pre-lubricated.*

1. With the oil pan removed, observe the position of the throttle cable cam in the transmission, in relation to the accelerator pedal position.

2. With the accelerator fully released and the carburetor lever at the idle stop, the heel of the cam must contact the full diameter of the downshift valve, taking up all of the slack in the inner throttle cable.

3. With the accelerator fully depressed and the carburetor lever at the full open stop, the constant radius area of the cam must be the point of contact with the downshift valve.

4. Make sure that the outer cable (cable housing) is correctly positioned in its adjuster.

Converter Stall Speed Chart

Year	Model (Engine Type)	Transmission Type	Identification Plate Color	Stall Speed (rpm)
1970	140 (B 20 B)	AS 7 35 EN	Light buff	1800
1970	164 (B 30 A)	AS 5 35 EN	Blue	2100
1971	140 (B 20 B)	AS 13 35 EN	Silver grey	2100
	140 (B 20 E)	211 J	Golden yellow	2550
1971	164 (B 30 A)	AS 15 35 EN	Light blue	2100
1971	1800 (B 20 E)	AS 9 35 EN	Red	2550
1972	140 (B 20 B)	325	Light green	2100
	140 (B 20 F)	351 H	Orange	2450
1972	164 (B 30 A)	323	Light blue	2100
	164 (B 30 F)	319	Green	2200
1972	1800 (B 20 F)	351	Orange	2550
1973	140 (B 20 F)	351 H	Orange	2450

Driveline

The driveshaft is a two-piece, tubular unit, connected by an intermediate universal joint. The rear end of the front section of the driveshaft forms a splined sleeve. A splined shaft forming one of the yokes for the intermediate u-joint fits into this sleeve. The front section is supported by a ball bearing contained in an insulated rubber housing which is attached to the bottom of the driveshaft tunnel. The front section is connected to the transmission flange, and the rear section is connected to the differential housing flange by universal joints. Each joint consists of a spider with four ground trunnions carried in the flange yokes by needle bearings.

Driveshaft and Universal Joint Removal and Installation

1. Jack up the vehicle and install safety stands.
2. Mark the relative positions of the driveshaft yokes and transmission and differential housing flanges for purposes of assembly. Remove the nuts and bolts which retain the front and rear driveshaft

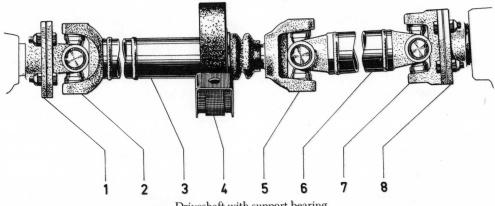

Driveshaft with support bearing

1. Flange on transmission	4. Support bearing	7. Rear universal joint
2. Front universal joint	5. Intermediate universal joint	8. Flange on rear axle
3. Front section of drive shaft	6. Rear drive shaft	

sections to the transmission and differential housing flanges, respectively. Remove the support bearing housing from the driveshaft tunnel, and lower the driveshaft and universal joint assembly as a unit.

3. Pry up the lock washer and remove the support bearing retaining nut. Pull off the rear section of the driveshaft with the intermediate universal joint and splined shaft of the front section. The support bearing may now be pressed off from the driveshaft.

4. Remove the support bearing from its housing.

5. For removal of the universal joints from the driveshaft, consult "Universal Joint Overhaul."

6. Inspect the driveshaft sections for straightness. Using a dial indicator, or rolling the shafts along a flat surface, make sure that the driveshaft out-of-round does not exceed 0.010 in. Do not attempt to straighten a damaged shaft. Any shaft exceeding 0.010 in. out-of-round will cause substantial vibration, and must be replaced. Also, inspect the support bearing by pressing the races against each other by hand, and turning them in opposite directions. If the bearing binds at any point, it must be discarded and replaced.

7. Install the support bearing into its housing.

8. Press the support bearing and housing onto the front driveshaft section. Push the splined shaft of the front section, with the intermediate universal joint and rear driveshaft section, into the splined sleeve of the front section. Install the retaining nut and lock washer for the support bearing.

9. Taking note of the alignment marks made prior to removal, position the driveshaft and universal joint assembly to its flange connections and install but do not tighten its retaining nuts and bolts. Position the support bearing housing to the driveshaft tunnel and install the retaining nut. Tighten the nuts which retain the driveshaft sections to the transmission and differential housing flanges to a torque of 25–30 ft lbs.

10. Remove the safety stands and lower the vehicle. Road test the car and check for driveline vibrations.

Universal Joint Overhaul

1. Remove the driveshaft and universal joint assembly as outlined in "Driveshaft and Universal Joint Assembly Removal and Installation."

2. Place the driveshaft section in a vise so that the joint being removed comes as close as possible to the vise jaws. Do not tighten the vise any more than is necessary as the driveshaft is of tubular construction, and easily deformed.

3. Remove the snap rings, which secure the needle bearings in the yokes, with a snap ring pliers.

4. With a hammer and a metal punch, drive the spider as far as it will go in one direction. The needle bearing should come about half way out. Then, drive the spider as far as it will go in the other direction.

5. Drive out one of the needle bearings with a thinner punch. Remove the spider, and then drive out the other needle bearing.

Universal joint disassembled

6. Clean the spider and needle bearings completely. Check the frictional surfaces for wear. Replace any worn or broken parts. If the old needle bearings and spider are to be reused, fill them with molybdenum disulphide chassis grease, and make sure that the rubber seals are not damaged. If new needle bearings are used, fill them half-way with the grease.

7. To install, position the spider in the yoke and push the spider in one direction as far as it will go, so that the needle bearing can be fitted onto the spider trunnion. Then, using a drift of a slightly smaller diameter than the needle bearing sleeve, press the needle bearing in until the bearing sleeve and snap ring can be fitted.

8. Install the other needle bearing, bearing sleeve, and snap ring as outlined in step 7.

9. Remove the driveshaft section from the vice and repeat steps 2–8 for the other universal joints.

10. Install the driveshaft and universal joint assembly as outlined under "Driveshaft and Universal Joint Removal and Installation."

Rear Axle

All 1970–73 Volvos utilize a solid rear axle housing carried in two support arms. Two torque rods, connected between the axle shaft tubes and the body, limit the rear axle wind-up. A track bar controls lateral movement of the axle housing. Final drive is of the hypoid design, with the drive pinion lying below the ring gear. Each axle shaft is indexed into a splined sleeve for the differential side gears, and supported at its outer end in a tapered roller bearing. Bearing clearance is not adjustable by use of shims as on earlier model Volvos, but instead is determined by bearing thickness. Both sides of the axle bearings are protected by oil seals.

Axle Shaft Removal and Installation, Bearing and Oil Seal Replacement

1. Raise the vehicle and install safety stands.
2. Remove the applicable wheel and tire assembly.
3. Place a wooden block beneath the brake pedal, plug the master cylinder reservoir vent hole, and remove and plug the brake line from the caliper. Be careful not to allow any brake fluid to spill onto the disc or pads. Remove the two bolts which retain the brake caliper to the axle housing, and lift off the caliper. Lift off the brake disc.
4. Remove the thrust washer bolts through the holes in the axle shaft flange. Using a puller, such as SVO 2709, or a slide hammer, remove the axle shaft, bearing and oil seal assembly.

Axle shaft removal

5. Using an arbor press, remove the axle shaft bearing and its locking ring from the axle shaft. Remove and discard the old oil seal.
6. Fill the space between the lips of the new oil seal with wheel bearing grease. Position the new seal on the axle shaft. Using an arbor press, install the bearing with a new locking ring, onto the axle shaft.
7. Thoroughly pack the bearing with wheel bearing grease. Install the axle shaft into the housing, rotating it so that it indexes with the differential. Install the bolts for the thrust washer and tighten to 36 ft lbs.
8. Install the brake disc. Position the brake caliper to its retainer on the axle housing and install the two retaining bolts. Torque the caliper retaining bolts to 45–50 ft lbs.
9. Unplug the brake line and connect it to the caliper. Bleed the caliper of all air trapped in the system. Follow the instructions under "Bleeding" in chapter 9.
10. Position the wheel and tire assembly on its lugs and hand-tighten the lug nuts. Remove the jackstands and lower the vehicle. Torque the lug nuts to 70–100 ft. lbs.

Chapter Eight

Suspension and Steering

Rear Suspension

All Volvos use a coil spring rear suspension. The solid rear axle is suspended from the rigid frame member by a pair of support arms and damped by a pair of double-acting telescopic shock absorbers. A pair of torque rods control rear axle wind-up and a track rod limits the lateral movement of the rear axle in relation to the car. On 1800 series models, a pair of fiber straps limit the downward travel of the suspension. On 145 models, a rubber buffer prevents the suspension from bottoming under heavy loads.

Spring Removal and Installation

140 SERIES, 164

1. Remove the hub cap and loosen the lug nuts a few turns. Jack up the car and place jackstands in front of the rear jacking points. Remove the wheel and tire assembly.

2. Place a hydraulic jack beneath the rear axle housing and raise the housing sufficiently to compress the spring. Loosen the nuts for the upper and lower spring attachments.

CAUTION: *Due to the fact that the* spring *is compressed under several hundred pounds of pressure, when it is freed from its lower attachment, it will attempt to suddenly return to its extended position. It is therefore imperative that the axle housing be lowered with extreme care until the spring is fully extended. As an added safety measure, a chain may be attached to the lower spring coil and secured to the axle housing.*

3. Disconnect the shock absorber at its upper attachment. Carefully lower the jack and axle housing until the spring is fully extended. Remove the spring.

4. To install, position the retaining bolt and inner washer, for the upper attachment, inside the spring and then, while holding the outer washer and rubber spacer to the upper body attachment, install the spring and inner washer to the upper attachment (sandwiching the rubber spacer), and tighten the retaining bolt.

5. Raise the jack and secure the bottom of the spring to its lower attachment with the washer and retaining bolt.

3. Connect the shock absorber to its upper attachment. Install the wheel and tire assembly.

7. Remove the jackstands and lower the car. Tighten the lug nuts to 70–100 ft lbs and install the hub cap.

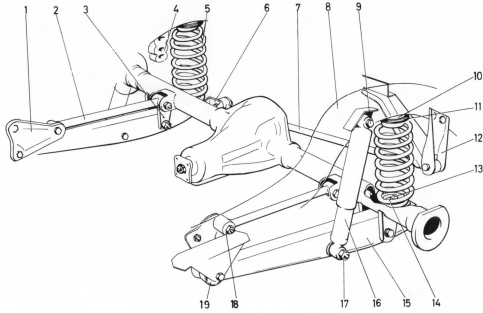

Rear suspension assembly—140 series, 164

1. Bracket	8. Rear side-member	14. Washer
2. Support stay	9. Shock absorber upper attachment	15. Support arm
3. Bracket		16. Shock absorber
4. Rubber buffer	10. Washer	17. Shock absorber lower attachment
5. Rear spring	11. Rubber spacer	
6. Bracket	12. Bracket	18. Front support stay attachment
7. Track bar	13. Screw, lower spring attachment	19. Front bushing support arm

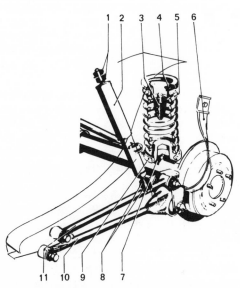

Rear suspension assembly—1800 series

1. Upper shock absorber bushings	7. Rubber cushion
2. Shock absorber	8. Lower shock absorber bushings
3. Rubber buffer	9. Spring attachment
4. Rubber spacer	10. Torque rod
5. Spring	11. Support stay
6. Suspension travel limiter	

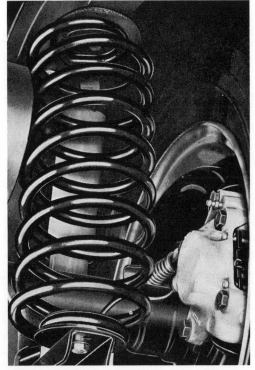

Rear spring

1800 Series

1. Remove the hub cap and loosen the lug nuts a few turns. Place blocks in front of the front wheels. Jack up the rear of the car and place jackstands in front of the rear jacking points.

2. Remove the wheel and tire assembly and release the parking brake.

3. Place a hydraulic jack beneath the rear axle housing and raise the jack and axle housing sufficiently to off-load the suspension downward travel limiter (shock absorber band).

4. Disconnect the shock absorber at its lower attachment. Also disconnect the suspension travel limiter (shock absorber band) at its upper attachment.

CAUTION: *Do not attempt to remove the spring until it is fully extended. As an added safety measure, a chain may be attached to the lower spring coil and secured to the axle housing.*

5. Carefully lower the jack and axle housing until the spring is fully extended. Remove the spring and rubber spacer.

6. To install, fit the rubber spacer to the top of the spring and position the spring into its upper attachment. Secure the bottom of the spring into its lower attachment, making sure that the rubber cushion on the axle housing is positioned correctly.

7. Raise the jack sufficiently so that the shock absorber may be connected to its lower attachment. Connect the suspension travel limiter to its upper attachment.

8. Install the wheel and tire assembly. Remove the jackstands and lower the car. Tighten the lug nuts to 70–100 ft lbs, and install the hub cap.

Shock Absorber Removal and Installation

140 Series, 164

1. Remove the hub cap and loosen the lug nuts a few turns. Place blocks in front of the front wheels. Jack up the rear of the car and place jackstands in front of the rear jacking points. Remove the wheel and tire assembly.

2. Remove the nuts and bolts which retain the shock absorber to its upper and lower attachments and remove the shock absorber. Make sure that the spacing sleeve, inside the axle support arm for the lower attachment, is not misplaced.

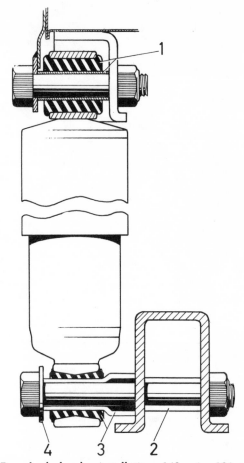

Rear shock absorber installation—140 series, 164

1. Bushing	3. Bushing
2. Spacing sleeve	4. Washer

3. The damping effect of the shock absorber may be tested by securing the lower attachment in a vise and extending and compressing it. A properly operating shock absorber should offer approximately three times as much resistance to extending the unit as compressing it. Replace the shock absorber if it does not function as above, or if its fixed rubber bushings are damaged.

4. To install, position the shock absorber to its upper and lower attachments. Make sure that the spacing sleeve is installed inside the axle support arm and is aligned with the lower attachment bolt hole. Install the retaining nuts and bolts.

5. Install the wheel and tire assembly. Remove the jackstands and lower the car. Tighten the lug nuts to 70–100 ft lbs, and install the hub cap.

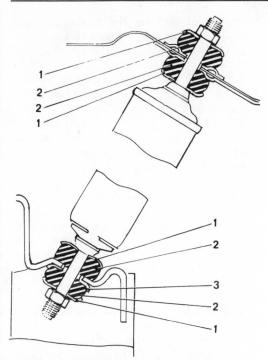

Rear shock absorber installation—1800 series

1. **Shock absorber washer (small hole)**
2. **Rubber bushing**
3. **Shock absorber washer (large hole)**

1800 SERIES

1. Fold the rear seat back forward. On 1800E models, remove the upholstery for the shelf under the rear window, and on 1800ES models, fold back the carpet for

the bed, which will reveal the shock absorber upper attaching points.

2. Remove the upper nut, washers, and outer rubber bushing from the top of the shock absorber.

3. Remove the lower nut, washers, and outer rubber bushing from the bottom of the shock absorber.

4. Compress and remove the shock absorber.

5. Test the damping action of the shock absorber. Extending the unit should offer about three times as much resistance as compressing the unit. If the shock absorber is operating properly and is being reinstalled, be sure to use new rubber bushings.

6. Install inner washers and new rubber bushings, if removed, on the unit. Compress the shock absorber and position it to its upper and lower attachments.

7. Install the outer nuts, washers, and new rubber bushings first to the top and then to the bottom, of the shock absorber.

8. Replace the package shelf upholstery or the bed carpet to its original position.

Front Suspension

All Volvos use a coil spring independent front suspension. A pair of upper and

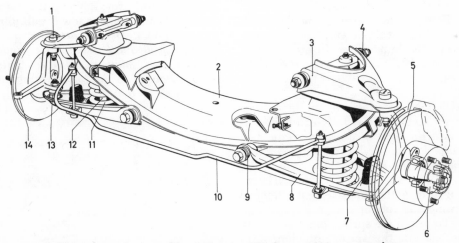

Front suspension assembly—140 series, 164 shown, 1800 series similar

1. **Upper ball joint**	6. **Hub**	11. **Coil spring**
2. **Front cross member**	7. **Rubber buffer**	12. **Shock absorber**
3. **Upper control arm**	8. **Lower control arm**	13. **Lower ball joint**
4. **Upper control arm bushing**	9. **Lower control arm bushing**	14. **Steering arm**
5. **Steering knuckle**	10. **Stabilizer**	

lower control arms are bolted to each side of the rigid front frame member. The coil springs and telescopic double-acting shock absorbers are bolted to the lower control arms at the bottom and seat in the cross-member at the top. A pair of steering knuckles are carried in ball joints between the upper and lower control arms. A stabilizer bar is attached to the lower control arms and to the body.

Spring Removal and Installation

140 SERIES, 164

1. Remove the hub cap and loosen the lug nuts a few turns.
2. Firmly apply the parking brake and place blocks in back of the rear wheels. Jack up the front of the car and place jackstands in back of the front jacking points. Remove the wheel and tire assembly.
3. Remove the shock absorber as outlined in the applicable "Shock Absorber Removal and Installation" procedure.
4. Remove the cotter pin and ball nut and disconnect the steering rod from the steering knuckle. Loosen the clamp for the flexible brake hoses. Remove the stabilizer attachment from the lower control arm.
5. Place a jack under the lower control arm. Raise the jack to unload the lower control arm. Remove the cotter pins and loosen the nuts for the upper and lower ball joints; then rap with a hammer until they loosen from the spindle. Remove the nuts and lower the jack slightly.
6. Remove the steering knuckle with the front brake caliper and disc still connected to the brake lines. In order not to stretch the brake lines, place the brake unit on a milk crate or other suitable stand.
CAUTION: *Do not attempt to remove the spring until it is fully extended. As an added safety measure, a chain may be attached to the lower spring coil and secured to the frame.*
7. Slowly lower the jack and lower control arm to the fullest extent. Remove the spring and rubber spacer.
8. To install the spring, place a jack directly beneath the spring attachment to the lower control arm. Place the spring with the rubber spacer in position, and lift up the lower control arm with the jack so that the steering knuckle and brake unit assembly may be installed.

9. Install and tighten the upper and lower ball joint nuts. Connect the stabilizer to its attachment on the lower control arm.
10. Install the shock absorber as outlined in the applicable "Shock Absorber Removal and Installation" section.
11. With the wheels pointing straight ahead, and the lower control arm unloaded, connect the steering rod to the steering knuckle and install the ball nut and cotter pin.
12. Clamp the brake hoses to the stabilizer bolt.
13. Install the wheel and tire assembly. Remove the jackstands and lower the car. Tighten the lug nuts to 70–100 ft lbs, and install the hub cap.

1800 SERIES

1. Remove the hub cap and loosen the lug nuts a few turns.
2. Firmly apply the parking brake and place blocks in back of the rear wheels.
3. Jack up the front of the car and place jackstands beneath the front crossmember. Remove the wheel and tire assembly.
4. Remove the shock absorber as outlined in the applicable "Shock Absorber Removal and Installation" procedure.
5. Position a jack directly beneath the lower spring attachment on the lower control arm, and raise the jack until the upper control arm rubber buffer is lifted.
6. Disconnect the stabilizer from the lower control arm. Remove the cotter pin and ball nut from the lower ball joint.
CAUTION: *Do not attempt to remove the spring until it is fully extended. As an added safety measure, a chain may be attached to the lower spring coil and secured to the frame.*

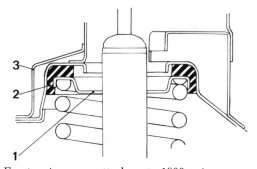

Front spring upper attachment—1800 series

**1. Front cross member   2. Rubber spacer
3. Washer**

7. Slowly lower the jack and lower control arm. If the lower ball joint does not release when the jack is lowered, it must be pressed out with a press tool such as SVO 2281. When the lower control arm is lowered sufficiently, carefully remove the spring, rubber spacer and washer assembly.

8. Reverse the above procedure to install, taking care to place the rubber spacer and washer correctly on top of the spring, prior to installation.

Shock Absorber Removal and Installation

140 SERIES, 164

1. Remove the upper nut, washer, and outer rubber bushing.

2. Remove the two lower attaching bolts beneath the lower control arm, and pull the shock absorber assembly down and out.

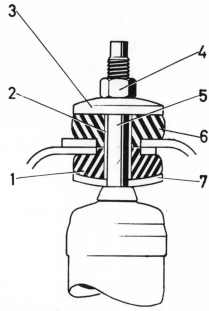

Front shock absorber upper attachment—140 series, 164

1. Rubber bushing	5. Spindle
2. Spacing sleeve	6. Rubber bushing
3. Washer	7. Washer
4. Nut	

Front shock absorber lower attachment—140 series, 164

3. Test the damping action of the shock absorber. Extending the unit should offer approximately three times as much resistance as compressing it. If the shock absorber is operating properly and is being reinstalled, be sure to use new rubber bushings on top.

4. Position the inner washer, spacing sleeve, and inner rubber bushing on top of the shock absorber.

5. Position the shock to its upper and lower attachments, and install the lower attaching bolts.

6. Install the outer rubber bushing, washer, and the upper nut on top of the

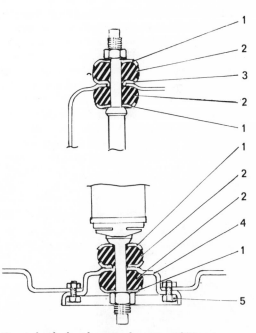

Front shock absorber attachments—1800 series

1. Shock absorber washer (small hole)
2. Rubber bushing
3. Shock absorber washer (large hole)
4. Lower attachment
5. Bolt for lower attachment

unit. Tighten the upper nut until it makes firm contact with the spacing sleeve.

1800 SERIES

1. Remove the upper nut, washer, and outer rubber bushing from the top of the shock absorber.

2. Remove the lower nut, washer, and outer rubber bushing from beneath the shock absorber.

3. Remove the two lower attaching bolts from beneath the lower control arm, and pull the shock absorber assembly down and out.

4. Test the damping action of the shock absorber. Extending the unit should offer approximately three times as much resistance as compressing it. If the shock absorber is operating properly and is being reinstalled, be sure to use new rubber bushings.

5. Reverse steps 1–3 to install.

UPPER BALL JOINT

Inspection

If the upper ball joint is worn, the wheel and tire assembly will exhibit excessive radial play when the joint is off-loaded. Place a jack beneath the lower control arm, and lift the wheel and tire assembly until clear of the ground. Make sure that the upper control arm is not making contact with the rubber stop. Firmly grasp the top and bottom of the tire and try to rock it in and out; that is, intermittently push the top of the tire towards the engine compartment, then pull it away from the car, while simultaneously doing the opposite to the bottom of the tire. Replace the upper ball joint if the radial play of the wheel and tire assembly is excessive.

NOTE: *Do not confuse possible wheel bearing play with ball joint play. It is advisable that the wheel bearing adjustment procedure in chapter nine be followed prior to replacing the ball joint.*

Removal and Installation

140 SERIES, 164

1. Remove the hub cap and loosen the lug nuts a few turns.

2. Jack up the front of the vehicle and place safety stands beneath the front jacking points. Remove the wheel and tire assembly.

3. Loosen, but do not remove the nut for the upper ball joint. With a hammer, rap around the ball joint stud on the steering knuckle until it loosens. Remove the nut, and safety wire the upper end of the steering knuckle to the stabilizer bar to avoid straining the flexible brake hoses.

4. Loosen the nuts for the upper control arm shaft ½ turn. Lift up the control arm slightly and press out the old ball joint with a press tool and a sleeve.

5. Make sure that the rubber cover of the new ball joint is filled with multipurpose grease. Bend the pin end over the slot, and make sure that the grease forces its way out, then fill as necessary.

6. Press the ball joint into the upper control arm using the press tool, a sleeve, and a drift. It is imperative that the ball joint be aligned so that the slot (A) comes in line with the longitudinal shaft of the control arm, either internally or externally,

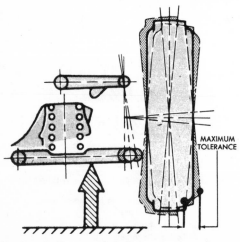

Checking ball joint radial play

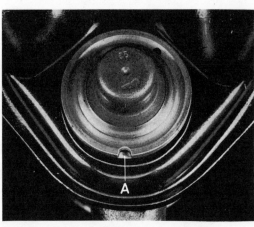

Location of upper ball joint—140 series, 164

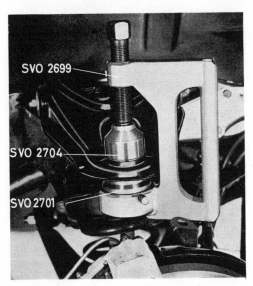

Installing upper ball joint—140 series, 164

as the pin has maximum movement along the line.

7. Lower the upper control arm to its operating position, and tighten the shaft nuts to 40–45 ft lbs. Remove the safety wire; place the steering knuckle in position; install and tighten the ball nut to 60–70 ft lbs. If the pin rotates during tightening, clamp it firmly with a screw vise.

8. Install the wheel and tire assembly. Remove the safety stands and lower the vehicle. Tighten the lug nuts to 70–100 ft lbs, and install the hub cap.

1800 Series

1. Remove the hub cap and loosen the lug nuts a few turns.

2. Jack up the front of the vehicle and place safety stands beneath the lower control arms. Remove the wheel and tire assembly.

3. Remove the two nuts (5) and bolts (8) which retain the ball joint to the upper control arm. Lift the upper control arm up and out of the way.

4. Remove the clamping nut (10) and bolt (9) which secure the ball joint to the steering knuckle. Remove the upper ball joint, sealing washers, and rubber cover assembly.

5. Make sure that the rubber cover of the new ball joint is filled with multipurpose (universal) grease. If the old ball joint is being reused, make sure that the rubber cover is not damaged, and fill it with grease.

6. After making sure that the sleeve and sealing washers (circlips) are positioned properly, place the ball joint assembly on the steering knuckle and install the clamping nut and bolt.

7. Lower the upper control arm into position over the ball joint and install the attaching nuts and bolts.

8. Install the wheel and tire assembly. Remove the safety stands and lower the vehicle. Tighten the lug nuts to 70–100 ft lbs, and install the hub cap.

LOWER BALL JOINT

Inspection

If the lower ball joint is worn, a measurement (A) taken from the ball stud to

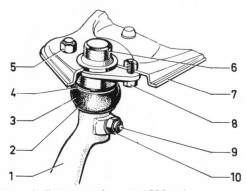

Upper ball joint attachment—1800 series

1. Spindle
2. Circlip
3. Rubber cover
4. Circlip
5. Nut
6. Upper ball joint
7. Upper wishbone
8. Bolt
9. Clamp bolt
10. Nut

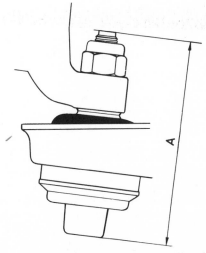

Spring type lower ball joint maximum allowable length

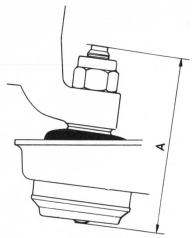

Non-spring type lower ball joint maximum allowable length

the cover of the ball joint will exceed the maximum allowable length for the ball joint when it is normally loaded. The check is made with the vehicle standing on the ground, wheels pointing straight ahead. Two types of lower ball joints have been used on late model Volvos: one utilizing a pressure spring, and the other not. The maximum allowable length for the spring type ball joint is 4.5 in. for the 140 series and 164, and 4.4 in. for the 1800 series. The maximum allowable length for the non-spring type ball joint is 3.91 in. for the 140 series and 164, and 3.76 in. for the 1800 series.

Removal and Installation

140 SERIES, 164

1. Remove the hub cap and loosen the lug nuts a few turns.

2. Jack up the front of the vehicle and place jackstands beneath the front jacking points. Remove the wheel and tire assembly.

3. Remove the cotter pin and ball stud nut, and press the steering rod ball stud from the steering knuckle. Remove the brake lines from their bracket at the stabilizer bolt.

4. Remove the cotter pins and loosen but do not remove the nuts for both the upper and lower ball joints. Rap with a hammer until the ball joints loosen from the spindle. Place a jack beneath the lower control arm and raise it to off-load the control arm. Remove the ball joint nuts.

5. Remove the steering knuckle with the front brake unit still connected to the brake lines. In order not to stretch the brake lines, place the brake unit on a milk crate or other suitable stand.

6. Press the lower ball joint out of the lower control arm with a press tool and sleeve.

Removing lower ball joint—140 series, 164

7. Make sure that the rubber cover of the new ball joint is filled with multipurpose grease. Bend the pin end to the side, and make sure that the grease forces its way out, then fill as necessary.

8. To install, press the lower ball joint into its control arm with a press tool, sleeve, and drift. Make sure that the ball joint is not loose in the control arm.

9. Position the steering knuckle and brake unit assembly in between the upper and lower control arms and tighten the ball joint stud nuts to 60–70 ft lbs (upper ball joint), and 75–90 ft lbs (lower ball joint). If the pins rotate during tightening, clamp them firmly with a screw vise.

10. Install the steering rod ball stud into the steering knuckle and tighten the stud nut. Lower the jack beneath the lower control arm slightly and with the front wheels pointing straight ahead, attach the brake lines to their bracket at the stabilizer bolt.

11. Install the wheel and tire assembly. Remove the jackstands and lower the vehicle. Tighten the lug nuts to 70–100 ft lbs, and install the hub cap.

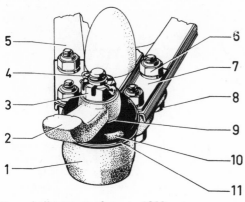

Lower ball joint attachment—1800 series

1. Lower ball joint	7. Bracket
2. Spindle	8. Bolt
3. Castle nut	9. Circlip
4. Cotter pin	10. Rubber cover
5. Lower wishbone	11. Circlip
6. Nut	

1800 SERIES

1. Remove the hub cap and loosen the lug nuts a few turns.

2. Jack up the front of the car and place safety stands beneath the lower control arms. Remove the wheel and tire assembly.

3. Remove the four nuts (6) and bolts (8) which retain the ball joint to the lower control arm. Remove the cotter pin and ball stud nut which secure the steering knuckle to the ball joint.

4. Disconnect and plug the brake hoses at their retainer. Remove the ball joint from the steering knuckle by lightly rapping its attachment with a hammer while backing up the knuckle with another hammer.

5. Make sure that the rubber cover of the new ball joint is filled with multipurpose (universal) grease.

6. Place the ball joint, sealing washers (circlips), and sleeve into position on the steering knuckle and install the ball stud nut. Tighten the nut to 35–40 ft lbs.

7. Place the ball joint and steering knuckle assembly into position on the lower control arm and install the four retaining nuts and bolts.

8. Unplug and connect the brake hoses. Bleed the brake caliper as outlined in chapter 9.

9. Install the wheel and tire assembly. Remove the safety stands and lower the

vehicle. Tighten the lug nuts to 70–100 ft lbs, and install the hub cap.

WHEEL ALIGNMENT

Front wheel alignment is the position of the front wheels relative to each other and to the vehicle. Correct alignment must be maintained to provide safe, accurate steering, vehicle stability, and minimum tire wear. The factors which determine wheel alignment are interdependent. Therefore, when one of the factors is adjusted, the others must be adjusted to compensate.

Caster angle is the number of degrees that a line, drawn through the center of the upper and lower ball joints and viewed from the side, can be tilted forward or backward. Positive caster means that the top of the upper ball joint is tilted toward the rear of the car, and negative caster means that it is tilted toward the front. A car with a slightly positive caster setting will have its lower ball joint pivot point slightly ahead of the tire's center. This will assist the directional stability of the car by causing a drag at the bottom center of the wheel when it turns, thereby resisting the turn and tending to hold the wheel steady in whatever direction the car is pointed. The car is therefore less susceptible to crosswinds and road surface deviations. A car with too much (positive) caster will be hard to steer and shimmy at

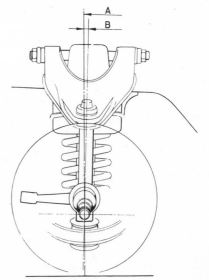

Caster angle

A = Vertical line
B = Caster

low speeds. A car with insufficient (negative) caster may tend to be unstable at high speeds and may respond erratically when the brakes are applied.

Camber angle is the number of degrees that the wheel itself is tilted from a vertical line, when viewed from the front. Positive camber means that the top of the wheel is slanted away from the car, while negative camber means that it is tilted toward the car. A car with a slightly positive camber setting will have the center of its tire directly beneath the lower pivot point. Placing the weight of the car directly above the pivot point allows for easier steering, and alleviates some of the load on the outer wheel bearing.

Steering axis, inclination is the number of degrees that a line drawn through the upper and lower ball joints and viewed from the front, is tilted to the left or right. This, in combination with caster, is responsible for the directional stability and self-centering of the steering. As the steering knuckle swings from lock to lock, the spindle generates an arc, causing the car to be raised when it is turned from the straight ahead position. The weight of the car acts against this lift, and attempts to return the spindle to the straight ahead position when the steering wheel is released.

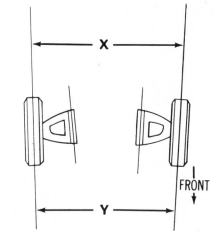

X − Y = Toe-in

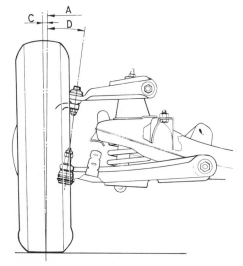

Camber angle

A = Verticle line
C = Camber
D = Steering axis inclination

Toe-in is the difference (in inches) between the front and rear of the front tires, measured at the spindle (hub) height of opposite tires. As the car is driven at increasingly faster speeds, the steering linkage joints expand, allowing the front wheels to turn out and away from each other. Therefore, initially setting the front wheels so that they are pointing slightly inward (toe-in), allows them to turn straight ahead when the car is underway.

When checking the front wheel alignment, first check the caster and camber then measure the toe-in. Steering axis inclination is fixed into the front end design and is non-adjustable. Several items which affect steering geometry should be inspected prior to making any adjustments: worn or loose tie rod ends, steering linkage joints, ball joints, improperly adjusted or worn wheel bearings, incorrect air pressure in all four tires, and unevenly worn front tires. It should be remembered that caster and camber adjustments require sophisticated alignment equipment and should not be attempted unless such a machine is available.

Caster and Camber Adjustment

The procedures for adjusting caster and camber are grouped together here because they may be performed at the same time on all Volvos. Both adjustments are made by inserting shims between the upper control arm shaft and the sheet metal of the shock absorber tower. Loosen the bolts which retain the control arm shaft to the shock tower and insert the shims. Before

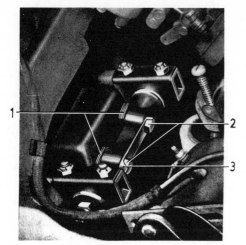

Adjusting caster and camber at upper control arm shaft

1. Shims   2. Bolts   3. Lock plate

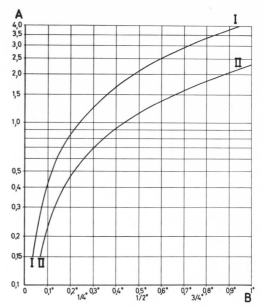

Alteration of angle graph—140 series, 164

I = Camber
II = Caster
A = Shims (mm)
B = Alteration of angle

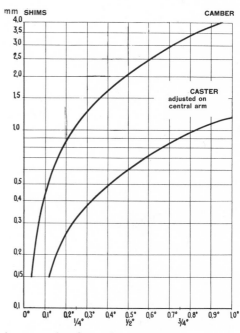

Alteration of angle graph—1800 series

each adjustment is completed, the bolts must be tightened or an erroneous measurement will be obtained. A special SVO tool (no. 2713) is available from dealers for loosening or tightening the control arm shaft bolts on the 140 series and 164 models, because gaining access to these bolts is difficult.

Caster is adjusted by either removing a shim at one of the bolts, adding a shim at the other bolt, or by transferring half of the required shim thickness from one bolt to another. Caster is adjusted to the positive side, for example, by inserting shims at the rear bolt or removing shims at the front bolt.

Camber is adjusted by either removing or adding shims of equal thickness at both bolts. Camber is increased toward the positive by removing shims, and decreased toward the negative by adding shims.

Shims are available in sizes of 0.15, 0.5, 1.0, 3.0, and 6.0 mm (0.006, 0.020, 0.039, 0.12, and 0.24 in.). Consult the alteration-of-angle graph for the applicable model when correcting the caster and camber angles by adding or removing shims. Remember to torque the control arm shaft bolts to 40–50 ft lbs after making the adjustment.

Toe-In Adjustment

Toe-in may be adjusted after performing the caster and camber adjustments. With a wheel spreader, measure the distance (X) between the rear of the right and left front tires, at spindle (hub) height, and then measure the distance (Y) between the front of the right and left front tires, also at spindle (hub) height. Subtract the front distance (Y) from the rear distance (X), and compare that to the specifications table. $X - Y$ = toe-in. If the adjustment is

Wheel Alignment

Year	Model	Caster Range (deg)	Camber Range (deg)	Toe-in (in.)	Steering Axis Inclination (at 0° camber)	WHEEL PIVOT RATIO (deg) Inner Wheel	Outer Wheel
1970–71	140 series, 164	0–1P	0–½P	0–0.16	7.5	20	21.5–23.5
1970–71	1800 series	0–1P	0–½P	0–0.16	8.0	20	21.5–23.5
1972	140 series, 164	0–1P	0–½P	0.08–0.20	7.5	20	21.5–23.5
1972–73	1800 series	①	0–½P	0–0.12	8.0	20	21.5–23.5
1973	140 series, 164	1½P–2P	0–½P	0.08–0.20	7.5	20	21.5–23.5

P = Positive
N = Negative
① 0–1P—165HR15 Tires
   2P–2½P—185/70HR15 Tires

not correct, loosen the locknuts on both sides of the tie rod, and rotate the tie rod itself. Toe-in is increased by turning the tie rod in the normal forward rotation of the wheels, and reduced by turning it in the opposite direction. After the final adjustment is made, torque the locknuts to 55–65 ft lbs, being careful not to disturb the adjustment.

Steering

Driver input is transmitted to the front wheels via the divided steering column, the steering box, the pitman arm, the tie

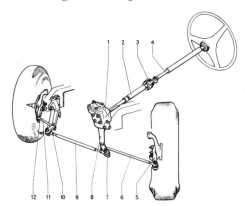

Steering linkage assembly—1800 series shown, 140 series, 164 similar

1. Steering box
2. Safety device
3. Rubber flange
4. Steering column
5. Left steering arm
6. Left steering rod
7. Ball joint
8. Pitman arm
9. Tie rod
10. Relay arm
11. Right steering rod
12. Right steering arm

rod, the steering rods and the steering knuckles. The idler arm moves in conjunction with the pitman arm.

All 1970–73 Volvos use divided steering columns that protect the driver during front end collisions. The system used on the 140 series utilizes a flange connection that breaks on impact, allowing the lower portion to travel backward but keeping the upper portion stable. The 164 uses a telescoping column and a breakaway flange at the steering box. The 1800 series utilizes the telescoping column. All 1973 models are designed to allow the entire column to be pushed forward if, for example, the driver is thrown against the steering wheel.

The manual steering gear used on the 140 series, and 1800 series models is the Gemmer worm and roller type. The power steering gear used on the 164 series, and some late production 1973 automatic transmission equipped 145 models, is the ZF worm and roller type with an integral hydraulically operated recirculating nut and ball assist.

Steering Wheel Removal and Installation

NOTE: *The use of a knock-off type steering wheel puller, or the use of a hammer may damage the collapsible column.*

140 SERIES, 164

1970–71

Due to the fact that the steering wheel hub, on these models, is not provided with a pair of threaded holes, the steering wheel must be removed with a special outside circumference puller.

1. Disconnect the negative battery cable.

2. Remove the retaining screw from the upper half of the molded turn signal switch housing, and the three retaining screws from the lower half. Remove both halves from the column.

3. Remove the two screws which retain the horn ring to the steering wheel. Turn and lift up the horn ring and disconnect the plug contact.

4. Remove the steering wheel nut.

5. With the front wheels pointing straight ahead, and the steering wheel centered, install a steering wheel puller, such as SVO 2711, and pull off the steering wheel.

6. To install, make sure that the front wheels are pointing straight ahead, then place the centered steering wheel on the column and install the nut. Tighten the steering wheel nut to 25–30 ft lbs.

7. Connect the horn plug contact and install the horn ring.

8. First install the lower and then the upper turn signal housing halves and their retaining screws.

9. Connect the negative battery cable and check the operation of the horn.

1972

A special outside circumference steering wheel puller must be used on these models.

1. Disconnect the negative battery cable.

2. Remove the retaining screw for the upper half of the molded turn signal switch housing and lift off the housing.

3. Pry up and remove the impact protection badge from the horn ring. Disconnect the plug contact for the horn and remove the four retaining screws for the horn ring. Lift off the horn ring, noting the positions of the various springs and washers.

4. Remove the steering wheel nut.

5. With the front wheels pointing straight ahead, and the steering wheel centered, install a steering wheel puller, such as SVO 2972, and pull off the steering wheel.

6. Remove the turn signal switch flange.

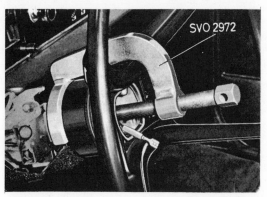
Removing steering wheel—140 series, 164; 1972 shown, 1970–71 similar

7. To install, make sure that the front wheels are pointing straight ahead, then position the turn signal switch flange onto the column and place the centered steering wheel on the column. Install the steering wheel nut and tighten to 20–30 ft lbs.

8. Making sure that the springs and washers are positioned correctly, install the horn ring on the steering wheel and tighten the four retaining screws. Connect the horn plug contact.

9. Install the upper turn signal housing half.

10. Connect the negative battery cable and test the operation of the horn.

1973

Due to the fact that the steering wheel hubs, on these models, are provided with two threaded holes, a standard universal steering wheel puller may be used.

1. Disconnect the negative battery cable.

2. Remove the retaining screws for the upper half of the molded turn signal housing and lift off the housing.

3. Pry off the steering wheel impact pad.

4. Disconnect the horn plug contact.

5. Remove the steering wheel nut.

6. With the front wheels pointing straight ahead, and the steering wheel centered, install a steering wheel puller, such as SVO 2263, and pull off the steering wheel.

7. To install, make sure that the front wheels are pointing straight ahead, then place the centered steering wheel on the column with the plug contact to the left. Install the nut and tighten to 20–30 ft lbs.

8. Connect the horn plug contact and install the impact pad.

9. Install the upper turn signal housing half.

10. Connect the negative battery cable and test the operation of the horn.

1800 SERIES

1970–73

A standard universal steering wheel puller may be used on these models.

1. Disconnect the negative battery cable.

2. Pry off the steering wheel impact pad.

3. Disconnect the horn plug contact. Remove the three retaining screws and lift off the horn ring, noting the placement of the springs and washers.

4. Remove the steering wheel nut. Mark the relative positions of the steering wheel to the column. Slacken the horn wire.

5. Install a steering wheel puller and pull off the wheel.

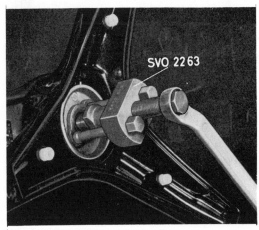

Removing steering wheel—1800 series shown, 1973 140 series, 164 similar

6. To install, place the steering wheel on the column so that the alignment marks made prior to removal line up. Install the nut and tighten to 20–30 ft lbs.

7. Connect the horn plug contact, and install the horn ring, springs, and washers with the three retaining screws.

8. Snap on the impact pad.

9. Connect the negative battery cable and test the operation of the horn.

Power Steering Pump Removal and Installation

1. Remove all dirt and grease from around the suction line connections and from around the delivery line on the pump housing.

2. Using a container to catch any power steering fluid that might run out, disconnect the oil lines, and plug them to prevent dirt from entering the system.

3. Remove the tensioning bolt and the attaching bolts.

4. Clear the pump free of the fan belt and lift it out.

5. If a new pump is to be used, the old brackets, fittings, and pulley must be transferred from the old unit. The pulley may be removed with a puller, and pressed on the pump shaft with a press tool. Under no circumstances should the pulley be hammered on, as this will damage the pump bearings.

6. To install, place the pump in position and loosely fit the attaching bolts. Connect the oil lines to the pump with new seals.

7. Place the fan belt onto the pulley and adjust the fan belt tension as outlined in chapter one.

8. Tighten the tensioning bolt and the attaching bolts.

9. Fill the reservoir with Type "A" automatic transmission fluid and bleed the system as outlined under "Power Steering System Bleeding."

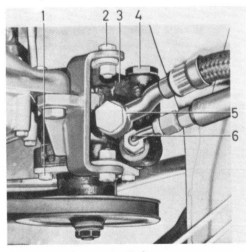

Power steering pump installed

1. Tension bolt	4. Plug for control valve
2. Attaching bolt	5. Suction line
3. Power steering pump	6. Delivery line

Power Steering System Bleeding

1. Fill the reservoir up to the edge with Automatic Transmission Fluid Type "A". Raise the front wheels off the ground, and install safety stands. Place the transmission in neutral and apply the parking brake.

2. Keeping a can of ATF Type "A" within easy reach, start the engine and fill the reservoir as the level drops.

3. When the reservoir level has stopped dropping, slowly turn the steering wheel from lock to lock several times. Fill the reservoir if necessary.

4. Locate the bleeder screw on the power steering gear. Open the bleeder screw ½–1 turn, and close it when oil starts flowing out.

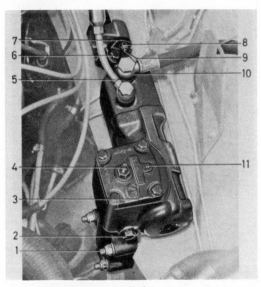

Power steering gear installed

1. Bolt	6. Clamping bolt	
2. Drain plug	7. Flange	
3. Steering box	8. Nut	
4. Adjusting screw	9. Screw	
5. Delivery line (early prod.)	10. Return line	
	11. Bleeder screw	

5. Continue to turn the steering wheel slowly until the fluid in the reservoir is free of air bubbles.

6. Stop the engine and observe the oil level in the reservoir. If the oil level rises more than ¼ in. past the level mark, air still remains in the system. Continue bleeding until the level rise is correct.

7. Remove the safety stands and lower the car.

Pitman Arm Adjustment

On a steering gear with a marked pitman arm and pitman arm shaft (on the steering gear), make sure that the marks align.

On a steering gear without the marks, lift up the front of the vehicle so that the front wheels are free. Turn the steering wheel to its center position (count the number of turns). Lower the vehicle. If the vehicle is correctly loaded, the wheels should now point straight forward. If the wheels do not, remove the pitman arm from the shaft with a puller. Then set the left wheel straight ahead and replace the pitman arm. The steering wheel should be in its center position. Tighten the pitman arm nut to 100–120 ft lbs.

Steering and Tie Rod Reconditioning

Bent or otherwise damaged steering rods and tie rods must be replaced, never straightened. All components of the steering linkage, including the pitman arm and idler arm, are connected by means of ball joints. Ball joints cannot be disassembled or adjusted, so they must also be replaced when damaged.

The ball joints of the steering rods are made in unit with the rods, therefore the entire rod assembly must be replaced when their ball joints become unserviceable. Maximum permissible axial (vertical) play is .120 in. After removing the cotter pins and ball stud nuts at the rod's connections, press the ball joint out of its connecting socket.

The ball joints of the tie rod may be replaced individually. After the ball joint is disconnected, the lock nut on the tie rod is loosened and the clamp bolt released. The ball joint is then screwed out of the tie rod, taking note of the number of turns. The new ball joint is screwed in the same number of turns, and the clamp bolt and lock nut tightened. The ball joint is locked to the rod with 55–65 ft lbs of torque. The new ball joint is pressed into its connection and the ball stud nut tightened to 23–27 ft lbs.

After reconditioning of the rods and joints, the wheel alignment must be adjusted.

Brake System

All 1970 and later model Volvos are equipped with a four wheel power-assisted disc brake system. The system utilizes a pair of four-piston, fixed calipers at the front, and a pair of two-piston fixed calipers at the rear. The calipers are either

Ate front brake unit

1. Hub	3. Brake disc
2. Front brake caliper	4. Cover plate

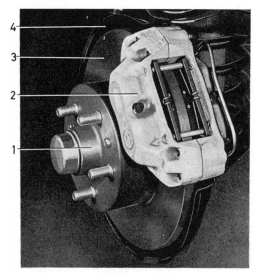

Girling front brake unit

1. Hub	3. Brake disc
2. Front brake caliper	4. Cover plate

Girling or Ate (Alfred Teves) manufacture, so when ordering disc pads or caliper rebuilding kits, you must identify which you have. The discs are one-piece castings. Since 1972, 164 models have been equipped with internally vented discs.

Braking is achieved in a manner similar to the way that you would squeeze a spinning phonograph record between your fingers. When the brake pedal is depressed,

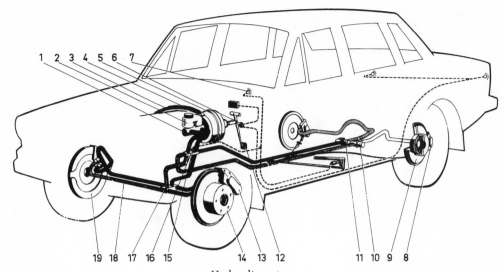

Hydraulic system

1. Tandem master cylinder
2. Brake fluid container
3. Vacuum line
4. Check valve
5. Vacuum booster
6. Brake switch
7. Warning lamp

8. Rear brake caliper
9. Brake disc with drum
10. Brake valve, secondary circuit
11. Brake valve, primary circuit
12. Brake pedal
13. Front brake caliper
14. Brake disc

15. Warning switch
16. Warning valve
17. 6-branch union, (double
    3-branch union)
18. Brake pipe
19. Cover plate

the master cylinder pistons move forward, displacing the brake fluid. Because the fluid cannot be compressed, the displacement results in hydraulic pressure being exerted on the caliper pistons, thus forcing the brake pads against the discs. When the pedal is released, hydraulic pressure drops. The wobbling action of the discs, and the piston seals retracting from their stretched positions return the brake pads to their released positions and force the displaced fluid back into the master cylinder. All disc brakes are inherently self-adjusting.

The hydraulic system is divided into a primary circuit and a secondary circuit. One of the circuits is connected to the right rear wheel, and the lower cylinders of both front wheels. The other circuit is connected to the left rear wheel, and the upper cylinders of both front wheels. The circuits are connected to separate sections of the tandem master cylinder, so that in case of a failure in one of the circuits, the other circuit will still provide 80% of full braking power with full directional stability during stopping.

Whenever adding to or replacing brake fluid, it is imperative that the fluid be of SAE 70 R3 (SAE J 1703) quality or better. Fluid meeting DOT 3 or DOT 4 specifications is also acceptable. Using inferior brake fluids may result in premature failure of the hydraulic components, or in braking effect. Fluids not meeting specifications may not withstand the great temperatures generated by the disc pad clamping action or may deteriorate chemically allowing water and, later, air to form in the system. Avoid mixing brake fluids from different manufacturers and never reuse old brake fluid.

Hydraulic System

MASTER CYLINDER

Removal and Installation

140 Series

1. To prevent brake fluid from spilling onto and damaging the paint, place a protective cover over the fender apron, and rags beneath the master cylinder.

2. Disconnect and plug the brake lines from the master cylinder.

Master cylinder installation—140 series shown, 164 similar

1. To left brake valve
2. To 6-branch union, lower
3. From secondary circuit (master cylinder)
4. Warning valve
5. Warning switch
6. To 6-branch union, upper
7. From primary circuit (master cylinder)
8. To right brake valve
9. Master cylinder
10. Attaching nut

3. Remove the two nuts which retain the master cylinder and reservoir assembly to the vacuum booster, and lift the assembly forward, being careful not to spill any fluid on the fender. Empty out and discard the brake fluid.

CAUTION: *Do not depress the brake pedal while the master cylinder is removed.*

4. In order for the master cylinder to function properly when installed to the vacuum booster, the adjusting nut for the thrust rod of the booster must not prevent the primary piston of the master cylinder from returning to its resting position. A clearance (C) of 0.020–0.059 in. on 1970 models, and 0.004–0.04 in. on 1971 and later models, is required between the thrust rod and primary piston with the master cylinder installed. The clearance may be adjusted by rotating the adjusting nut for the booster thrust rod in the required direction. To determine what the clearance (C) will be when the master cylinder and booster are connected, first measure the distance (A) between the face of the attaching flange and the center of the primary piston on the master cylinder, then measure the distance (B) that the

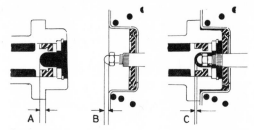

Adjusting thrust rod

thrust rod protrudes from the fixed surface of the booster (making sure that the thrust rod is depressed fully with a partial vacuum existing in the booster). When measurement (B) is subtracted from measurement (A), clearance (C) should be obtained. If not, adjust the length of the thrust rod by turning the adjusting screw to suit. After the final adjustment is obtained, apply a few drops of locking compound, such as Loctite, to the adjusting nut.

5. Position the master cylinder and reservoir assembly onto the studs for the booster, and install the washers and nuts. Tighten the nuts to 17 ft lbs.

6. Remove the plugs and connect the brake lines.

7. Bleed the entire brake system, as outlined in this chapter.

164, 1800 Series

1. Follow steps 1–3 under "Master Cylinder Removal and Installation" for the 140 series.

CAUTION: *Do not depress the brake pedal while the master cylinder is removed.*

2. To install, place a new sealing ring onto the sealing flange of the master cylinder. Position the master cylinder and reservoir assembly onto the booster studs, and install the washers and nuts. Tighten the nuts to 8.7–10.8 ft lbs.

3. Remove the plugs and loosely connect the brake lines. Have a friend depress the brake pedal to remove air from the cylinder. Tighten the nuts for the lines when brake fluid (free of air bubbles) is forced out.

4. Bleed the entire brake system, as outlined in this chapter.

Master Cylinder Overhaul

140 Series

1. Remove the master cylinder from the booster as outlined in the applicable

"Master Cylinder Removal and Installation" section.

2. Firmly fasten the flange of the master cylinder in a vise.

3. Position both hands beneath the reservoir and pull it free of its rubber seals. Remove the filler cap and strainer from the reservoir, as well as the rubber seals and nuts (if so equipped) from the cylinder.

4. Remove the stop screw. Using a pair of snap-ring pliers, remove the snap-ring from the primary piston and shake out the piston. If the secondary piston remains lodged in the bore, it may be forced out by blowing air into the stoplight switch hole.

Master cylinder disassembled (with type 1 secondary piston)—140 series

2. Piston seal	12. Circlip
3. Secondary piston	13. Cylinder housing
4. Piston seal	17. Sealing washer
9. Primary piston (assembled)	18. Stop screw
11. Thrust washer	19. Return spring

5. Remove both seals from the secondary piston, taking care not to damage or score the surfaces of the plunger. The old primary piston should be discarded and replaced.

6. Clean all reusable metal parts in clean brake fluid or methylated alcohol. The parts may be allowed to thoroughly air dry, or compressed air may be used. At any rate, all alcohol must be removed from the parts, as alcohol lowers the boiling temperature of brake fluid. If the inside of the cylinder is scored or scratched, the cylinder must be replaced. Minor pitting or corrosion may be removed by honing. Remember to flush the cylinder clean after honing, and make sure that the passages are clear.

Check the piston for damage and proper clearance in the bore. The cylinder diameter may not exceed 0.881 in., while the piston diameter may not be less than 0.870 in.

7. Install new seals on the secondary piston, making sure that they are positioned in the proper direction.

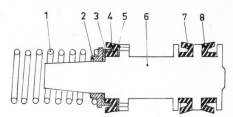

Type 2 secondary piston—140 series

1. Spring	5. Washer
2. Spring plate	6. Piston
3. Back-up ring	7. Piston seal
4. Piston seal	8. Piston seal

8. Coat the cylinder bore with brake fluid and dip the secondary piston and seals in brake fluid prior to installation. Slide the spring, spring plate, and washer onto the secondary piston and install the assembly in the bore, taking care not to damage the seals. Dip the new primary piston and seal assembly in brake fluid. Press the primary piston assembly into the bore and install a new washer and snap-ring.

9. Make sure that the hole for the stop screw is clear and install the new stop screw and sealing washer. Torque the screw to 9.5 ft lbs on 1970–71 models, and 7–9 ft lbs on 1972 and later models.

10. Check the movement of the pistons and make sure that the flow-through holes are clear. The equalizing hole is checked by inserting a 25 gauge soft copper wire through it and making sure that it is not blocked by the secondary piston seal. If it is blocked, then the master cylinder is incorrectly assembled, and you must take it through the numbers once more.

11. Install the nuts (if so equipped), new rubber seals, and washers onto the master cylinder at the reservoir connections. After making sure that the venting hole in the cap is open, install the cleaned strainer and cap. Press the reservoir into the master cylinder by hand. If the stoplight switch was removed, reinstall it.

12. Install the master cylinder as outlined in the applicable "Master Cylinder Removal and Installation" section.

164, 1800 Series

1. Remove the master cylinder from the booster as outlined in the applicable "Master Cylinder Removal and Installation" section.

2. Follow steps 2–4 under "Master Cylinder Overhaul" for the 140 series.

3. Discard both the primary and secondary pistons.

4. Clean all reusable metal parts in clean brake fluid or methylated alcohol. The parts must be thoroughly dried with filtered, water-free compressed air, or air dried. All cleaning alcohol must be removed from the parts, as it lowers the boiling temperature of brake fluid. If the inside of the cylinder is scored or scratched, the cylinder must be replaced. Minor pitting and corrosion may be removed by honing. Remember to flush the cylinder clean after honing, and make sure that the passages are clear.

Check the cylinder bore for excessive wear. On 1800 series models, the bore must not exceed 0.881 in., and on 164 models, no more than 0.942 in.

5. Make sure that new rubber seals, a new brass washer and back-up ring are installed on the new secondary piston. Make sure that the rubber seals are pointing in the right direction.

6. Coat the cylinder bore with brake fluid and dip the secondary piston and seals in brake fluid prior to installation. Install the secondary piston and spring in the bore, taking care not to damage the rubber seals.

7. Make sure that the new rubber seals, metal washers, plastic washer, back-up ring, sleeve, and spring are installed on the new primary piston. Make sure that the seals are facing in the right direction.

8. On 1800 models, compress the primary piston spring and tighten the screw for the sleeve until it bottoms. Torque the screw to 1.5–2.2 ft lbs.

9. Dip the primary piston assembly in brake fluid and install it in the bore, taking care not to damage the rubber seals. While holding the piston in the bore, install the snap-ring.

10. Check that the hole for the stop screw is clear, and install the new stop screw and sealing washer. Torque the screw to 3.5–5.7 ft lbs on all 164 models and 1972 and later 1800 series models, and 7–8.5 ft lbs on 1971 and earlier 1800 series models.

11. Check the movement of the pistons and make sure that the flow-through holes are clear. The equalizing hole is checked by inserting a 25 gauge (1800) or 22 gauge (164) soft copper wire through it and making sure that it is not blocked by the secondary piston seal. If it is blocked, the master cylinder will not function properly and must be reassembled.

12. Install the nuts (if so equipped), new rubber seals and washers onto the master cylinder at the reservoir connections. After making sure that the venting hole in the cap is open, install the cleaned strainer and cap. Press the reservoir into the master cylinder by hand. If the stoplight switch was removed, reinstall it.

13. Install the master cylinder as outlined in the applicable "Master Cylinder Removal and Installation" section.

BRAKE SYSTEM WARNING VALVE

The brake system warning valve is located near the master cylinder in the engine compartment. The valve is centered by hydraulic pressure from the primary circuit on one side and the secondary circuit on the other. When a hydraulic imbalance exists, such as a leak in one of the calipers, the valve will move off-center toward the system with the leak and, there-

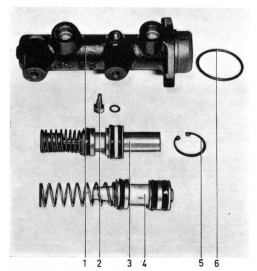

Master cylinder disassembled—164, 1800 series

1. Cylinder housing	4. Secondary piston
2. Stop screw	5. Circlip
3. Primary piston	6. Sealing ring

fore, the lowest pressure. When the valve moves off-center, it closes a circuit to a warning light on the dashboard, warning the driver of the imbalance. Sometimes, the valve will actuate the warning light when one of the systems is bled during normal maintenance. When this happens, the valve has to be reset.

Valve Resetting

1. Disconnect the plug contact and screw out the warning switch so that the pistons inside the valve may return to their normal position.
2. Repair and bleed the faulty hydraulic circuit.
3. Screw in the warning switch and tighten it to a torque of 10–14 ft lbs. Connect the plug contact.

Valve Replacement

1. Placing a rag beneath the valve to catch the brake fluid, loosen the pipe connections, and disconnect the six brake lines. Disconnect the electrical plug contact, and lift out the valve.
2. Connect the new warning valve in the reverse order of removal, and connect the plug contact.
3. Bleed the entire brake system.

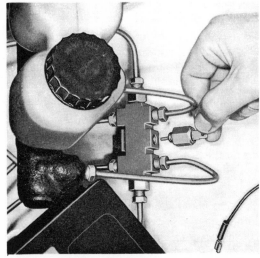

Removing warning switch

BRAKE SYSTEM PROPORTIONING VALVES

Each of the brake circuits has a proportioning (relief) valve located in-line between the rear wheels. The purpose of

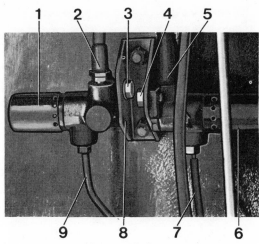

Proportioning valves installed

1. Left brake valve
2. Brake hose to left rear wheel
3. Attaching screw
4. Attaching screw
5. Brake hose to right rear wheel
6. Right brake valve
7. From the master cylinder
8. Bracket
9. From the master cylinder secondary circuit

these valves is to ensure that brake pressure on all four wheels compensates for the change in weight distribution under varied braking conditions. The harder the brakes are applied, the more weight there is on the front wheels. The valves regulate the hydraulic pressure to the rear wheels so that under hard braking conditions, they receive a smaller percentage of the total braking effort. This prevents premature rear wheel lock-up when the brakes are applied in emergency situations.

Valve Replacement

Sophisticated pressure testing equipment is required to troubleshoot the dual hydraulic system in order to determine if the proportioning valves are in need of replacement. However, if the car is demonstrating signs of rear wheel lock-up under moderate to heavy braking pressure, and other variables such as tire pressure, tread depth, etc. have been ruled out, the valve(s) may be at fault. Rebuilding kits are available from the dealer for the valves in 1972 and earlier model Volvos. However, the valves installed in 1973 and later models are not rebuildable, and must be replaced as a unit.

1. Unscrew, disconnect and plug the brake pipe from the master cylinder, at the valve connection.

2. Slacken the connection for the flexible brake hose to the rear wheel a *maximum* of ¼ turn.

3. Remove the bolt(s) which retain the valve to the underbody, and unscrew the valve from the rear brake hose.

4. To install the valve, place a new seal on it, and screw the valve onto the rear brake hose and hand tighten. Secure the valve to the underbody with the retaining bolt(s).

5. Connect the brake pipe and tighten both connections, making sure that there is no tension on the flexible rear hose.

6. Bleed the brake system.

BLEEDING HYDRAULIC SYSTEM

Whenever a spongy brake pedal indicates that there is air in the system, or when any part of the hydraulic system has been removed for service, the system must be bled. In addition, if the level in the master cylinder reservoir is allowed to go below the minimum mark for too long a period of time, air may enter the system, necessitating bleeding.

If only one brake caliper is removed for servicing, it is usually only necessary to bleed that unit. If, however, the master cylinder, warning valve, or any of the main brake lines are removed, the entire system must be bled.

Be careful not to spill any brake fluid onto the brake disc or pads and, of course, the paintwork. When bleeding the entire system, the rear of the car should be raised higher than the front. Only use brake fluid bearing the designation SAE 1703 (SAE 70

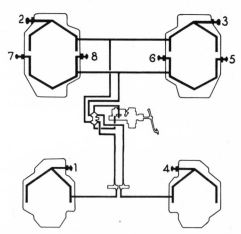

Bleeding sequence—140 series, 164, with Ate brakes

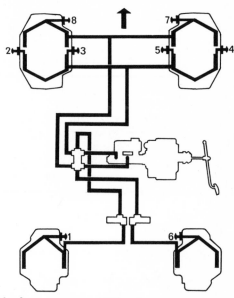

Bleeding sequence—1800 series

R3), DOT 3, or DOT 4. Never reuse old brake fluid.

1. Check to make sure that there are no mats or other materials obstructing the travel of the brake pedal. During bleeding, the full pedal travel should be 6 in. for the 140 series, and 5.5 in. for the 164 and 1800 series (providing that both circuits are bled simultaneously).

2. Disconnect the plug contact, and unscrew the electric switch from the warning valve.

3. Clean the cap and the top of the master cylinder reservoir, and make sure that the vent hole in the cap is open. Fill the reservoir to the maximum mark, if neces-

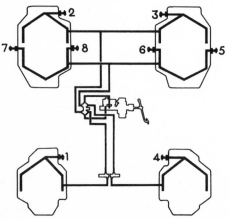

Bleeding sequence—140 series, 164, with Girling brakes

sary. Never allow the level to dip below the minimum mark during bleeding, as this will allow air into the system.

4. If only one brake caliper was removed, it will usually suffice to bleed only that wheel. Otherwise, prepare to bleed the entire system according to the numbered sequence in the bleeding diagrams.

Bleeding front wheel caliper, rear caliper similar

5. Remove the protective cap for the bleeder screw, and fit a 5/16 in. ring spanner wrench on the nipple. Install a tight fitting plastic hose onto the nipple, and insert the other end of the hose into a glass bottle containing clean brake fluid. The hose must hang down below the surface of the fluid, or air will be sucked into the system when the brake pedal is released. Open the bleeder screw a maximum of ½ turn. Slowly depress the brake pedal until it bottoms, pause a second or two, and then quickly release the pedal. This should be repeated until the fluid flowing into the bottle is completely free of air bubbles. Then have a friend press the pedal to the bottom and hold it there while you tighten the bleeder screw to 3–4.5 ft lbs. Install the protective cap.

6. If the entire system is to be bled, follow the above procedure for the remaining 7 nipples. Generally, it is sufficient to

bleed each circuit once. However, if the pedal continues to feel spongy, repeat the bleeding sequence. Remember to keep the master cylinder reservoir level above the minimum mark.

7. Fill the reservoir with the specified brake fluid to the maximum mark.

8. Screw the electric switch into the warning valve and connect the plug contact. Tighten the switch to 10–14 ft lbs. Make sure that the warning light is actuated only when the parking brake is applied.

Stoplight Switch Adjustment

With the brake pedal in the released position, the distance (A) between the brass hub of the switch and the pedal lever should be 0.08–0.24 in. To adjust, loosen the attaching screws for the switch bracket and move the switch in the required direction.

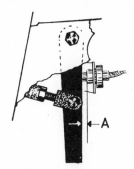

Stoplight switch adjustment

Power Booster System

Vacuum Booster Removal and Installation

140 SERIES

1. Remove the master cylinder as outlined in the applicable "Master Cylinder Removal and Installation" section.

2. Loosen the fork from the pedal by removing the cotter pin and bolt.

3. Disconnect the vacuum hose at the check valve. Remove the ignition coil and position it to one side.

4. Remove the nuts which retain the booster mounting bracket onto the firewall and remove the support bracket.

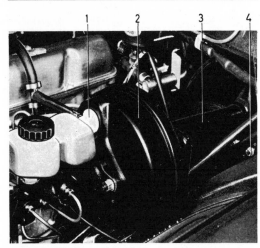

Power booster installed—140 series

1. Check valve
2. Vacuum booster
3. Bracket
4. Attaching bolt

5. Lift off the booster and place it on a bench. Loosen the locknut (2) and screw off the fork. Remove the rubber cover (4) and the mounting bracket (5). Unscrew the thrust rod (3) from the rear thrust rod of the booster.

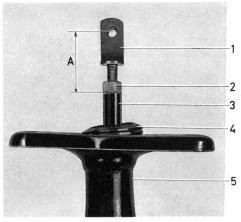

Removing thrust rod—140 series

1. Fork
2. Locknut
3. Thrust rod
4. Rubber cover
5. Bracket
6. A = approx. 45 mm
   (1.8")

6. Apply locking compound, such as Loctite® type B, to the booster thrust rod. Then screw in the thrust rod (3) that runs inside of the bracket, as far as possible onto the booster thrust rod.

7. Position the brackets on the booster, but do not tighten the attaching nuts at this time.

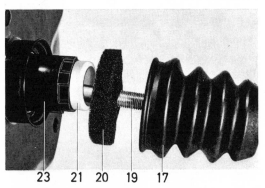

Replacing booster air filter—140 series

17. Rubber cover
19. Ingoing thrust rod
20. Filter
21. Plastic
23. Valve housing

8. Place a new filter on the sleeve of the thrust rod and place the rubber cover in position. Screw in the fork with locknut so that the distance (A) from the center of the fork hole to the end of the thrust rod is 1.8 in.

9. Place the booster with brackets in the vehicle and install, but do not tighten the attaching nuts. After all of the nuts are loosely fitted, tighten them.

10. Install the ignition coil, and connect the vacuum hose to the check valve.

11. Connect the fork to the brake pedal and install the cotter pin.

12. Install the master cylinder as outlined in the applicable "Master Cylinder Removal and Installation" section.

164

1. Remove the master cylinder as outlined in the applicable "Master Cylinder Removal and Installation" section.

2. Disconnect the vacuum hose at the booster.

3. Disconnect the link arm from the brake pedal. Remove the bracket with the clutch pedal stop from the firewall.

4. Remove the four nuts which retain the booster to the firewall.

5. Pull the booster forward, and from the engine compartment, disconnect the fork from the link arm. Lift out the unit.

6. Lift the rubber cover and pry up the protective washer from the booster. Lift out the old damper and filter, and replace them with new ones, making sure that they are installed with their slots positioned 180° opposite each other. Install the protective washer and rubber cover, making

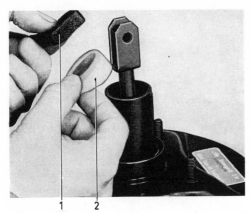

Replacing booster air filter—164

1. Damper   2. Air filter

2. Disconnect the vacuum hose from the booster.

3. Disconnect the support clamp and remove the nuts which attach the booster to the firewall.

4. Unscrew the locknut on the thrust rod and unscrew the yoke.

5. Pull forward and lift out the booster.

6. Lift the rubber cover and pry up the washer from the booster. Lift out the old damper and filter, and install new ones, making sure that they are installed with their slots positioned 180° opposite each other. Install the washer and rubber cover, making sure that the cover is correctly positioned onto the washer and booster.

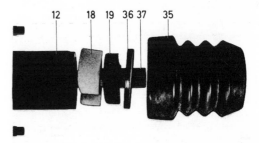

Replacing booster air filter—1800 series

12. Guide housing   35. Rubber cover
18. Filter   36. Washer
19. Silencer   37. Rear thrust rod

sure that the rubber cover is pressed down properly at the inner edge of the washer.

7. Place the booster in the engine compartment, and connect the fork to the link arm. Push in the booster so that the attaching bolts are positioned.

8. Secure the booster to the firewall with the lock washers and nuts.

9. Install the clutch pedal bracket on the inside of the firewall, and connect the link arm to the brake pedal.

10. Connect the vacuum hose to the booster, with the connection facing downward.

11. Install the master cylinder as outlined in the applicable "Master Cylinder Removal and Installation" section.

1800 SERIES

1. Remove the master cylinder as outlined in the applicable "Master Cylinder Removal and Installation" section.

7. Position the booster in the engine compartment and screw the yoke to the bottom of the thrust rod. Tighten the locknut. Install the lock washers and nuts which secure the booster to the firewall and to the support clamp.

8. Connect the vacuum hose to the booster.

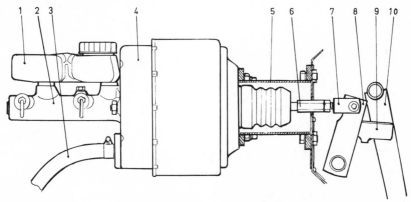

Power booster installed—1800 series

1. Brake fluid container   4. Vacuum booster   7. Yoke   10. Brake pedal
2. Master cylinder   5. Bracket   8. Double lever
3. Vacuum hose   6. Thrust rod   9. Thrust link

9. Install the master cylinder as outlined in the applicable "Master Cylinder Removal and Installation" section.

Vacuum Booster Filter Replacement

Under normal driving conditions, the filter in the vacuum booster should be replaced every three years. The booster must be removed to replace the filter. Consult the applicable "Vacuum Booster Removal and Installation" section for the procedure.

Disc Brakes

BRAKE DISCS

Inspection and Replacement

Remove the hub cap, loosen the lug nuts, raise the car, and remove the wheel and tire assembly. The friction surface on both sides of the disc should be examined for surface deviations such as scoring or corrosion. Minor radial scratches and small rust spots may be removed by turning or fine polishing the disc. The lateral run-out of the disc must not exceed 0.004 in. for the front, and 0.006 in. for the rear, measured at the outer edge of the disc. Do not mistake a faulty wheel bearing adjustment, or an improperly mounted disc for lateral runout. Actual disc thickness, which varies from model to model (see specifications), should not vary more than 0.0012 in. when taken at several points on the same disc. If the disc is worn at any point to less than the minimum permissible thickness (see specifications), it must be replaced.

Checking brake disc lateral run-out, front shown

When removing the disc, either to have it machined or replaced, the brake line must be disconnected from the caliper and plugged, the two bolts attaching the caliper to its retainer removed, and the caliper lifted off. The disc is then removed by unscrewing its two phillips head retaining screws and rapping on the inside of the disc with a plastic hammer or rubber mallet. Machining should be performed in unit with the hub, and should be equal on both sides. After machining, recheck the disc thickness and compare it to the minimum permissible thickness value on the specifications chart. To install the disc, reverse the removal procedure, taking care to bleed the brake caliper as outlined in this chapter.

BRAKE PADS

Removal and Installation

GIRLING BRAKES

1. Remove the hub caps and loosen the lug nuts a few turns.

2. Raise the vehicle and place jackstands beneath the rear axle and the front jack attachments. Remove the wheel and tire assemblies.

3. Remove the hairpin-shaped locking

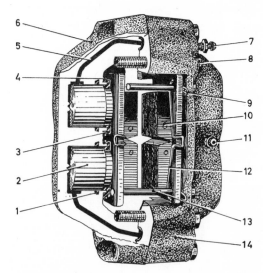

Girling front caliper

1. Sealing ring	8. Bolt
2. Piston	9. Retaining clip
3. Rubber dust cover	10. Brake pad
4. Retaining ring	11. Lower bleeder nipple
5. Channel	12. Damping spring
6. Outer half	13. Retaining pin
7. Upper bleeder nipple	14. Inner half

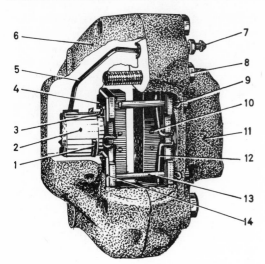

Girling rear caliper

1. Sealing ring
2. Piston
3. Rubber dust cover
4. Retaining ring
5. Channel
6. Outer half
7. Bleeder nipple

8. Bolt
9. Retaining clip
10. Brake pad
11. Inner half
12. Damping spring
13. Retaining pin
14. Washer

clips, one lock pin then the other, together with the damping springs for the brake pads. Pull out the pads. Discard them if they are worn down to a lining thickness of ⅛ in. or less. If they are reusable, mark them for ease of assembly.

4. Carefully clean out the pad cavity. Replace any damaged dust covers. If any dirt has contaminated the cylinders, the caliper must be removed for overhaul. Inspect the brake disc as described under "Brake Discs—Inspection and Replacement."

5. Carefully depress the pistons in their cylinders so that the new pads will fit. This may be done with a screwdriver, but extra care must be exercised not to dam-

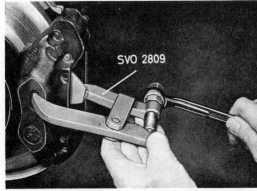

Depressing pistons

age the rubber piston seals, the pistons, or the new pads themselves. A piston depressing tool (SVO 2809) is available from the dealer that accomplishes the job without danger to the caliper components. Remember that when the pistons are depressed in their bores, brake fluid is displaced causing the level in the master cylinder to rise, and perhaps, overflow.

6. Install the new pads and secure them with first one lock pin, then the other pin with the damping springs. Install new locking clips on the lock pins. Make sure that the pads are able to move and that the linings do not project outside of the brake disc.

7. Depress the brake pedal several times and make sure that the movement feels normal. Bleeding is not usually necessary after pad replacement.

8. Clean the contact surfaces of the wheel and hub. Install the wheel and tire assemblies. Remove the jackstands and lower the vehicle. Tighten the lug nuts to 70–100 ft lbs, and install the hub cap.

NOTE: *If at all possible, braking should be moderate for the first 25 miles or so until the new pads seat correctly. Avoid panic stops in the beginning, unless necessary.*

ATE BRAKES

1. Remove the hub caps and loosen the lug nuts a few turns.

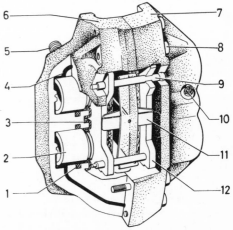

Ate front caliper

1. Sealing ring
2. Piston
3. Rubber dust cover
4. Channel
5. Upper bleeder nipple
6. Outer half

7. Inner half
8. Bolt
9. Guide pin
10. Inner bleeder nipple
11. Damping spring
12. Brake pad

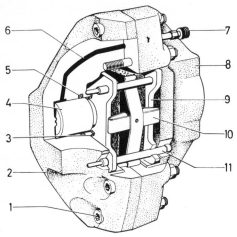

Ate rear caliper

1.	Bolt	7.	Bleeder nipple
2.	Outer half	8.	Inner half
3.	Rubber dust cover	9.	Brake pad
4.	Piston	10.	Damping spring
5.	Sealing ring	11.	Guide pin
6.	Channel		

2. Raise the vehicle and place jackstands beneath the rear axle and the front jack attachments.

3. Using a $9/64$ in. drift, tap out the upper guide pin for the pads and remove and discard the tensioning spring. Tap out the lower pin. Pull out the pads. Discard them if they are worn down to a lining thickness of $1/8$ in. or less. If they are reusable, mark them for ease of assembly.

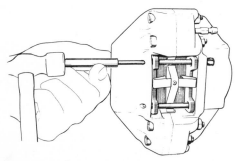

Removing guide pin—Ate brakes

4. Carefully clean out the pad cavities. Replace any damaged dust covers. If any dirt has contaminated the cylinders, the caliper must be removed for overhaul. Inspect the brake disc as described under "Brake Discs—Inspection and Replacement."

5. Carefully depress the pistons in their cylinders so that the new pads will fit. This may be done with a screwdriver, but

extra care must be exercised not to damage the rubber piston seals, the pistons, or the new pads themselves. A piston depressing tool (SVO 2809) is available from the dealer that accomplishes the job without danger to the caliper components. Remember that when the pistons are depressed in their bores, brake fluid is displaced, causing the level in the master cylinder to rise, and perhaps, overflow.

6. Install the new pads. Using only a hammer, tap one of the guide pins into position. Place a new tensioning spring into position, and while pushing it in against the pads, tap the other guide pin into position. Make sure that the pads can move.

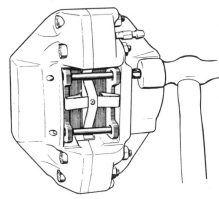

Installing guide pin—Ate brakes

7. Depress the brake pedal several times and make sure that the movement feels normal. Bleeding is not normally necessary after pad replacement.

8. Clean the contact surfaces of the wheel and hub. Install the wheel and tire assemblies. Remove the jackstands and lower the vehicle. Tighten the lug nuts to 70–100 ft lbs, and install the hub cap.

NOTE: *If at all possible, avoid hard or lengthy braking for the first 25 miles or so, until the new pads seat correctly.*

FRONT BRAKE CALIPER

Removal and Installation

1. Remove the hub cap and loosen the lug nuts a few turns. Block the reservoir cap vent hole to reduce leakage of brake fluid when the lines are disconnected. Firmly apply the parking brake.

2. Raise the front end and place jackstands beneath the front jack attachments. Remove the wheel and tire assembly.

3. On 140 series and 164 models, remove the brake hose retaining clip from the stabilizer bar, and disconnect the lower hose and secondary circuit brake pipe from their inboard connection underneath the car. Disconnect the upper hose from the caliper. Plug all brake connections to prevent leakage.

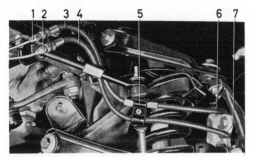

Front brake hose connections—140 series, 164

1. Connection for the primary circuit
2. Connection for the secondary circuit
3. Upper brake hose
4. Lower brake hose
5. Clip
6. Connection for lower wheel unit cylinder
7. Connection for upper wheel unit cylinder

4. On 1800 series models, disconnect both brake lines at the caliper and plug them.

5. Remove the two caliper attaching bolts and lift the unit off the retainer.

6. To install, first check the mating surfaces of the caliper and its retainer to make sure that they are clean and not damaged. Coat the threads of the attach-

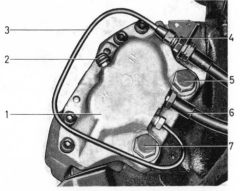

Front caliper installed—Ate shown, Girling similar

1. Front wheel brake caliper
2. Lower bleeder nipple
3. Upper bleeder nipple
4. Connection for lower wheel unit cylinder
5. Attaching bolt
6. Connection for upper wheel unit cylinder
7. Attaching bolt

ing bolts with a locking compound such as Loctite®. Position the caliper to its retainer over the disc and install the two attaching bolts. Tighten the bolts to 65–70 ft lbs. Make sure that the caliper is parallel to the disc, and that the disc can rotate freely in the brake pads.

7. On 140 series and 164 models, connect the lower brake hose and the secondary circuit brake pipe to their inboard connection and install the brake hose retaining clip to the stabilizer bar. Connect the upper brake hose to the caliper.

8. On 1800 series models, connect both brake lines to the caliper.

9. Unplug the reservoir cap vent hole. Install the wheel and tire assembly. Remove the jackstands and lower the car. Tighten the lug nuts to 70–100 ft lbs and install the hub cap.

10. Bleed the brake system as outlined under "Bleeding Hydraulic System" in this chapter.

REAR BRAKE CALIPER

Removal and Installation

1. Remove the hub cap and loosen the lug nuts a few turns. Block the reservoir cap vent hole to reduce leakage of brake fluid when the line is disconnected.

2. Place blocks in front of the front wheels. Raise the rear of the car and place jackstands beneath the rear axle. Remove the wheel and tire assembly. Release the parking brake.

Rear caliper installed—Girling shown, Ate similar

1. Attaching bolt
2. Brake line
3. Attaching bolt
4. Rear wheel brake caliper
5. Bleeder nipple

3. Disconnect the brake line from the caliper and plug it to prevent leakage.

4. Remove the two caliper attaching bolts and lift the unit off the retainer.

5. To install, first check the mating surfaces of the caliper and its retainer to make sure that they are clean and not damaged. Coat the threads of the attaching bolts with locking compound, such as Loctite type AV. Position the caliper to its retainer and install the two attaching bolts. Tighten the bolts to 45–50 ft lbs. Make sure that the caliper is parallel to the disc, and that the disc can rotate freely in the brake pads.

6. Connect the brake line to the caliper. Unplug the reservoir cap hole.

7. Install the wheel and tire assembly. Remove the jackstands and lower the car. Tighten the lug nuts to 70–100 ft lbs, and install the hub cap.

8. Bleed the applicable rear brake caliper as outlined under "Bleeding Hydraulic System" in this chapter.

Caliper Overhaul

The following procedure applies to four piston front calipers and two piston rear calipers of both Girling and Ate design.

1. Remove the brake caliper from the car as outlined in the applicable "Caliper Removal and Installation" section.

2. Remove the brake pads as outlined in step 3 of the applicable "Brake Pad Removal and Installation" section.

3. Remove the retaining rings and the rubber dust covers. Place a wooden block between the pistons. Using compressed air applied through the brake line connection, force the pistons in toward the wooden

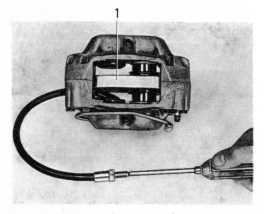

Removing pistons with compressed air

1. Wooden disc

block. Remove the pistons from their bores, taking care not to burr or scratch them.

4. Remove the sealing rings with a blunt plastic tool. Be careful not to damage the edges of the grooves. Screw out the bleeder nipple(s), and on front calipers, remove the external connecting pipe.

NOTE: *It is not necessary to separate the caliper halves. Assembling the halves would require special pressure testing equipment.*

5. Clean all reusable metal parts in clean brake fluid or methylated alcohol. Dry all parts with compressed air or allow to air dry. Make sure that all of the passages are clear. All alcohol must be removed from the parts as alcohol lowers the boiling temperature of brake fluid. If any of the cylinders are scored or scratched, the entire housing must be replaced. Minor scratching may be removed from the pistons by fine polishing. Replace any piston that is damaged or worn.

6. Coat the mating surfaces of the pistons and cylinders with brake fluid.

7. Install new sealing rings in the cylinders.

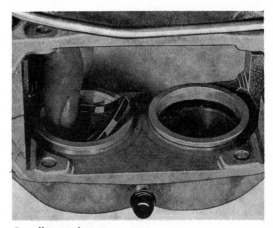

Installing sealing rings

8. On Girling brakes and ATE front brakes, press the pistons into their bores with the large diameter end facing inward. Make sure that the pistons are installed straight and are not scratched in the process.

9. On ATE rear brakes, check to make sure that the pistons are in the proper positions to prevent brake squeal. The piston recess should incline 20° in relation to the lower guide area on the caliper. Check the

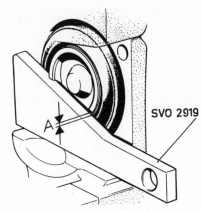

Checking location of rear caliper pistons—Ate brakes

location of the piston with template SVO 2919. When the template is placed against the one recess, the distance (A) to the other recess may be no greater than 0.039 in. If the location of the piston needs adjusting, press SVO 2918 against the piston and force out the shoes by screwing in the handle. Turn the piston in the required direction, release the tool, and re-measure with the template. Repeat this operation for the other piston.

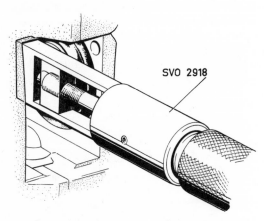

Adjusting location of rear caliper pistons—Ate brakes

10. Place the new rubber dust covers on the pistons and housing. Install the new retaining rings.

11. Install the brake pads as outlined in step 6 of the applicable "Brake Pad Removal and Installation" section.

12. Screw in the bleeder nipple(s).

13. Install the caliper as outlined in the applicable "Caliper Removal and Installation" section.

FRONT WHEEL BEARINGS

Replacement and Adjustment

1. Remove the hub cap and loosen the lug nuts a few turns.

2. Firmly apply the parking brake. Jack up the front of the car and place jackstands beneath the lower control arms. Remove the wheel and tire assembly.

3. Remove the front caliper as outlined in "Front Caliper Removal and Installation."

4. Pry off the grease cap. Remove the cotter pin and castle nut. Use a hub puller to pull off the hub. If the inner bearing remains lodged on the stub axle, remove it with a puller.

Removing front hub.

5. Using a drift, remove the inner and outer bearing rings.

6. Thoroughly clean the hub, brake disc, and grease cap.

7. Press in the new inner and outer bearing rings with a drift.

8. Press grease into both bearings with a bearing packer. If one is not available, pack the bearings with as much wheel bearing grease as possible by hand. Also coat the outsides of the bearings and the outer rings pressed into the hub. Fill the recess in the hub with grease up to the smallest diameter on the outer ring for the outer bearing. Place the inner bearing in position in the hub and press its seal in with a drift. The felt ring should be thoroughly coated with light engine oil.

9. Place the hub onto the stub axle. Install the outer bearing, washer, and castle nut.

10. Adjust the front wheel bearings by tightening the castle nut to 50 ft lbs to seat the bearings. Then, back off the nut ⅓ of a turn counterclockwise. If the nut slot does not align with the hole in the stub axle, loosen the nut until the cotter pin may be installed. Make sure that the wheel spins freely without any side play.

11. Fill the grease cap halfway with wheel bearing grease, and install it on the hub.

12. Install the front caliper as outlined in "Front Caliper Removal and Installation."

13. Install the wheel and tire assembly. Remove the jackstands and lower the car. Tighten the lug nuts to 70–100 ft lbs, and install the hub cap.

Adjusting parking brake

Parking Brake

The parking brake is mechanically actuated by a cable which is connected, by means of a pull rod and linkage, to a lever mounted on the floor to the left of the driver's seat. The brake consists of two miniature duo-servo drum brakes, one mounted at each end of the rear axle housing inside the hub of the rear brake discs.

Adjustment

The parking brake should be fully engaged when the lever is pulled up to the third or fourth notch. If it does not, adjust as follows.

1. Apply the parking brake. Remove the rear hub caps and loosen the lug nuts a few turns.

2. Place blocks in front of the front wheels. Jack up the rear end and place jackstands beneath the rear axle. Remove the wheel and tire assemblies. Release the parking brake.

3. Make sure that the brake pads are not stuck to their discs. Disconnect the cable from the lever.

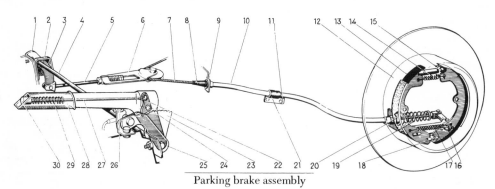

Parking brake assembly

1. Inside support attachment	11. Attachment	21. Rubber cable guide
2. Rubber cover	12. Brake drum	22. Pawl
3. Lever	13. Brake shoe (secondary shoe)	23. Ratchet segment
4. Shaft	14. Return spring	24. Rivet
5. Pull rod	15. Adjusting device	25. Outside support attachment
6. Block	16. Lever	26. Warning valve switch
7. Cable	17. Movable rod	27. Push rod
8. Rubber cover	18. Anchor bolt	28. Parking brake lever
9. Front attachment	19. Return spring	29. Spring
10. Cable sleeve	20. Rear attachment	30. Push button

4. Rotate the disc until the adjusting screw hole aligns with the serrations on the adjusting screw. Insert a screwdriver, and adjust the shoes by moving the handle of the screwdriver upward. When the disc cannot be rotated easily, stop adjusting the shoes. Turn the adjusting screw back 4 or 5 serrations. Make sure that the shoes do not drag by hand turning the disc in its normal direction of rotation. A slight drag is permissible. However, if there is a heavy drag, back off the adjusting screw 2 or 3 serrations more. Connect the cable to the lever.

5. Repeat the adjusting procedure for the other wheel.

6. Apply the parking brake lever and make sure that the parking brake is fully engaged with the lever at the third or fourth notch. If not, tighten the cable. This is accomplished by loosening the locknuts and screwing in the block on the pull rod. After adjusting, tighten the locknuts. Make sure that there is approximately the same braking effect on both rear wheels.

7. Install the wheel and tire asssemblies. Remove the jackstands and lower the car. Tighten the lug nuts to 70–100 ft lbs and install the hub caps.

Cable Replacement

1. Apply the parking brake. Remove the hub caps for the rear wheels and loosen the lug nuts a few turns.

2. Place blocks in front of the front wheels. Jack up the rear end and place jackstands beneath the rear axle. Remove the wheel and tire assembly. Release the parking brake.

3. Remove the bolt and the wheel from the pulley.

4. Remove the rubber cover for the front attachment of the cable sleeve and nut, as well as the attachment for the rubber suspension ring on the frame. Remove the cable from the other side of the attachment in the same manner.

5. Hold the return spring in position. Pry up the lock and remove the lock pin so that the cable releases from the lever.

6. Remove the return spring with washers. Loosen the nut for the rear attachment of the cable sleeve. Lift the cable forward, after loosening both sides of the attachments, and remove it.

7. To install, first adjust the rear brake shoes of the parking brake as outlined in steps 3, 4, and 5 under "Parking Brake Adjustment."

Brake Specifications

(all measurements are given in inches)

Year	Model	Master Cylinder Bore	Wheel Cylinder Bore		Min Pad Thickness	Front Disc			Rear Disc		
			F	R		Diameter	Max Runout	Min Thickness	Diameter	Max Runout	Min Thickness
1970	140 series	0.882	1.422	1.5	0.125	10.7	0.004	0.457	11.60	0.006	0.331
	164	0.950	1.422	1.5	0.125	10.7	0.004	0.457	11.60	0.006	0.331
	1800 series	0.882	1.422	1.422	0.125	10.6	0.004	0.517	11.60	0.006	0.331
1971	140 series	0.882	①	②	0.125	10.7	0.004	③	11.63	0.006	0.331
	164	0.950	1.422	1.5	0.125	10.7	0.004	0.517	11.63	0.006	0.331
	1800 series	0.882	1.422	1.422	0.125	10.6	0.004	0.517	11.63	0.006	0.331
1972	140 series	0.882	①	②	0.125	10.7	0.004	0.457	11.63	0.006	0.331
	164	0.950	1.5	1.7	0.125	10.7	0.004	0.900	11.63	0.006	0.331
	1800 series	0.882	1.422	1.422	0.125	10.6	0.004	0.517	11.63	0.006	0.331
1973	140 series	0.882	①	②	0.125	10.7	0.004	0.457	11.63	0.006	0.331
	164	④	1.5	1.7	0.125	10.7	0.004	0.900	11.63	0.006	0.331

① 1.6 Girling
  1.5 ATE
② 1.8 Girling
  1.7 ATE
③ 0.457 B20B
  0.557 B20E
④ Up to chassis no. 79020—0.950
  Starting chassis no. 79021—0.875

8. Install new rubber cable guides for the cable suspension. Place the cable in position in the rear attachment and tighten the nut. Install the washers and return spring. Oil the lock pin and install it, together with the cable, on the lever. Install the attachment and rubber cable guide on the frame.

9. Install the cable in the same manner on the side of the vehicle.

10. Place the cable sleeve in position in the front attachments and install the rubber covers.

11. Lubricate and install the pulley on the pull rod. Adjust the pulley so that the parking brake is fully engaged with the lever at the third or fourth notch.

12. Install the wheel and tire assemblies. Remove the jackstands and lower the vehicle. Tighten the lug nut to 70–100 ft lbs and install the hub caps.

Doors

Removal and Installation

140 SERIES, 164

1. Remove the window handle, arm rest, and door upholstery as outlined under the applicable "Door Panel Removal and Installation" procedure.

2. Remove the bolt that attaches the door stop to the post, and remove the rubber sealing.

3. Remove the three bolts which retain the door stop to the door. Lift out the door stop through the upper opening in the door.

4. Open the door and remove the bolts which retain the hinges to the door. Carefully lift the door from the hinges.

5. Reverse the above procedure to install, taking care to align the door. The door can be adjusted laterally at the hinge attachments at both the door and the post, and adjusted vertically at the door post.

1800 SERIES

1. Remove the window handle, door handle, arm rest, and door upholstery as outlined under the applicable "Door Panel Removal and Installation" procedure.

2. Remove the six bolts which retain the

door stop and hinge to the door. Carefully lift the door from the hinges.

3. Reverse the above procedure to install, taking care to align the door. Longitudinal and vertical adjustment is made at the bolt holes in the body. Lateral adjustment is made by inserting shims.

DOOR PANELS

Removal and Installation

140 SERIES, 164

1. Remove the front door arm rest by first prying out the plastic covers for the attaching screws, and removing the arm rest attaching screws. Then, turn the plastic locking ring at the front of the arm rest several turns counterclockwise until the arm rest can be released and lifted out. The rear door arm rest, if so equipped, is removed by prying out the plastic covers and removing its attaching screws.

2. Remove the window regulator handle by pressing its washer in against the upholstery, and then in the direction of the handle.

3. Remove the phillips screws which retain the top of the upholstery to the door. Using a screwdriver pry around the edge of the upholstery to release the clips, then lift off the door panel.

4. Reverse the above procedure to install, taking care to position the spring clip

217

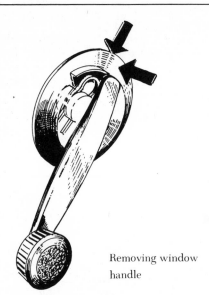

Removing window handle

for the regulator with its open end facing in the direction of the handle.

1800 SERIES

1. Remove the window regulator handle by pressing its washer in against the upholstery, and then pushing the washer in the direction of the handle.

2. On 1971 and earlier models, remove the two phillips screws which retain the upper half of the upholstery to the door. Pry with a screwdriver around the edge of the upper upholstery section, and lift upward. Then remove the four phillips screws which retain the lower section to the door, and pry it free of the door. Remove the lower upholstery section and the arm rest as a unit. Remove the plastic and paper insulation from the door. Release the door handle by tapping out its retaining pin with a drift.

3. On 1972 and later models, remove the arm rest by first prying out the pastic covers for the attaching screws, and removing the arm rest attaching screws. Then, turn the plastic locking ring at the front of the arm rest several turns counterclockwise until the arm rest can be released and lifted out. Release the door handle by tapping out its retaining pin with a drift. Pry with a screwdriver around the edge of the upholstery to release the clips, then lift off the door panel.

4. Reverse the above procedure to install, taking care to position the spring clip for the regulator with its open end facing in the direction of the handle.

Striker Plate Adjustment

140 SERIES, 164

The front door striker plate should have an inward inclination (A) of 1.5° from the horizontal. The striker plate for the rear door, if so equipped, should be tilted inward to an angle (A) of 2.5°. If the plate is not tilted correctly, loosen the four screws and make the necessary adjustment.

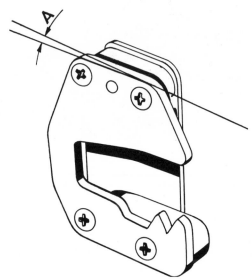

Striker plate inclination

1800 SERIES

Check the vertical position of the striker plate by shutting the door with the outside door handle button depressed and determining if the guide pin may glide straight into the striker plate. If the plate does not receive the guide pin correctly, loosen the three screws and make the necessary adjustment.

Hood

Hood Alignment

140 SERIES, 164

The hood may be aligned laterally and longitudinally by adjusting the position of the hood bolts in the oval hinge holes. The hood may be aligned vertically by adjusting the rubber stops at the front corners.

1800 Series

The hood may be aligned laterally and longitudinally by moving the hinges in the slotted holes. Vertical hood alignment may be accomplished by placing shims between the hood and hinges at the front and placing shims between the hood and lock bracket. In addition, the hood may be aligned at the rear corners by adjusting the rubber stops.

Sunroof

Sunroof Adjustment

140 Series, 164

1. Open the sunroof and remove the clips which secure the roof upholstery.

2. Close the sunroof and make sure that it is level with the roof. To adjust vertically, turn the screws at the front adjustment (7) in the appropriate direction, and raise or lower the lifts at the rear adjustment (12). Also, make sure that the lifts remain vertical when the roof is closed.

3. Secure the roof upholstery.

Tailgate

Tailgate Replacement

145

1. Remove the tailgate upholstery panel.
2. Remove the left-hand license plate lamp, and disconnect its cable.
3. Disconnect all electrical plug contacts inside the tailgate.

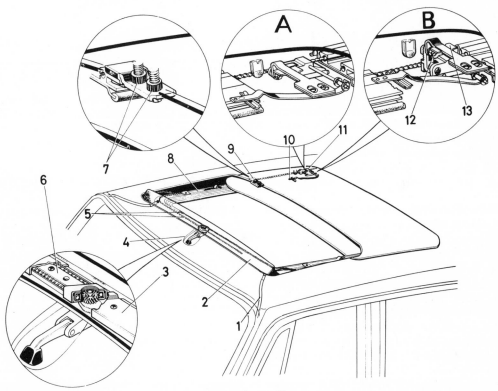

Sunroof assembly

A. Rear attachment when roof is open
B. Rear attachment when roof is closed

1. Drain hose	6. Front guide rail	11. Rear attachment
2. Wind deflector	7. Front adjustment	12. Rear adjustment
3. Covering strip	8. Intermediate piece	13. Reinforcing plate
4. Crank housing with crank	9. Front attachment	
5. Cables	10. Blade spring	

4. Remove the gas spring on the right side from its attachment on the tailgate, then remove it from the car.

5. Remove the screws which retain the two hinges to the tailgate, and carefully remove it.

6. Reverse the above procedure to install, taking care to adjust the play of the gas spring.

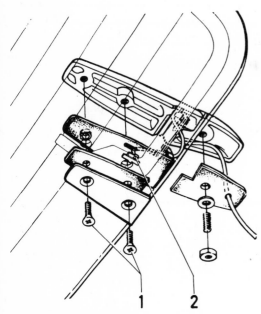

Tailgate hinges—1800ES

1. Phillips head screw   2. Soldering point

1800 ES

CAUTION: *Remember that you are working with a large piece of hardened glass and a sensitive rear window defroster.*

1. Remove the two gas springs by removing their safety catches and then pulling them straight out from the bolt. Disconnect the negative battery cable.

2. If you are more adept at soldering connections than gluing headliners, use the following procedure. With the tailgate closed, release the two phillips screws (1) for each hinge, and their rubber spacers. Then, being careful not to melt the window, heat the soldering point (2) for the window defroster wire thereby disconnecting it. Then carefully free the glass from its hinges at the top, open the latch, and lift off the glass.

3. If you feel more competent with a bottle of glue than a soldering iron, use the following procedure. With the tailgate closed, loosen the headliner at the rear edge, and remove the nut and washer for each hinge. Then, disconnect the defroster cable connections at the plug contact. Then lift the glass, hinges and all, from the body after opening the latch.

4. Reverse the procedure to install, taking care to install the rubber spacers on the roof and/or on both sides of the glass at the hinges. If the soldering procedure is used, make sure that the connection is clean as any excess solder contacting the hinge screw will result in a short circuit. Tighten the hinge screws to a torque of 3–6 ft lbs, *and no greater*. The tailgate is properly aligned when the distance between the moulding strip screws in the window is a minimum 1.4 in. all around. Connect the negative battery cable and test the operation of the rear window defroster.

Bumpers

Bumper Replacement

140 Series, 164

1970–72

The one piece aluminum bumpers on the front and rear are each attached to the side members by four support bars. The front bumper is removed by unscrewing the bolts inside the bumper and then lifting it from its support rails. The rear bumper is removed together with its support rails, by unscrewing the bolts which secure the rails to the body.

1973

The new energy absorbing bumpers, designed to protect the car from damage in a 5 mph front or 2.5 mph rear collision, are attached to the body by two gelatin filled shock absorbers which must be replaced after they compress in an accident. Remove the bumper after taking off the rubber cover washers for the cover strip above the bumper, and then removing the two nuts (1) and pulling out the two bolts (2).

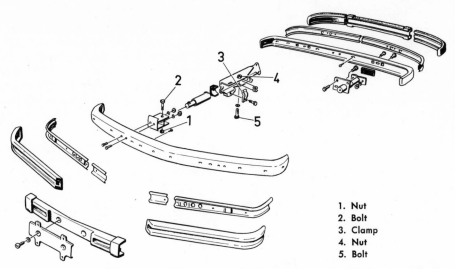

1. Nut
2. Bolt
3. Clamp
4. Nut
5. Bolt

Bumper and shock absorber assemblies—1973 140 series, 164

1800 Series

1970–72

The front bumpers of the 1800E and 1800ES, as well as the rear bumper of the 1800E, are three-piece units attached to the body by four support bars each. The rear bumper of the 1800ES is a five-piece unit attached with six support bars. Removal is a simple task of unbolting the bumpers from the support bars.

Appendix

General Conversion Table

Multiply by	To convert	To	
2.54	Inches	Centimeters	.3937
30.48	Feet	Centimeters	.0328
.914	Yards	Meters	1.094
1.609	Miles	Kilometers	.621
.645	Square inches	Square cm.	.155
.836	Square yards	Square meters	1.196
16.39	Cubic inches	Cubic cm.	.061
28.3	Cubic feet	Liters	.0353
.4536	Pounds	Kilograms	2.2045
4.546	Gallons	Liters	.22
.068	Lbs./sq. in. (psi)	Atmospheres	14.7
.138	Foot pounds	Kg. m.	7.23
1.014	H.P. (DIN)	H.P. (SAE)	.9861
——	To obtain	From	Multiply by

Note: 1 cm. equals 10 mm.; 1 mm. equals .0394".

Conversion—Common Fractions to Decimals and Millimeters

INCHES			INCHES			INCHES		
Common Fractions	Decimal Fractions	Millimeters (approx.)	Common Fractions	Decimal Fractions	Millimeters (approx.)	Common Fractions	Decimal Fractions	Millimeters (approx.)
1/128	.008	0.20	11/32	.344	8.73	43/64	.672	17.07
1/64	.016	0.40	23/64	.359	9.13	11/16	.688	17.46
1/32	.031	0.79	3/8	.375	9.53	45/64	.703	17.86
3/64	.047	1.19	25/64	.391	9.92	23/32	.719	18.26
1/16	.063	1.59	13/32	.406	10.32	47/64	.734	18.65
5/64	.078	1.98	27/64	.422	10.72	3/4	.750	19.05
3/32	.094	2.38	7/16	.438	11.11	49/64	.766	19.45
7/64	.109	2.78	29/64	.453	11.51	25/32	.781	19.84
1/8	.125	3.18	15/32	.469	11.91	51/64	.797	20.24
9/64	.141	3.57	31/64	.484	12.30	13/16	.813	20.64
5/32	.156	3.97	1/2	.500	12.70	53/64	.828	21.03
11/64	.172	4.37	33/64	.516	13.10	27/32	.844	21.43
3/16	.188	4.76	17/32	.531	13.49	55/64	.859	21.83
13/64	.203	5.16	35/64	.547	13.89	7/8	.875	22.23
7/32	.219	5.56	9/16	.563	14.29	57/64	.891	22.62
15/64	.234	5.95	37/64	.578	14.68	29/32	.906	23.02
1/4	.250	6.35	19/32	.594	15.08	59/64	.922	23.42
17/64	.266	6.75	39/64	.609	15.48	15/16	.938	23.81
9/32	.281	7.14	5/8	.625	15.88	61/64	.953	24.21
19/64	.297	7.54	41/64	.641	16.27	31/32	.969	24.61
5/16	.313	7.94	21/32	.656	16.67	63/64	.984	25.00
21/64	.328	8.33						

Conversion—Millimeters to Decimal Inches

mm	inches	mm	inches	mm	inches	mm	inches	mm	inches
1	.039 370	31	1.220 470	61	2.401 570	91	3.582 670	210	8.267 700
2	.078 740	32	1.259 840	62	2.440 940	92	3.622 040	220	8.661 400
3	.118 110	33	1.299 210	63	2.480 310	93	3.661 410	230	9.055 100
4	.157 480	34	1.338 580	64	2.519 680	94	3.700 780	240	9.448 800
5	.196 850	35	1.377 949	65	2.559 050	95	3.740 150	250	9.842 500
6	.236 220	36	1.417 319	66	2.598 420	96	3.779 520	260	10.236 200
7	.275 590	37	1.456 689	67	2.637 790	97	3.818 890	270	10.629 900
8	.314 960	38	1.496 050	68	2.677 160	98	3.858 260	280	11.032 600
9	.354 330	39	1.535 430	69	2.716 530	99	3.897 630	290	11.417 300
10	.393 700	40	1.574 800	70	2.755 900	100	3.937 000	300	11.811 000
11	.433 070	41	1.614 170	71	2.795 270	105	4.133 848	310	12.204 700
12	.472 440	42	1.653 540	72	2.834 640	110	4.330 700	320	12.598 400
13	.511 810	43	1.692 910	73	2.874 010	115	4.527 550	330	12.992 100
14	.551 180	44	1.732 280	74	2.913 380	120	4.724 400	340	13.385 800
15	.590 550	45	1.771 650	75	2.952 750	125	4.921 250	350	13.779 500
16	.629 920	46	1.811 020	76	2.992 120	130	5.118 100	360	14.173 200
17	.669 290	47	1.850 390	77	3.031 490	135	5.314 950	370	14.566 900
18	.708 660	48	1.889 760	78	3.070 860	140	5.511 800	380	14.960 600
19	.748 030	49	1.929 130	79	3.110 230	145	5.708 650	390	15.354 300
20	.787 400	50	1.968 500	80	3.149 600	150	5.905 500	400	15.748 000
21	.826 770	51	2.007 870	81	3.188 970	155	6.102 350	500	19.685 000
22	.866 140	52	2.047 240	82	3.228 340	160	6.299 200	600	23.622 000
23	.905 510	53	2.086 610	83	3.267 710	165	6.496 050	700	27.559 000
24	.944 880	54	2.125 980	84	3.307 080	170	6.692 900	800	31.496 000
25	.984 250	55	2.165 350	85	3.346 450	175	6.889 750	900	35.433 000
26	1.023 620	56	2.204 720	86	3.385 820	180	7.086 600	1000	39.370 000
27	1.062 990	57	2.244 090	87	3.425 190	185	7.283 450	2000	78.740 000
28	1.102 360	58	2.283 460	88	3.464 560	190	7.480 300	3000	118.110 000
29	1.141 730	59	2.322 830	89	3.503 903	195	7.677 150	4000	157.480 000
30	1.181 100	60	2.362 200	90	3.543 300	200	7.874 000	5000	196.850 000

To change decimal millimeters to decimal inches, position the decimal point where desired on either side of the millimeter measurement shown and reset the inches decimal by the same number of digits in the same direction. For example, to convert .001 mm into decimal inches, reset the decimal behind the 1 mm (shown on the chart) to .001; change the decimal inch equivalent (.039″ shown) to .00039″).

Tap Drill Sizes

National Fine or S.A.E.			National Coarse or U.S.S.		
Screw & Tap Size	Threads Per Inch	Use Drill Number	Screw & Tap Size	Threads Per Inch	Use Drill Number
No. 5	44	37	No. 5	40	39
No. 6	40	33	No. 6	32	36
No. 8	36	29	No. 8	32	29
No. 10	32	21	No. 10	24	25
No. 12	28	15	No. 12	24	17
$1/4$	28	3	$1/4$	20	8
$5/16$	24	1	$5/16$	18	F
$3/8$	24	Q	$3/8$	16	$5/16$
$7/16$	20	W	$7/16$	14	U
$1/2$	20	$29/64$	$1/2$	13	$27/64$
$9/16$	18	$33/64$	$9/16$	12	$31/64$
$5/8$	18	$37/64$	$5/8$	11	$17/32$
$3/4$	16	$11/16$	$3/4$	10	$21/32$
$7/8$	14	$13/16$	$7/8$	9	$49/64$
$1 1/8$	12	$1 3/64$	1	8	$7/8$
$1 1/4$	12	$1 11/64$	$1 1/8$	7	$63/64$
$1 1/2$	12	$1 27/64$	$1 1/4$	7	$1 7/64$
			$1 1/2$	6	$1 11/32$

Decimal Equivalent Size of the Number Drills

Drill No.	Decimal Equivalent	Drill No.	Decimal Equivalent	Drill No.	Decimal Equivalent
80	.0135	53	.0595	26	.1470
79	.0145	52	.0635	25	.1495
78	.0160	51	.0670	24	.1520
77	.0180	50	.0700	23	.1540
76	.0200	49	.0730	22	.1570
75	.0210	48	.0760	21	.1590
74	.0225	47	.0785	20	.1610
73	.0240	46	.0810	19	.1660
72	.0250	45	.0820	18	.1695
71	.0260	44	.0860	17	.1730
70	.0280	43	.0890	16	.1770
69	.0292	42	.0935	15	.1800
68	.0310	41	.0960	14	.1820
67	.0320	40	.0980	13	.1850
66	.0330	39	.0995	12	.1890
65	.0350	38	.1015	11	.1910
64	.0360	37	.1040	10	.1935
63	.0370	36	.1065	9	.1960
62	.0380	35	.1100	8	.1990
61	.0390	34	.1110	7	.2010
60	.0400	33	.1130	6	.2040
59	.0410	32	.1160	5	.2055
58	.0420	31	.1200	4	.2090
57	.0430	30	.1285	3	.2130
56	.0465	29	.1360	2	.2210
55	.0520	28	.1405	1	.2280
54	.0550	27	.1440		

Decimal Equivalent Size of the Letter Drills

Letter Drill	Decimal Equivalent	Letter Drill	Decimal Equivalent	Letter Drill	Decimal Equivalent
A	.234	J	.277	S	.348
B	.238	K	.281	T	.358
C	.242	L	.290	U	.368
D	.246	M	.295	V	.377
E	.250	N	.302	W	.386
F	.257	O	.316	X	.397
G	.261	P	.323	Y	.404
H	.266	Q	.332	Z	.413
I	.272	R	.339		

ANTI-FREEZE INFORMATION

Freezing and Boiling Points of Solutions
According to Percentage of Alcohol or Ethylene Glycol

Freezing Point of Solution	Alcohol Volume %	Alcohol Solution Boils at	Ethylene Glycol Volume %	Ethylene Glycol Solution Boils at
20°F.	12	196°F.	16	216°F.
10°F.	20	189°F.	25	218°F.
0°F.	27	184°F.	33	220°F.
−10°F.	32	181°F.	39	222°F.
−20°F.	38	178°F.	44	224°F.
−30°F.	42	176°F.	48	225°F.

Note: above boiling points are at sea level. For every 1,000 feet of altitude, boiling points are approximately 2°F. lower than those shown. For every pound of pressure exerted by the pressure cap, the boiling points are approximately 3°F. higher than those shown.

To Increase the Freezing Protection of Anti-Freeze Solutions Already Installed

Cooling System Capacity Quarts	Number of Quarts of **ALCOHOL** Anti-Freeze Required to Increase Protection													
	From +20°F. to					From +10°F. to					From 0°F. to			
	0°	−10°	−20°	−30°	−40°	0°	−10°	−20°	−30°	−40°	−10°	−20°	−30°	−40°
10	2	2¾	3½	4	4½	1	2	2⅓	3¼	3¾	1	1¾	2½	3
12	2½	3¼	4	4¾	5¼	1¼	2¼	3	3¾	4½	1¼	2	2¾	3½
14	3	4	4¾	5½	6	1½	2½	3½	4½	5	1¼	2½	3¼	4
16	3¼	4½	5½	6¼	7	1¾	3	4	5	5¾	1½	2¾	3¾	4¾
18	3¾	5	6	7	7¾	2	3¼	4½	5¾	6½	1¾	3	4¼	5¼
20	4	5½	6¾	7¾	8¾	2	3¼	5	6¼	7¼	1¾	3½	4¾	5¾
22	4½	6	7½	8½	9½	2¼	4	5½	6¾	8	2	3¾	5¼	6½
24	5	6¾	8	9¼	10½	2½	4½	6	7½	8¾	2¼	4	5½	7
26	5¼	7¼	8¾	10	11¼	2¾	4¾	6½	8	9½	2½	4½	6	7½
28	5¾	7¾	9½	11	12	3	5¼	7	8¾	10¼	2½	4¾	6½	8
30	6	8¼	10	11¾	13	3	5½	7½	9¼	10¾	2¾	5	7	8¾

Test radiator solution with proper tester. Determine from the table the number of quarts of solution to be drawn off from a full cooling system and replace with concentrated anti-freeze, to give the desired increased protection. For example, to increase protection of a 22-quart cooling system containing Alcohol anti-freeze, from +10°F. to −20°F. will require the replacement of 5½ quarts of solution with concentrated anti-freeze.

Cooling System Capacity Quarts	Number of Quarts of **ETHYLENE GLYCOL** Anti-Freeze Required to Increase Protection													
	From +20°F. to					From +10°F. to					From 0°F. to			
	0°	−10°	−20°	−30°	−40°	0°	−10°	−20°	−30°	−40°	−10°	−20°	−30°	−40°
10	1¾	2¼	3	3½	3¾	¾	1½	2¼	2¾	3¼	¾	1½	2	2½
12	2	2¾	3½	4	4½	1	1¾	2½	3¼	3¾	1	1¾	2½	3¼
14	2¼	3¼	4	4¾	5½	1¼	2	3	3¾	4½	1	2	3	3½
16	2½	3½	4½	5¼	6	1¼	2½	3½	4¼	5¼	1¼	2¼	3¼	4
18	3	4	5	6	7	1½	2¾	4	5	5¾	1½	2½	3¾	4¾
20	3¼	4½	5¾	6¾	7½	1¾	3	4¼	5½	6½	1½	2¾	4¼	5¼
22	3½	5	6¼	7¼	8¼	1¾	3¼	4¾	6	7¼	1¾	3¼	4½	5½
24	4	5½	7	8	9	2	3½	5	6½	7½	1¾	3½	5	6
26	4¼	6	7½	8¾	10	2	4	5½	7	8¼	2	3¾	5½	6¾
28	4½	6¼	8	9½	10½	2¼	4¼	6	7½	9	2	4	5¾	7¼
30	5	6¾	8½	10	11½	2½	4½	6½	8	9½	2¼	4¼	6¼	7¾

Test radiator solution with proper hydrometer. Determine from the table the number of quarts of solution to be drawn off from a full cooling system and replace with undiluted anti-freeze, to give the desired increased protection. For example, to increase protection of a 22-quart cooling system containing Ethylene Glycol (permanent type) anti-freeze, from +20°F. to −20°F. will require the replacement of 6¼ quarts of solution with undiluted anti-freeze.

ANTI-FREEZE CHART

Temperatures Shown in Degrees Fahrenheit
+32 is Freezing

Quarts of ALCOHOL Needed for Protection to Temperatures Shown Below

Cooling System Capacity Quarts	1	2	3	4	5	6	7	8	9	10	11	12	13
10	+23°	+11°	−5°	−27°									
11	+25	+13	0	−18	−40°								
12		+15	+3	−12	−31								
13		+17	+7	−7	−23								
14		+19	+9	−3	−17	−34°							
15		+20	+11	+1	−12	−27							
16		+21	+13	+3	−8	−21	−36°						
17		+22	+16	+6	−4	−16	−29						
18		+23	+17	+8	−1	−12	−25	−38°					
19		+24	+17	+9	+2	−8	−21	−32					
20			+18	+11	+4	−5	−16	−27	−39°				
21			+19	+12	+5	−3	−12	−22	−34				
22			+20	+14	+7	0	−9	−18	−29	−40°			
23			+21	+15	+8	+2	−7	−15	−25	−36°			
24			+21	+16	+10	+4	−4	−12	−21	−31			
25			+22	+17	+11	+6	−2	−9	−18	−27	−37°		
26			+22	+17	+12	+7	+1	−7	−14	−23	−32		
27			+23	+18	+13	+8	+3	−5	−12	−20	−28	−39°	
28			+23	+19	+14	+9	+4	−3	−9	−17	−25	−34	
29			+24	+19	+15	+10	+6	−1	−7	−15	−22	−30	−39°
30			+24	+20	+16	+11	+7	+1	−5	−12	−19	−27	−35

+ Figures are above Zero, but below Freezing.

− Figures are below Zero. Also below Freezing.

Quarts of ETHYLENE GLYCOL Needed for Protection to Temperatures Shown Below

Cooling System Capacity Quarts	1	2	3	4	5	6	7	8	9	10	11	12	13	14
10	+24°	+16°	+4°	−12°	−34°	−62°								
11	+25	+18	+8	−6	−23	−47								
12	+26	+19	+10	0	−15	−34	−57°							
13	+27	+21	+13	+3	−9	−25	−45							
14			+15	+6	−5	−18	−34							
15			+16	+8	0	−12	−26							
16			+17	+10	+2	−8	−19	−34	−52°					
17			+18	+12	+5	−4	−14	−27	−42					
18			+19	+14	+7	0	−10	−21	−34	−50°				
19			+20	+15	+9	+2	−7	−16	−28	−42				
20				+16	+10	+4	−3	−12	−22	−34	−48°			
21				+17	+12	+6	0	−9	−17	−28	−41			
22				+18	+13	+8	+2	−6	−14	−23	−34	−47°		
23				+19	+14	+9	+4	−3	−10	−19	−29	−40		
24				+19	+15	+10	+5	0	−8	−15	−23	−34	−46°	
25				+20	+16	+12	+7	+1	−5	−12	−20	−29	−40	−50°
26					+17	+13	+8	+3	−3	−9	−16	−25	−34	−44
27					+18	+14	+9	+5	−1	−7	−13	−21	−29	−39
28					+18	+15	+10	+6	+1	−5	−11	−18	−25	−34
29					+19	+16	+12	+7	+2	−3	−8	−15	−22	−29
30					+20	+17	+13	+8	+4	−1	−6	−12	−18	−25

For capacities over 30 quarts divide true capacity by 3. Find quarts Anti-Freeze for the 1/3 and multiply by 3 for quarts to add.

For capacities under 10 quarts multiply true capacity by 3. Find quarts Anti-Freeze for the tripled volume and divide by 3 for quarts to add.

THE LIFE OF THE PARTY IS DEAD.

He killed himself.

He didn't mean to. But he had lost control of his drinking. And after the party, he lost control of his driving and killed himself.

Now his friends shake their heads and stare at the ground and wonder why. But the sad fact is his friends weren't friends. His friends let him die.

They knew he didn't drink only at parties. They knew he was a problem drinker. And still, they let him drive.

Last year, problem drinkers were responsible for 19,000 highway deaths. If one of your friends has a drinking problem, there are many ways you can help him. But first you must help him stay alive.

If you are really his friend, don't help him drink.

If he has been drinking, don't let him drive. Drive him yourself. Call a cab. Take his car keys. Everything you think you can't do, you must do.

We were lucky this time. The life of the party killed only himself.

Write Drunk Driver, Box 2345, Rockville, Maryland 20852.

WHEN A PROBLEM DRINKER DRIVES, IT'S YOUR PROBLEM.

U.S. DEPARTMENT OF TRANSPORTATION • NATIONAL HIGHWAY TRAFFIC SAFETY ADMINISTRATION

Space for this public service message contributed by CHILTON BOOK COMPANY